Women of the Pioneer Trail

Women of the Pioneer Trail

Two Women of the American Westward
Expansion During the 19th Century

By Ox Team to California

Lavinia Honeyman Porter

Days on the Road: Crossing the Plains in
1865

Sarah Raymond Herndon

LEONAUR

Women of the Pioneer Trail
Two Women of the American Westward Expansion During the 19th Century
By Ox Team to California
by Lavinia Honeyman Porterl
Days on the Road: Crossing the Plains in 1865
by Sarah Raymond Herndon

FIRST EDITION

Leonaur is an imprint of Oakpast Ltd

Copyright in this form © 2023 Oakpast Ltd

ISBN: 978-1-916535-16-9 (hardcover)
ISBN: 978-1-916535-17-6 (softcover)

http://www.leonaur.com

Publisher's Notes

Contents

By Ox Team to California

Contents

TO MY SISTER
CHARLOTTE DUNNING BAKER
WHOSE CONSTANT NAGGING INDUCED
ME TO UNDERTAKE THE WRITING OF MY
MEMORIES OF MY LIFE ACROSS
THE PLAINS

Introductory

When my two great, stalwart grandsons were little shavers, it was their favourite habit in the early hours of the morning to come creeping into bed with grandmother. Their soft little arms would twine lovingly about my neck and kisses from their dewy lips were pressed upon my cheek and brow. And were I ever so far away in slumber land their sweet voices clamouring for a story would banish all sleep from my drowsy eyelids. Usually, they selected their own stories from the numbers I had so often repeated, but invariably wound up, when I had exhausted my fund, by saying, "Now, grandmother, tell us about crossing the plains."

The true stories appealed more strongly to them than all the illusory conceptions of fancy, from the fact, perhaps, that I could relate what really had occurred better than I could draw from my imagination. Be that as it may, they never wearied of hearing how I crossed the plains, climbed the Rocky Mountains and travelled many months on my way to California. To gratify them and their dear mother I have consented to write up for them the history of my overland journey.

Those who may favour the succeeding pages with their perusal must not expect any attempt at fine writing, or glowing descriptions. The author's intention is to furnish a plain, unvarnished tale of actual occurrences and facts relating to her long journey. Nothing not strictly true will be admitted into its pages, and if some of the incidents related be found of a thrilling character the reader will experience satisfaction in knowing that they are not the results of imaginary picturing. Whenever a personal adventure is narrated, it will be found to illustrate some particular phase of character, and none are recounted which do not convey information.

As I recall those years after the lapse of time, they are as vivid as the memory of yesterday's events. It has been a positive delight in the midst of this modern life, to live over some of those scenes. Those peculiar conditions no longer exist, for the advent of the overland railway and the customs and usages of more civilized life have done away with much of the fascinations of romance and adventure.

If I have not laid sufficient emphasis on the difficulties and discouragement which we encountered, it is not because there were not numerous obstacles to overcome, but in turning the mind upon the past, the more pleasant memories stand out in bolder relief; even when the cares and responsibilities weighed most heavily upon us, we had that saving grace of humour which enabled us to meet situations otherwise insuperable, and to gather courage whereby we might endure them all.

Necessarily in recounting these events so closely identified with our life on the plains this narrative has assumed an autobiographical character to a larger extent than the author could wish, and I humbly beg pardon of the reader if I have exceeded the canons of good taste.

All through that tedious and extended time I kept a journal of every day's happenings as they occurred, but after our arrival in California we settled on a remote ranch, and in those early and primitive days, books, magazines or literature of any kind were rare among the farming community where we were located. My journal proving interesting to our neighbours, was loaned and re-loaned from one family to another until at last it fell into the hands of some careless persons who allowed it to be partially destroyed, particularly that part relating to the first months of our journey. Many names of rivers, streams and different points and places have slipped from my memory, but the principal places and events of our journey were so strongly impressed upon my then young mind, that they have become indelible and time cannot efface them. Perhaps the repetition of them over and over to my little grandsons and their young playmates served to strengthen them in my memory, and, while I may be lacking in ability to embellish this humble history, I can still give the plain facts and incidents of that never to be forgotten journey.

Chapter 1

The Start

It was in the fall and winter of eighteen fifty-nine that my husband and I decided to emigrate to the far West. Imprudent speculations and other misfortunes had embarrassed us financially to such an extent that our prospects for the future looked dark and forbidding; we then determined to use the small remnant of our fortune to provide a suitable outfit for a lengthy journey toward the setting sun. We were both young and inexperienced, my husband still in his twenties, and I a young and immature girl scarce twenty years of age. I had been raised south of "Mason's and Dixon's line." My parents were well-to-do Southern people, and I had hitherto led the indolent life of the ordinary Southern girl.

My husband, educated for a profession, knew nothing of manual labour, and had no idea of any other vocation outside of his profession; nor had he the training to make a living on the plains of the West, or the crossing of the continent in an ox team a successful venture. However, we had youth in our favour, and an indomitable will to succeed, and I have since learned by experience that a kind providence watches over fools and children. Since that long ago time when I look back at the temerity of our undertaking I have wondered why, and how, our older and wiser friends permitted us to be turned loose upon the wilds of the West without a guardian. We were two such precious dunces, but with a most exalted ego, and the utmost confidence in our ability to brave the dangers of the undertaking.

A journey across the plains of the West was considered a great event in those early days. It was long thought of and planned seriously with and among the various members of the family to which the would-be traveller belonged. Whoever had the temerity to propose turning their backs on civilized life and their faces toward the far-off Rocky Mountains were supposed to be daring with a boldness bordering on recklessness. Emigration then meant the facing of unknown dangers in a half-savage country.

After many lengthy debates over the manner of transportation, and a diversified quantity of advice from our numerous friends, as to the merits of horses, mules or oxen, we at last decided (and it proved to be a wise decision) to purchase three yoke of strong, sturdy oxen and a large well-built emigrant wagon; roomy enough to hold all we wanted to take with us, and in which we might travel with some degree of comfort. In due time the oxen were bought. The six animals were young and had never been broken, to the yoke. When they were driven to our home, turned loose in our barnyard, they were as formidable a lot of wild brutes as the eye ever gazed upon, as agile as deer, and as handy with their heels as with their horns.

Not one of us was brave enough to venture into the corral with them, and we soon realised that we had six white elephants on our hands. Finally, my husband found a negro man who agreed to break them to yoke and chain. It proved to be rare sport to our neighbours watching them in, the somewhat difficult task of training that bunch of young steers. But with time and patience they became more amenable to yoke and chain, and sullenly submitted to be attached and to draw the wagon.

I shall never forget the first time I ventured to ride behind them, we had invited some of our neighbours who were brave enough to risk their necks to ride with us. There were several ladies and children and a man or two included. It was our intention to drive our new team a short distance into the country and give our friends a foretaste of what a journey would be behind the slow-moving cattle, but before we had driven a block our skittish and newly-broken team took it into their heads to run away down the hilly streets of our village, pell-mell, first on one side of the street then the other.

In vain my husband called "Whoa, Buck, whoa, Jill" to the leaders. It only seemed to add to their fury, and as they recklessly sped along in their blind rage, the way proper matrons and prudish maids climbed and scrambled out of the rear end of that wagon was a sight to behold if not to describe. After repeated trials and much patience on our part, our wild oxen became tractable, and long before the end of our journey we had become very much attached to them, and they in turn had learned to love us, becoming docile and kind as kittens, any one of them would follow me wherever I led, eat out of our hands, or allow me or our little son to ride on his back.

The strong wagon with which we had provided ourselves had a staunch canvass covering, made water tight and firm enough to defy the ravages of wind and storm. Then came the loading and packing of provisions, raiment, and all the other paraphernalia necessary for a long trip. What to take and what to leave behind us was the problem that confronted us every day. Many times, was the wagon loaded and unloaded before it proved satisfactory. Many of our most cherished treasures had to be left behind to give place to the more necessary articles.

The report of fabulous mines just discovered in the Rocky Mountains had extended far and near, and the Pike's Peak excitement was then at fever heat It was at this time that thousands of people had set their faces westward towards that mecca of their hopes. While our friends imagined that we, too, would make that point the end of our pilgrimage, yet we had decided and promised each other that if Pike's Peak and its environments did not come up to our expectations we would push on to California. With that final objective point in view, we provided ourselves with provisions sufficient to last us for six months or even longer.

Young as I was at that time, we had been married nearly five years. We had a dear little fair-haired son, Robert, who was the pride and joy of our hearts. I began at once to prepare an outfit for both him and myself which I thought suitable to wear on the plains. In this I showed the callow ideas of an immature mind which would not be guided by older and wiser heads—proving also that my conception of roughing it for six months was very primitive. Among the other necessary garments in my outfit, I had made two blue cloth traveling dresses with an array of white collars and cuffs. When a sensible elderly neighbour suggested home-spun or linsey Woolsey as being far more appropriate, I scorned her advice. These fabrics were worn only by the negroes in the South. I assured her that I intended to look as neatly and well-dressed on the plains as at home. However, I soon discarded my cloth gowns and my collars and cuffs, as I will relate farther on.

When our plans were fully matured and all our arrangements nearly completed for an early departure there was revealed to me a most startling discovery that in the course of a few months the stork intended to make us another visit. Welcome as he might have been under more favourable circumstances, his promised coming in the near future brought consternation to our hearts, and we were afraid our plans would all have to be changed. We feared the perils of our journey might prove to be too hard for me to endure under these new circumstances. But I was well, young and strong; had the courage and bravery of ignorance, besides, we hoped to reach the end of our destination and find a home and resting place before the final advent of the stork's promised visit, which I was careful to conceal from my friends.

I did not wish to give my dear parents any unnecessary worry; they were already filled with dread and anxiety at the undertaking we had so lightly assumed. We concluded to make the best of what could not be helped, and with stout hearts still continued our final, preparations.

Everything being now in readiness, we waited impatiently for the warm days of spring, as we were to depend mostly on the wild grass of the prairie for food for our stock which now consisted of the aforesaid three yoke of oxen, a full-blooded Arabian saddle horse and a milch cow.

It was the third day of April, 1860, that my husband and eldest brother, Sam, who accompanied us as far as Pike's Peak, left the little town of Hannibal, on the Mississippi river, and started overland across the state of Missouri for St. Joseph, where by rail and train myself and little son joined them. We remained in St. Joseph a day or two to make my farewell visit to my dear sister who resided there.

On the fourteenth day of April, we left St. Joseph, driving aboard the ferry for the farther shore of the muddy Missouri river, accompanied by my sister, her husband and a few other friends. We landed in a little village on the Kansas shore, and drove our friends out a few miles on the prairie, and made our first halt for our noonday meal in which our friends were to join us for the last time. It was a sorrowful picnic, for our parting hour was near at hand.

Seven and forty years ago it was a serious thing to say goodbye to all that was nearest and dearest, to uproot ourselves from home and go forth into the wilderness into many and unknown dangers.

My sister and friends were to return by the ferry to St. Joseph. My husband and brother were too tender-hearted to remain and witness our sad parting. They hurriedly gathered the cattle from where they were feeding on the short grass, yoked them to the wagon, put my little son into the wagon beside them and drove slowly away, leaving me to bid my friends a long and last farewell.

I never recall that sad parting from my dear sister on the plains of Kansas without the tears flowing fast and free. Even now as I write, although so many long years have passed since then, I cannot restrain them. We were the eldest of a large family and the bond of affection and love that existed between us was strong indeed. It was like tearing our heart strings asunder. But such sorrows are to be endured not described. As she with the other friends turned to leave me for the ferry which was to take them back to home and civilization, I stood alone on that wild prairie. Looking westward I saw my husband driving slowly over the plain; turning my face once more to the east, my dear sister's footsteps were fast widening the distance between us.

For the time I knew not which way to go, nor whom to follow. But in a few moments, I rallied my forces, and waiving a last *adieu* to my beloved sister, turned my dim and tear-stained eyes westward and soon overtook the slowly moving oxen, who were bearing my husband and child over the green prairie. Climbing into the wagon beside them, with everything we possessed piled high behind us, we turned our faces toward the land of golden promise, that lay far beyond the Rocky Mountains. Little idea had I of the hardships, the perils, the deprivation awaiting me.

When the reality proved to be more than my most vivid imagination had pictured it, I was still able to endure it with a staunch heart, but often as I walked ahead of the team and alone, thoughts of home and my dear father and mother would almost overwhelm me with grief. As each step bore me farther from them, the unbidden tears would flow in spite of my brave resolve to be the courageous and valiant frontierswoman. I had been taught that a wife owed her first duty to her husband, and hard as it seemed I had the courage to do what I had promised under the highest and most solemn sanction.

We had been several days on our journey before I began to realise the immolation and sacrifice, I was to endure; giving up my comfortable home and all my dear ones, cut off from the congenial society of my associates and personal friends, the ease, luxuries and comforts of civilized life. Enduring the disagreeable drudgery of camp work, the constant exposure to the elements, the glare of the scorching sun, the furious and fearful thunder storms that so often overtook us, the high winds, and blinding, pitiless sand storms that blew for days without cessation, the dread that settled down upon us at nightfall for fear of wild beasts and the other dangers that so often menaced us in our utter loneliness, the necessity of still moving onward, each day, whether we were in the humour for traveling or not.

At first the novelty attending the starting out on such a trip and the continuous change of our environment kept up our interest. But as the days wore on the irksome monotony of the journey began to pall upon me, and I spent many unhappy hours which I tried to conceal within my own breast, sometimes confiding to my journal my woes and disappointments, but managed to keep up a cheerful exterior before my husband and brother. Gradually, however, I became used to the peculiar situations by which I was surrounded and learned by daily experience how to surmount the trials and difficulties, and with a naturally cheerful and optimistic temperament soon became philosophical enough to take things as I found them and make the best of the situation.

CHAPTER 2

Camping in Kansas

Our first night in camp was near a small stream. On the banks were a few stunted and wind-blown trees. The forage for our stock was not good. During the night the cattle strayed from camp in search of better grazing, or the inclination for the old pastures, and turned backwards toward home. When morning dawned, we had nothing left but our "Arabian steed," which fortunately we had securely picketed, or he too, might have deserted us. James, my husband, took the horse and went back rapidly over the road we had travelled the day before. My brother, taking the field-glasses, went on foot in another direction to find traces of our wandering herd. With my little son I was left alone in camp to wrestle with the campfire and breakfast.

I must admit that my first experience with real cooking was on this journey. Like many other Southern girls, I had learned how to make a delicate cake or a fancy pudding, but never before had I tried to cook a meal. You can well imagine what a difficult task it must have been for me to build a campfire, get my kettle to stand upright on the rolling wood, keep the smoke out of my eyes and ashes out of the food, hampered as I was with my blue cloth traveling dress and the great effort required to keep my white cuffs clean. A short distance from our camp an old man and his two sons had set up their tent. I learned that they also were *en route* for Pike's Peak, coming from their thrice remote New England home. I was conscious that they were watching my poor efforts very closely, and after I had upset my coffee pot, and the camp kettle had turned over and put out the little fire I had at last got started, the elderly man came to my assistance, rebuilt my fire, adjusted my kettle in the proper way, expressed his kindly sympathy in our dilemma, and then bidding me a polite good day returned to his own camp.

As the morning advanced my Yankee neighbours soon did up their camp work, folded their tent, and moved along on their way, leaving me alone on that forlorn prairie, with not a soul in sight anywhere. Had I been a timid creature I might have wailed my lonely plight. My little son and I ate our poorly cooked and joyless breakfast alone, after waiting long for the return of my husband and brother. Not until the noonday sun was high in the heavens were my tired and strained eyes gladdened by the sight of them afar off driving the lost cattle before them. After that experience the stock was herded until bed time, and then securely staked to prevent another occurrence of that kind.

I very soon discarded the blue cloth dress and white collars and cuffs, fully realising that they were not just the proper thing for camp life. Fortunately, I had with me some short wash dresses which I immediately donned, tied my much-betrimmed straw hat up in the wagon, put on my big shaker sun-bonnet and my heavy buckskin gloves, and looked the ideal emigrant woman. The first days of such a journey, however commonplace, were interesting to us. Every faculty was on the alert. Even so trivial a thing as a jack-rabbit rising out of the grass, scared, and scampering with long leaps, striving to widen the distance between us, was able to hold our attention. Or we watched the misfortunes of a fellow traveller by the wayside, who, in his great haste, had neglected to lubricate his running gear properly; hence a hotbox which he was vainly trying to cool off with a wet blanket.

Crossing a deep stream on whose opposite side were a few rough houses and the usual saloon, the entire population turned out to see us drive through the village. As we passed the last house, an old crone was bending over her tub busily washing, but she stopped her labours long enough to ask us in drawling tones, "be you gwine to Pike's Peak?" Answering her in the affirmative, we inquired the name of the village we were just leaving. "Oh," she replied, "this is Mason City." Anywhere through Kansas three or four log huts constituted a city.

My young brother who travelled with us was a youth of susceptible proclivities, fresh from the restraints of college life, and with the exhilaration of his new found freedom unusually elated. For was not his face turned towards the wonderful land of the Golden West? While we were yet children around the home fireside, we had planned a life of travel and adventure, and now our childish longings were to be realised. He had an absorbing passion for nature, for every curious formation of rock or stone, a quick eye for all the beauties of the unfolding landscape, a ready ear, too, for every touch of humour, and was hilarious over the interminable picnic that he imagined we had begun.

Nature had also endowed him with a nimble tongue, and he was constantly telling us funny stories of college life. Often we would laughingly accuse him of drawing the long bow, on relating some very unusual experience. In vain we would try to outwit him and play our own jokes upon him, but his lively retorts were nearly always to our complete discomfiture. Generous hearted boy was he, and round the camp fires and over many of the wearisome stretches of our journey he made the hours seem shorter with his cheerful badinage.

Part of my work when in camp was cooking. I have already acknowledged my great deficiency in that accomplishment. The bread-making at first was a total failure. When I attempted to make light rolls for breakfast, they were leaden. My husband, wise man that he was, ate them in silence, but my humorous brother, less polite, called them sinkers. I felt chagrined at my failure, but persisting in my efforts I soon overcame the mysteries of the dried yeast cakes with which I had been supplied, and in a short time learned to make sweet and wholesome light bread.

As we had no tent we slept in the wagon, my brother taking the rear end for his "Pullman," spreading his blankets above the bales and boxes, never seeming to mind the ridges and uneven surface of his couch. James, myself and our little son, occupied the front of the wagon. We had a huge old-fashioned feather bed, that made sleeping above the boxes and barrels a trifle more comfortable. During the day it was necessary to stow away the beds more compactly to enable us to get at the stores beneath them. This also was my work while the men brushed and curried the stock, lubricated the wheels of the wagon, and reloaded the various camp equipage. James was kindly solicitous for the welfare of his cattle, giving the oxen the same careful grooming that our horse received, and they fared much better for this attention, looking sleek and fine for the extra care.

When I had finished my part of the camp work, I would wrap myself in a warm shawl and start out on the road ahead of the team. The early spring mornings were keen and cold and I felt the need of brisk exercise. I had always been an enthusiastic pedestrian and greatly enjoyed walking over the gently undulating plains of Kansas. It was our endeavour to make from twenty to thirty-five miles' progress westward every day. If the weather permitted and the roads were not too heavy from the frequent rains, it was my habit to walk the entire distance. As I grew accustomed to the continued exercise, I could accomplish the long walk with ease. At other times, mounting my horse,

I would enjoy a gallop over the prairies, occasionally getting a bad fall.

My horse was a kind and gentle animal; but I soon discovered that he was possessed of one most treacherous fault, namely, when frightened instead of swaying or shying sidewise, he would suddenly squat, and the best rider would become unseated. I had been thrown from his back once or twice in this manner, luckily without injury, and Sam, my brother, made great sport of my failure to stay in the saddle on these occasions. This mortified me exceedingly, as from my early childhood I had ridden horseback. There were few horses that I dared not mount, and I was extremely vain of my skill as an equestrienne. However, one fine day. he too, came to grief. I had been riding for several hours and becoming weary dismounted.

My brother vaulted lightly on the horse and rode swiftly away. While I stood admiring his graceful pose and the fearless manner in which he rode, suddenly I saw him go flying out of the saddle and quickly strike the ground, and not on his feet either. After his own failure, he ceased to vex me with his jests and raillery. We had only been a few days out on our journey when we witnessed an electrical storm, something unusual at this time of the year. This storm was frightful in the extreme for us as we were so unprotected from its fury.

The sky was overcast with dark and threatening clouds, a low sullen murmur as of distant wind filled the air. The lightning blamed incessantly as it lit up the darkening horizon. The thunder burst forth in peal after peal of deafening reverberation. We hurriedly drove our frightened team into camp as this storm continued. By midnight a furious gale swept over the bare prairie. Our wagon, exposed to the fury of the wind, shook and rocked in such a manner, that every moment we feared it would be overturned. Yet with all this flurry of the elements scarcely a drop of rain fell in our vicinity. Farther on we discovered next day by the condition of the roads there must have been heavy showers. For the first two or three weeks it rained almost daily, which made the conditions very uncomfortable and with difficulty we made our fires from the water-soaked wood and cooked our meals under the falling rain.

When the days were bright and clear the travel through Kansas was delightful. The aspect of the prairies in the early morning sunshine was most alluring. The air was fresh and bracing, filled with the fragrance of countless spring flowers, and every little blade of grass hung with drops of dew that scintillated like jewels as they waved in the gentle breeze of morning. The sweet note of the meadow lark was music to the listening ear. On every side was high waving grass that covered these vast stretches of undulating land. I rode or walked over the tufted plain, seeing, unvexed by sound of wheel or human voice the pleasant sights along the way.

The solitude upon this wide expanse of open plain was absolute. No smoke arose in the clear air from any habitation. No cattle browsed upon the succulent grasses. No whistling ploughboy tore the sod-grown turf with his shining plough, nor uprooted the tinted blue star flower that sprang up on every hand. There were numerous winding streams fringed here and there with miniature forests. Our cattle grew sleek and fat with the nourishing food nature so lavishly provided. And just within the woodland that fringed the banks of some small stream, we would halt for the night, happy to find both wood and waiter, the two great essentials for a comfortable camp.

When we had been two weeks or more on the road, we came to one of the largest streams in Kansas, the Big Blue, timbered with sycamores, cottonwood, oaks and occasional elms. After breakfast one morning, my brother loaded his gun and took a short excursion in search of prairie hens. We had seen numbers of them along the road. Much to his great disappointment and ours also, he was unable to start a single one in the high grass. This we learned was the fate of most huntsmen at this hour of the morning and season of the year. These birds wait until the sun gets high and warm before they come forth from their hiding places to strut and coquette with each other. This led Sam to take a much longer detour than he had anticipated and it was nearly noon before he presented himself wet and bedraggled, but triumphantly bearing one prairie hen.

Only wounded by his shot, it had weakly flown just beyond his reach, until it led him near the shelving banks of the Big Blue, when in a last successful effort to reach his fluttering victim he had stepped too near the edge of the crumbling banks of the river, and huntsman and bird disappeared beneath the waters of the stream. Luckily grasping a willow sapling as he went down and still holding on to his feathered victim, he pulled himself on shore and came back to camp elated with his adventure. We enjoyed the flavour of the wild bird, as our appetites had palled on salt meat. Up to this time wild game had been scarce near the road. As we proceeded prairie chickens, quail and the ringdove became more plentiful and proved a grateful addition to our larder.

Here and there along our way, we saw numerous dugouts which

we were told were occupied by herdsmen. These were supposed to be a secure shelter from the cyclones that came so suddenly upon these vast plains which were treeless; and as lumber was scarce, they also afforded cheap homes for the pioneer emigrants who occasionally settled here. Anything that looked like a home attracted us and brought to our minds the association of home life from which we were going farther and farther away.

While we were camping on the Big Blue, we were in the midst of a large company, who like ourselves, were bound for Pike's Peak. The beautiful undulating meadow lands were dotted here and there with tents. The blue smoke from numerous camp fires arose on all sides, while huge prairie schooners were anchored within hailing distance; in many instances like our own serving for tent and shelter. Cattle were leisurely feeding on the luxuriant grass, campers were fishing or hunting along the stream, while the women were on duties bent or sitting by their camp fires. The children of the emigrants, released from the strain of travel, were romping over bush and briar, and their shouts of glee resounded as some unfortunate stubbed his brown, uncovered toes and fell face forward on the soft earth.

As we approached Nebraska, the country became wild and somewhat more sterile. All signs of human habitation disappeared entirely, and with them the wild game became less abundant. No longer the prairie hen or the quail flew from the grass as we approached, though plovers and doves still seemed plentiful.

Between Big Sandy and the Little Blue River was a monotonous drive, hot and uncomfortable, with only a few cottonwoods to enliven the landscape. Here we found a settler who's humble, but comfortable cabin was filled with children of all ages; they seemed to overflow from doors and windows; their brown and sun-burned faces forming a strange contrast to their tow white hair. We were invited to visit them in their humble home and were surprised to find so much culture and marks of refinement in this far away land. The mother was an educated eastern woman, and in spite of the hard work necessary on a new farm and the encumbrance of a large and growing family, she, without the assistance of either maid or servant performed all the labours of her household, and still found time to instruct her children in the rudiments of a good education.

Her courtesy and good manners I never saw excelled in the best society. While the cabin was very meagrely furnished, yet on the cheap wooden shelves that adorned the walls were many good books of standard authors, which bore the marks of being well read. The children were clean and well clad although their clothing did not need the services of a French laundry; neither did the mother have time to dawdle away her time at bridge or go to card clubs, even if these things had existed or been thought of in that isolated home on the plains of Nebraska. The father was a typical sturdy rancher, both horseman and herdsman, with a rich vein of humour combined with strong common sense. He proved to be most interesting, amusing and instructive. His fund of back-woods stories and his inexhaustible humour kept us in a constant roar of laughter. We left these cheerful people with feelings of regret.

CHAPTER 3

Settlers in Nebraska

To the inexperienced traveller the approach of nightfall is hailed with joy, for the camp fire is among the chief pleasures of out-door life. We vied with each other in replenishing its cheerful blaze. There was always a fascination in watching it kindle from its little glimmering light into the roaring flame. The flicker and glow illuminating the countenance of those nearest the fire for a brief moment, bringing out every feature with a peculiar distinctness and just as suddenly obliterating them with an intense shadow. Then, too, if the night was bleak and the wind blew his frosty breath, you were reminded by your freezing back that picturesqueness and comfort did not always go together. The brilliant tongues of flame and the innumerable sparks floating off into the air, had no charms for those who were roasted on one side and frozen on the other.

The flying sparks on windy nights would blister any exposed surface of the skin, while the smoke with every change of the breeze was whirled into your eyes. For all that, in many of our lonely halting places, the bright and cheerful glow of the camp fire served to drive away the gloom that surrounded us, and keep the wolf and howling coyote at a respectful distance. When we were far out on the great plains, with no wood or tree in sight, our main dependence for any sort of fire was on the despised buffalo chips. These emitted scarcely any flame, and we hurriedly cooked our evening meal before its unsatisfactory glow dissolved into a few light ashes. Then we appreciated fully, in spite of its minor drawbacks, our bright wood camp fire.

In the early stages of our journey before we had grown wise by experience, it had been our custom when we came to a stream at evening to camp before crossing it. Storms that occurred so frequently at night caused these streams to rise suddenly and overflow their banks. These shallow brooklets which we could wade easily at night, would become angry, rushing torrents before morning, filled with drift wood and debris. While these floods were raging, we had no alternative but to swim our cattle across or wait for the stream to subside. We had made this mistake once too often and at last found ourselves, as the rain continued, waiting in camp for several days for the waters to fall. But we were not alone.

Each day brought us more company and before the water had subsided there were fifty or sixty other emigrant wagons in view, their tents dotting the landscape on all sides, while their stock was grazing on the rolling prairie around us. The emigrants worked about their camps, the women busily employed in cooking or in trying to dry their clothing that had been drenched by the continual rain. Sitting around their wagons were other unkempt, soiled and bedraggled women, most of them lean, angular and homely, nearly every one of them chewing on a short stick, which they occasionally withdrew and swabbed around in a box containing some black powder, while a muddy stream oozed from the corners of their polluted mouths. It was evident to the most casual observer that they were snuff dippers from Arkansas or Tennessee.

A number of ragged and half-clothed children of both sexes swarmed around their camp, bare-footed and bare-legged. One of the women, to whom my attention was particularly called, sat disconsolately apart from all the others, who were pottering around their camp work or gossiping in little groups. Her thin knees were clasped by her bonier hands, and her tousled head drooped forward. There was a most tragic expression on her care-worn countenance and she looked as if she cared for nothing on earth. A strong measure of human suffering was depicted on her hopeless face, and it seemed as if nothing would rouse her. But in this I was much mistaken.

Two of her bare-footed boys had committed some childish prank which roused the fierce anger of one of the men who stood idly by smoking his short pipe. In a voice thick with sudden rage, he called the boys to him. The terror and the panic depicted on their faces plainly showed their great fear and instead of obeying the surly call they started to run. The man, seizing an ox goad, soon overtook them, and quickly applying it to their naked legs caused them to emit screams of anguish with the severity of the blows. Then in another instant I saw that mother aroused from her seeming apathy. With one bound, like an enraged tigress, she cleared the wagon, catching up a horse whip as she ran, and soon reached the man, who was so unmercifully beating her children.

Her attack was so sudden that he was unprepared for the onslaught. She rained quick and sturdy blows on his head, face, arms, anywhere in her blind fury. It required the combined efforts of two men of the company to make her desist. The man whom she had beaten was wild to chastise her in return, but those who had separated the angry couple protected the woman. The boys in the meantime had scampered out of sight. After many hot words, a truce was declared and the commotion soon died down. I comforted myself with the thought that we were not obliged to travel with such an inharmonious company.

We were now being continually overtaken by numerous trains of the faster horse and mule teams, many of them bearing on their painted wagon covers such fanciful legends as "Pike's Peak or Bust," "Root Hog or Die." Long before our slow-moving oxen reached Denver, we met those same teams coming back, and underneath their legends was the brief word "Busted" or "The Hog's Dead." The wild rush was not confined to wagons alone. Hundreds of men had pack animals which were loaded with blankets, provisions, coffee pots and frying pans. A few even had hand carts which they pushed with their light outfit before them.

Travelling alone with our one wagon, independent of the numerous caravans that overtook us, we were passed by most of them, for our oxen were much slower than the horse and mule teams, which seemed to predominate. Yet the days were full of excitement, as we came into contact with such a diversified lot of human nature. Nearly every state in the union was represented, all looking forward with eager eyes toward the rich mines of the Rocky Mountains.

These vast prairies of Kansas and Nebraska were sadly deficient in bridges. While at low water many of the streams were not difficult to cross, yet often we found ourselves at the brink of others whose steep and slippery banks looked very formidable. Down the precipitous incline the wagon would seem almost to topple over on the oxen, then into the deep stream and up the difficult pull on the opposite side. We had been on the road nearly a month, owing to the delays of wet weather and the high water we encountered, when we came to a large stream too deep and treacherous to ford, called the Republican River, where arrangement was provided to cross by a rope ferry.

At this place we found a large number of families, with an immense herd of horses and cattle, migrating from Illinois and Missouri to California by the way of Fort Kearney, where they would strike the old military road. They had been trying to swim their stock over this stream. This was slow and difficult and their patience was well-nigh exhausted. It was impossible to get such a large number of animals ferried over in a hurry. Consequently, we had to wait our turn and nearly two days went by before we could take this primitive ferry across the deep stream.

One often hears the plains of the West spoken of as monotonous levels. But here and there they rise and fall in gentle undulations, sometimes crossed by narrow streams fringed by the homely and ragged Cottonwood. One morning, while climbing a rather high divide, we caught sight of our first antelope, and my impulsive brother wanted to give them a chase at once; but they soon showed us by their swift flight that they had no desire for a closer acquaintance with us. We were sadly disappointed, for by this time we were beginning to grow tired of bacon and salt pork, and longed for a taste of fresh meat.

In a day or two they became more frequent and less wary, and one afternoon we sighted several in a group so intently feeding that my brother laid one of the beautiful creatures low with his rifle. The others soon sped out of range. They were beautiful, graceful creatures; in colour a yellowish brown on the upper portions of the body and almost white on the under parts. The nose, horns and hoofs were black, with eyes bright and most beautifully expressive. We afterwards saw numbers of them in the distance, but this was the only one we ever came near enough to shoot. I could not forget the startled look in the beautiful eyes of the timid creature as it fell to the ground wounded and dying, and I did not relish the meat prepared from it as I had anticipated.

One Sunday while resting in camp, my husband accompanied me and our son to a small stream some distance from our wagon, where we could take a refreshing dip in the clear water. We had enjoyed our bath greatly. Leaving the middle of the stream. I seated myself on its banks and as I was drawing forth my foot from its depths, a huge snake came gliding out of the water close by my side. With true feminine instinct I uttered a shrill scream and started on a swift run toward camp in my scanty bathing attire. Before my husband could overtake me, however, I had recovered from my fright and went back for the remainder of my clothing.

Frequently when walking the sight of a huge rattler would cause me to make a sudden jump into the air to avoid coming in contact with the repulsive creature. James, who ever kept a watchful eye on me as I walked ahead of the team, would jokingly ask, "Why did you jump so high and run so swiftly at intervals?" These reptiles were quite numerous on our route, rattlesnakes predominating, with many others not so venomous, but just as repulsive.

CHAPTER 4

Returning Gold Seekers

By the frequency of the trails that continually crossed our road, we found we were nearing the land of the buffalo. Now and then the heads and skeletons of buffaloes dotted the plains, and in certain localities the ground was fairly white with the bleached bones. We never imagined that any use could be made of them, but many years after that time I was informed that a regular trade had sprung up for these bones, and that a number of Eastern firms did a large business in shipping them to their markets, where they were used in manufacturing buttons or ground into a fertilizer. As yet we had not seen a herd of buffaloes. We had listened to many tales of how they loped over the plains, coming swiftly with bended heads, tearing the turf in their mad rush, which no obstacle could oppose. They had been known to run directly through and over trains of emigrant wagons leaving scarcely a vestige, and while we were now constantly on the lookout for a sight of these animals, it was with fear and trembling.

One morning we had just finished our breakfast of salt pork, fried mush and coffee, of which I had partaken with little relish. My hitherto pampered appetite had begun to rebel at the coarse and homely fare. I was hungry for some fresh meat. Nearly a quarter of a mile beyond us was another camp of emigrants, men, women and children, with their full complement of tents and wagons. Suddenly from this camp I saw a man come running toward us, and as he came nearer, pointing and gesticulating madly, I heard him shouting "buffaloes." Looking quickly in the direction he was pointing, I saw a large herd of a hundred or more. They seemed to be making a wild dash for our camp, bellowing, as they ran with lowered heads in a long awkward gallop. Several of the men were running on foot to get a shot at them.

My brother levelled his Sharp's rifle and fired, but it seemed rather to hasten than arrest their flight. On they came with rapid strides, and crossed the stream almost beside our camp. One shaggy headed old fellow, shambling up the bank, was fired at several times by a number of the men just as he entered the water. Falling to the ground as he emerged on the bank near our side, he caused the rest of the shaggy herd to veer suddenly in their course, taking their way between the two camps, and quickly disappeared around a group of low rolling mounds just beyond us. My little boy and myself had taken refuge in the wagon, expecting every moment to feel the trampling of their hoofs, for we had heard much of their rushing through and over trains in their mad flight, leaving them wrecked and their occupants mangled beyond recognition.

The buffalo the marksmen had wounded so that he could no longer follow the herd was quickly dispatched. The men dressed the carcass, and each one of the campers took a portion of the animal. When we received our share, I immediately raked together the coals and embers of my breakfast fire, and broiled thereon a piece of the fresh meat to satisfy my craving appetite. It proved a great disappointment, for it was tough, strong and dry. I had heard that no meat could equal or excel that of the buffalo, but the piece I had cooked was not relished. I also learned that this was the meat of an old bull, and we had not even taken the best part of the animal, which was the hump on the shoulders and was considered a very choice morsel.

After this we saw many large droves of buffaloes in the distance. There must have been thousands, but they had grown wary. The overland traffic in 1860 was so enormous that the buffaloes kept too far from the main travelled road to give much sport to the skilful hunters. We never again fired a shot at one. Occasionally we were able to buy from the Indians a few pounds of what was then termed "jerked buffalo." This was strips of the wild meat dried in the sun and wind without salt. The tongues of the animals dried in this manner were fairly palatable, but one could chew for hours on one small piece of the dried meat, and the longer you chewed the bigger it grew. However, it was a change from salt pork and bacon.

We passed hundreds of new-made graves on this part of our route. One would imagine that an epidemic had broken out among those preceding us, so frequent were these tell-tale mounds of earth. One day we overtook a belated team on its way to one of the distant forts with only a man and his wife. The wife was quite ill in the little tent, having given birth to a child a day or two before, which lived only a day. The father had put it in a rude box and laid it away in its tiny grave by the wayside. The poor mother was grieving her heart out at leaving it behind on the lonely plain with only a rude stone to mark its resting place.

I think it must have been near the middle or last of May when we met our first Indians, a band of thirty or forty Cheyennes. They did not trouble us to any great extent, although we felt rather annoyed at their proximity. The first Saturday after we came into the neighbourhood of this tribe, we called an early halt in the afternoon. For several days the grazing for our stock had been very poor, but in this Indian country the buffalo grass was more plentiful, and while it was short yet it stood very thickly over the ground. The roots of this buffalo grass were long and sweet, and the cattle devoured them, with as much relish as the tops of the grass.

In all stages of ripeness it was very nutritious, and the stock throve upon it. Taking advantage of this good pasturage we concluded to wait over a day or two and let our cattle recruit, while James made some needed repairs to the wagon. It gave me a convenient time to do my necessary washing and baking. Continual moving on did not give much extra time for cooking, and bacon, beans and bread, day after day, became monotonous; so, I gladly embraced this opportunity to have a change of diet. I made dried-apple pies with bacon drippings for shortening; and some ginger cookies, with the same ingredient entering largely into their composition in place of butter. The latter was a scarce commodity, as all that we had was from the milk of our one little cow.

We had soon discovered that by pouring our morning's milk into a covered can in the wagon, the continual jolting would churn it as we moved along, and at night we would have butter enough for our evening meal if we used it very sparingly. For breakfast our bread was dipped in gravy as usual! These two days in camp near a stream gave us an opportunity for a bath, and me a chance to wash the alkali dust from my hair, and to do the necessary mending of our clothing.

We were now in the midst of numerous bands of roving Indians, not hostile to us, but intent on begging or stealing. Whenever or wherever we made our camp, they soon found us and never left us throughout the day. This Sunday I had discarded an old, worn-out hoop-skirt that I had worn thus far on my journey, and much to my amusement and amazement as well, it was immediately donned by a huge Indian brave, who strutted proudly among the group of Indians who were squatting around our camp. As the skeleton hoop composed the larger part of his attire he was a sight to behold. Even the stolid squaws were provoked to mirth at the ludicrous spectacle.

The following Monday found us ready to move on, and we began very soon to meet team after team of disappointed "Pike's Peakers" returning East. We talked with a number of them who had not even gone so far, but had been assured by many returning that the whole country was a vast humbug. They, too, had lost courage and faith and were going back to their homes. They told us of hundreds in Denver who would gladly work for their board, that men who were in the mines could not average a dollar a day, and all who could get away were leaving, urging us to go no farther. But we were not to be intimidated by their doleful tales. We would see for ourselves and continued on our way.

On the level lands and river bottoms of Kansas and Colorado were countless numbers of prairie dogs. These harmless little animals lived in villages, which we travelled through for weeks. These marmots made the air lively with their chattering, a peculiar short shrill squeak, rather than a bark, and the honeycombed soil was in motion with their antics. Sitting on their haunches on top of their pinnacled earth-burrows, they would peer curiously at us with their shining, beady eyes, until our approach jarred on their nerves, when they would suddenly disappear into the depths of their burrows. In many places there would be hundreds of them on an acre of ground. Beside the prairie dogs the coyote became familiar with us, never by day at close range however, but at nightfall he could be heard prowling about our pans and kettles.

Occasionally we passed a small settlement where a hardy pioneer had built for himself a rude home, partly and sometimes wholly of sod, with a rude forge and a primitive blacksmith shop and the inevitable whiskey mill. As we went farther west these little settlements were called cities, although consisting only of wretched little mud cabins, a few acres of land ploughed but unfenced, and sometimes beside these cabins a wayside house, from whose portals swung a wooden sign bearing the name Tavern. They were queer structures, partly tent and partly cabin. A few rough posts would be driven into the ground. These supported a ridgepole, across which some old pieces of canvas and ragged sailcloth formed a rude and primitive shelter, large enough, however to hold several barrels of whiskey.

On a dusty shelf above a counter made of boards resting on two empty barrels were a number of broken and cracked glasses, some half-emptied bottles, a few cans of oysters and sardines, and this constituted the entire outfit of the so-called "Tavern." Probably the Boniface of this crude establishment knew his business better than we did and had decided not to squander his capital in articles that were not considered a prime necessity.

And here I found as well as at other places on the road that whiskey was considered a prime necessity of every outfit on the plains. This had been the subject of many spirited discussions between my husband, brother and myself before and after starting on our trip. While laying in the supplies for our journey, everyone said we must take a barrel of that article with us. In spite of strenuous objections on my part, which were overruled, the whiskey was bought and duly stored with the rest of our provisions. At different points on our journey, I began to notice when we camped at night and also at our noon halt that our wagon had a drawing attraction for many of the other emigrants whose camps were in the vicinity, and it finally dawned on me that the barrel of whiskey was the alluring charm.

While my husband was a temperate man, yet he was socially and hospitably inclined, and many of the emigrants, taking undue advantage of these qualities, would too frequently for their own good and my peace of mind visit our camp. I knew it was useless to complain or interfere. But I patiently bided my time, and one day when no one was around, I quietly loosened the bung of the barrel of whiskey and by nightfall there was nothing left of the precious stuff, save the empty barrel and the aroma of its spilled contents. Not even a bottle was saved for emergencies and we never needed it.

The continual walking day after day over the hot, dry roads, the wading through heavy sand and dust for much of the distance, caused extreme suffering to the feet of many emigrants. My husband had not taken into consideration that he needed larger and roomier boots for this long tramp and continued to wear the same size he had been accustomed to wear at home. After a few weeks he began to complain that his feet hurt him. Every morning it required greater effort to get on his boots. At length, finding his feet continued to enlarge, he tried splitting his boots open to give his feet more room. This of course let in sand and alkali dust, which irritated them still more.

There was no store of any kind on the road where we could buy either boots or shoes or any other merchandise. Finally, his feet became so painful that he discarded boots altogether, and becoming too disabled to walk, was compelled to ride in the wagon for several days to allow the painful swelling to subside. My brother and I took turns in driving the oxen. Finally, we met a band of Indians from: whom we were able to buy some *moccasins* made from deer skin, which were large, soft, and comfortable, and afforded great relief. They proved to be strong and durable, and lasted until we reached Denver, where he was able to replenish his foot-gear in larger proportions.

CHAPTER 5

Indians

We gradually approached more desolate regions where we could look for miles over immense distances and see nothing but the long, dim perspective, and yet no sooner were we settled in our camp at evening and our fire lighted, when our Indian friends would appear, fathers, and mothers, and, judging from their appearance of old age, grandfathers and grandmothers, besides children of all ages, squatting as was their custom on the ground, watching silently though with greedy hungry eyes every mouthful that was cooked or eaten, sitting so near my fire that I was compelled to step over their feet in getting to and from the mess-box while I prepared my evening meal.

By many crude efforts in the sign language and an earnest use of a few Indian words that we had picked up among them, we attempted to carry on a sort of "Pigeon English" with the various tribes with whom we came in contact. There were two words we found that were thoroughly understood by them, and universally used wherever we met them, and they were "Bishket" and "Coffee." It would have been impossible for us to have fed any number of them, but frequently I gave an old man or old woman a cup of coffee and a biscuit, which they greedily swallowed, or a lump of sugar to a child, which was seized with extreme avidity.

After finishing our own meal and scraping off the remnants of food, bones, and meat rinds from our plates to the ground, there would be a mad rush of every Indian for the refuse, and it was amusing to see the scramble that would ensue for the discarded scraps. After lingering a while and finding there was no prospect of getting anything more to eat, they would slip away one by one as silently as they came, but there was no sign of any habitation, unless they burrowed in the ground.

When camping one Sunday near the Platte River we were surrounded by Indians as usual whenever we stopped for any length of time, and their continual attendance left us little, privacy. This Sunday I had washed my long hair to free it from the dust of travel and was engaged in brushing and combing out the tangles, having near me a small hand mirror. One brave who had been watching me so very intently that I wondered if he knew what he looked like. Without a moment's thought I took up the hand-glass and held it before him. I never saw such a look of surprise and consternation as came over his stolid countenance. He took the mirror in his hand, looked intently into it for some moment's turned it over, examined and looked again. Then taking it among the other Indians who were loitering in our camp, he showed them the mirror with their different reflections therein, which seemed to cause them much curious amusement, I think this must have been their first experience in seeing themselves as others saw them.

After a while he brought the mirror back to me. I had given up all hopes of having it in my possession again. At length this Indian with several of his tribe silently departed, but in a few hours returned with some new recruits, all decked in their paint, feathers, beads, and blankets. Approaching me he made signs for the mirror again. When I handed it to him, he burst forth in a guttural sort of laugh and immediately turned it on his new followers, who in turn expressed much amazement at this first view of themselves. The Indians generally were not voluble, but a wonderful flow of unintelligible sounds came to my ears as they discussed among themselves the merits or demerits of the strange little mirror.

A band of mounted Sioux met us one day. They were friendly in their advances and stopped to trade with us. I would state here that the Sioux Indians were the finest looking warriors we had seen. Their ponies and horses were richly caparisoned, and their blankets, which were supplied by the United States Government, were gay with bright colours. The headdress of the men was unique and imposing. Sable braids of hair fell down each side of their painted faces, and the crowns of their heads were decorated with the coloured feathers from the wild birds of the mountain and plain.

Their buckskin jackets were jewelled with beads and hung with the teeth of wild animals. Descending from their long braids of hair, were graduating discs of bright silver made from the half-dollars that were paid them by the government. These were hammered out very thin, until the first was as large as a small saucer, and the others grew gradually smaller as they reached nearly to the ground. These discs were hung on strong but slender strips of buckskin, and glittered gaily in the bright sunlight, as the warriors, mounted on their fleet ponies galloped over the plain.

We found the Sioux tribe very friendly, too friendly in fact, for my peace of mind, for one huge brave, gayly bedecked and most grotesquely painted, took a great fancy to me. Bringing a number of ponies to our camp, he at length made my husband understand that he wanted me in exchange. This was the first time I was really frightened at their advances. Though I knew they were a friendly band and under the care and protection of the government, yet I was filled with a fear that I could not wholly overcome, and urged my husband to move on as rapidly as possible, so we left our camp next morning before the break of day. About noon, as we ascended some low rolling hills, I looked back on the plain and saw a number of mounted Indians approaching us very rapidly and driving a large band of ponies before them.

My heart almost ceased beating, as we were completely at their mercy if they meant us harm. Finally, they overtook us. We halted our team and had a lengthy parley with them. They proved to be the brave and his followers of the day before. He had added more ponies to his band, thinking my husband had refused to trade because they had not offered a sufficient number. After numerous signs and shakes of the head, they at last understood there was no prospect of business. Very reluctantly they mounted their ponies and left us, to my great relief. The next few days I rode very closely in the wagon. Before they departed, however, I cooked them a good dinner, and James treated them liberally to his best tobacco, so we parted good friends.

Early in the forenoon of one eventful day we met the first warlike band of Indians. I was walking some distance ahead of the wagon, when in that clear bright atmosphere there appeared on the level plain a cloud of dust far off to the left of our road. I usually carried the field glasses with me and I quickly looked to see what I could discover. At first the dust was so dense that the eye could not penetrate it, but soon there was revealed the forms of many moving animals. My first thoughts were "buffaloes," and I hurriedly retraced my steps to the wagon and the protection of my husband and brother. I had scarcely reached the wagon before my ears were filled with the din of most uncanny character, and out of the cloud of dust on numerous ponies rode a formidable looking band of Indians, many of them arrayed in the most whimsical and barbarous style that one could imagine.

There was not the slightest attempt at uniformity in costume. Some of them wore the discarded and ragged clothes of emigrants, from which hung strings of buckskin knotted with gay beads and buttons, and interspersed here and there with a tin spoon or fork stolen from the emigrants. Their faces were painted in the most grotesque manner, and their coarse and matted hair, which grew long and scraggy, was ornamented with tufts of feathers from the wild birds of the plain and the tails of wild animals. Some were attired in the usual breech cloth, while many were wrapped in gaudy blankets of red and blue.

Among this motley crowd were several that might have been devils let loose from the so-called infernal regions, for on their beetle brows were crowns made from buffalo horns, their limbs naked to the knee, were covered with buckskin leggings and on their feet were *moccasins*. Others had made great effort to array themselves in fanciful attire of skins peculiarly painted and embroidered by their skilful squaws. Yet we discovered among the number some few who were not dressed at all.

As they bore down on us in their rapid approach, we were almost speechless with fright. Our first impression was that we were to be an-nihilated at once. We saw at a glance that they were warriors ready for the fray, and had made elaborate preparations to go forth on the war path. They were armed with all sorts of weapons, knives and shields of various and strange devices, but the bow and arrow, the natural weapon of the red man was most in evidence. They surrounded our wagon on all sides, making numerous signs and gestures and uttering words of Indian jargon that were Greek to us, for we could not un-derstand a syllable. Then despairing of making themselves understood, they pointed first east then west, then to their ponies and held up their hands with extended fingers.

All in vain. We could only shake our heads. At last, finding it was only a waste of time to parley with us, their chieftain gave the com-mand, and re-mounting their ponies, they sped away, giving voice again to their bloodcurdling yells and leaving us to recover slowly from our suspense. We drew a long breath of relief when we realised that we were still possessed of our usual amount of hair. We afterwards learned that they were in pursuit of some other marauding band of Indians who had stolen and run off with a large number of their ponies.

That night we camped near a few cottonwoods on the banks of a small stream. The wind blew in fitful gusts and the limbs of the cot-tonwoods rocked restlessly, making mournful sounds. From every side we were startled by noises we could not place; strange rustlings caused us to peer sharply into the shadows, footsteps seemed to stealthily approach and then skulk away; even the thin and scraggy bushes appeared to suddenly close together as if someone were behind them, and we feared that the Indians of the day, knowing that we were alone, might surround us in the hours of darkness, take us unawares, and massacre us. None of us slept through the long hours of that night. We were afraid to close our eyes for fear of their stealthy return, but dawn found us unmolested.

I have said that neither the Indians nor ourselves could understand each other in conversation. Yet we found on several occasions, that they had picked up and readily adopted a number of phrases from the emigrants, particularly the teamsters, whose vocabulary of profane words was extensive. The usual salutation of the Indians whom we first met was "How." But after hearing the irate teamsters from day to day cursing their overworked and often contrary cattle, the Indians very quickly adopted some of their pet phrases. Often when we met them, they saluted us in this manner, "Gee, Whoa, Haw. G-d d-n you," and did not appear to know that this was not the regular manner of saluting.

We saw but few Indian lodges. Those we did see were of the Sioux and Pawnee tribes. Usually, their camps were remote from the travelled highway. We had been induced to take a shorter cut that took us in sight of one of their encampments. These lodges were built in circular form, a number of light poles forming the support, around which were stretched buffalo hides which the squaws had ingeniously sewed together. Some of these lodges were unique in their way, decorated and painted in accordance with the red man's idea of art, with grotesque faces and queer figures of animals, and strange hieroglyphics emblematic of something in their creed.

Many of these tribes did not bury their dead. Perceiving at some distance poles set upright on the ground and what appeared to us like a huge shelf above them, we saw on approaching nearer the form of a human body well wrapped in blankets and buffalo skins, and found that it was the Indian manner of burial.

A little familiarity with these aborigines will convince one that it needs a very poetic mind to make them even bearable. We found them not only lazy but covered with vermin and while squatting around our camp it was the principal relaxation of the squaws to spend their time overlooking the heads of their papooses and catching and killing the insects that inhabited them', very much to my disgust. The Indian

43

man abhors labour, and they looked on the white man with scorn and derision whenever they performed any duties to relieve the labours of their wives. The squaw accepted her life of toil as her just due for being born a woman.

It was the squaw who dressed and tanned the skins and made the garments that the lazy Indian wore. It was she who manufactured the rough utensils in which the food was cooked. It was she who took down and pitched the rude wigwam and gathered the fuel, dressed and cooked the game, often walking for miles to bring it home, when her arrogant lord returned from the hunt. She made his rude tents after tanning and dressing the rough hides of which, they were made, his *moccasins* and his clothing.

In many of the tribes these women were exceedingly skilful, and it was wonderful what an amount of work they could accomplish with the most primitive tools. In addition to all this, when she felt the pangs of approaching motherhood, the squaw would betake herself to the banks of some nearby stream and there all alone without the aid of a nurse or accoucheur her babe would come into the world. After giving her new-born child a hasty dip in the cold stream, it was wrapped in a rough skin, strapped to a board and borne back to camp on the mother's shoulders. Then with all the stoicism for which the Indian character is noted, she resumed her interrupted duties.

CHAPTER 6

Sick on the Desert

Even to the most courageous there were hours of depression and discouragement. Our days were not always sunshine, nor our route through pleasant lands. The fertile soil covered but a small portion of our journey between the Missouri River and Denver. After the first month or six wrecks of our pilgrimage the change of vegetation became very apparent. The sage brush, that forerunner of sterile soil, began to crop out here and there. The farther we travelled the thicker it grew, particularly in the dry and sandy localities. Its only redeeming feature that I could discover was that it served for fuel in the absence of any other wood. We were amazed at the magnitude of these barren, unfenced plains. The occasional little hamlet was left behind and only at rare intervals did we come on the solitary cabin of some brave pre-emptor, who showed more courage than wisdom in settling on such a forlorn hope in Uncle Sam's domains.

The wind had full sweep over these barren plains. Many times, it was almost impossible for anyone to walk against it. Frequently we staked our wagon down with ropes and also our stock to keep them from stampeding, for the wind and showers of blinding sand came with such force that neither man nor beast could face it. At such times we could cook no food, but crawling into the wagon, tying down the covers on every side, were forced to content ourselves with dry crackers and molasses.

These winds tried my patience sorely and seemed to act directly on the nerves; and as for cooking around a camp-fire when the wind was blowing a gale, it required a greater amount of fortitude and self-control than I possessed. I tried to keep my hasty temper within bounds, but no matter on which side of the fire I stood when cooking, the ever-shifting smoke blinded me, and the gale whisked my short skirts over the fire, until I found not only my clothes but my temper ablaze. I would make a brave effort to be cheerful and patient until the camp work was done. Then starting out ahead of the team and my men folks, when I thought I had gone beyond hearing distance, I would throw myself down on the unfriendly desert and give way like a child to sobs and tears, wishing myself back home with my friends and chiding myself for consenting to take this wild-goose chase. But after a good cry I would feel relieved, and long before I was again visible to husband or brother, I had assumed a more cheerful frame of mind, whether I felt it or not.

Besides wind and rain storms we would often encounter great swarms of gnats, which would annoy our stock almost to the verge of madness, stinging our own faces and hands, getting into our food and making it impossible to drink our coffee, without first skimming them off. These swarms of insects would last two or three days before we would leave them behind us.

As we proceeded on our journey the streams of water grew smaller and farther apart and the great plains drier and dustier. There were days of travel with scarcely enough water for our stock, and that so strongly impregnated with alkali that a very small quantity would satisfy. Oh, how we longed for the sight of a cold, clear spring of water. We could sometimes see for miles ahead of us what looked to our longing eyes a lake of limpid water, but on coming nearer it we found it was only a thin alkali incrustation covering many acres of the smooth sands, and later on we were compelled to make a drive of nearly sixty miles without a drop of water for our stock.

Our poor cattle were choked and dry with the great thirst. When at last they scented water they were almost unmanageable, and struck a bee-line for it, paying not the slightest attention to the roadway, but speeding as fast as they could travel over hills and hummocks, caring naught for the safety or comfort of those riding in the wagon. While in this almost arid region we endeavoured to keep our small keg filled with water, but found it impossible to carry enough for our stock. Indeed, we had to use it very sparingly ourselves.

Through many parts of Kansas, Nebraska, and Colorado the question of fuel was constantly before us. Days and days passed without seeing a piece of timber as big as one's little finger. Our only fuel was buffalo chips. This was the sun-dried excrement of that animal. It was my custom in the early hours of the afternoon as I walked, to carry a basket or sack, and fill it with buffalo chips, often wandering a distance from the road to find a sufficient quantity with which to cook our evening meal and enough to bake our bread for the next day.

This proved at last to be quite a laborious task for me, because the numerous caravans ahead of us had gathered up all that lay near the roadway and I was compelled to cover considerable territory before finding a sufficient supply. The sack of buffalo chips became a heavy burden before I reached the wagon. I had been performing this task for days, when one afternoon we passed some low hills on which grew a few dwarfed and Stunted pine trees. They were only about a quarter of a mile from the road, and I asked James and my brother to drive to them, and cut me enough of the wood to last us for a day or two.

But men on the plains I had found were not so accommodating nor so ready to serve or wait upon women as they were in more civilized communities. Driving a lot of wayward cattle all day in the hot sun, over heavy roads of sand and dust was not conducive to politeness or accommodation. When the drivers were weary and foot-sore, they were none too ready to deviate a hand's breadth from the travelled road. Therefore, as it required almost half a mile of extra effort to get that wood for me, they thought it unnecessary trouble and refused.

I was feeling somewhat under the weather and unusually tired, and crawling into the wagon told them if they wanted fuel for the evening meal, they could get it themselves and cook the meal also, and laying my head down on a pillow, I cried myself to sleep. When I awakened, I found that we had camped and they were taking me at my word. The only fuel in sight was across the deep and cold stream of the Platte, but they waded across the stream hatchet in hand, the water coming up to their hips. On the farther side grew some small willows which they cut and bore on their shoulders back to camp, and after many efforts at last got the fire to burn and the supper cooked.

James came to the wagon where I was lying and meekly asked how much baking powder to put in the biscuits. I replied shortly, "Oh, as much as you please." I will admit that his biscuits that night were as light and nice as any that I have ever eaten, and both he and my brother were quite elated with their success in getting the evening meal, and said it did not matter whether I cooked any more for them as they could do just as well if not better than I did. The coffee also was fine, but the dried corn which they had tried to cook was not a complete success; This was a delicacy we did not indulge in every day. It was usually saved for a special treat for our Sunday dinner, and I had always put it to soak for several hours to soften it before cooking, a precaution the new cooks had not taken.

I was hungry and ate too heartily of the underdone corn. The consequence was that I was very ill with a severe and painful attack of dysentery for several days. Finally becoming so weakened that I could no longer climb in or out of the wagon, I was compelled to keep my bed as we journeyed along. The jolting motion of the wagon soon became a perfect torture to me, and at last became so unendurable that I implored my husband to take me out, make my bed on the sand and let me die in peace. He, poor man, was very much alarmed at my condition, and was at his wit's end to know what to do for me.

Complying with my wish, he had halted the team in the middle of the forenoon and was preparing my bed on the ground. We were in the meantime overtaken by another emigrant team, whose sole occupant was a blunt, old Missourian. He stopped to inquire the cause of our delay so early in the day. James told him of my illness, describing my symptoms The old man then said, "What your woman needs is a good, big dose of castor ile. That'll straighten her out all right."

Now one of the most peculiar oversights in preparing for this journey was that we had not provided ourselves with any medicine. Not one of us had ever been ill, nor had we been accustomed to illness in our families, and our friends believing in the hydropathic treatment, had not suggested such a need to us. We were also five hundred miles from a drug store, but after a moment's thought, I remembered that among the toilet articles in my trunk was a bottle containing castor oil, bergamot, and bay rum, put up specially for a hair tonic that was much in vogue at that time. This was sought for at once by my husband, and pouring out a tea cup full of the vile stuff in order to get enough of the oil, with grim determination I swallowed it down.

Oh, the horror of that draught! To this day I never smell the odours of bay rum or bergamot without the vision of a poor, sick emigrant woman lying on the sands of the desert. Offensive and obnoxious as the dose was, it had the desired effect and acted like a charm. I have since recommended the remedy a number of times. In a few days I was quite recovered and ready to continue our interrupted journey. I noticed that my men folks were only too willing to turn over the culinary department to me again, and really made quite commendable efforts to keep me supplied with fuel thereafter.

The United States Government sent out many trains of provisions to the different posts that were stationed far out on the plains, and these wagon trains would often travel near each other for help and protection, their white canvas-covered wagons sometimes reaching as far as the eye could see. Many of these trains were composed entirely of ox teams, and their drivers had a profane vocabulary that sent cold chills over me. Never in my life had I heard such strings of oaths come from the mouth of man. These immense caravans were called bull trains and their captains called bull-train bosses. The men who drove the teams were called bull whackers. All of these government teamsters in their moments of leisure were anxious for something to read.

Before leaving home, I had stowed away among my belongings a few favourite volumes to while away the hours of enforced leisure. My Shakespeare, Byron, and Burns and a few others that I could not part with I soon learned to hide very carefully and peruse with drawn curtains, or they would have disappeared from my eye. The few novels and magazines that I possessed were loaned and re-loaned until they were so tattered and torn as to be scarcely legible. It was astonishing how great was the demand for something to read in those days of overland travel. The majority of those crossing the plains had taken no books with them, burdening themselves with nothing save the bare necessities of life.

Anything in the shape of print was greedily devoured. Every scout, trapper, or other lone frontiersman with whom we came in contact would eagerly inquire for old newspapers, magazines or novels—anything to read. It was impossible to buy reading matter on the road in those days. In fact, over a stretch of five hundred miles there were only three or four post offices, and from the time we left St. Joseph on the Missouri River until we reached Denver, three long months, we had had no news from home and the dear ones left behind us.

At intervals we were electrified with a passing glimpse of the overland stage, bearing the mails and sometimes passengers from the East, but they flew by us with such break-neck speed, that it was impossible to even hail them. Yet I still watched for them day by day for they seemed to be a connecting link between us and civilization. Occasionally we would pass an overland stage station, a low hut or cabin constructed wholly of adobe or dried mud.

These huts were said to be very cool in summer and warm in winter, their walls being from two to three feet in thickness, and were considered proof against the severe blizzards that swept over the country, as well as bullet proof in attacks from hostile Indians. I often wished that I might look into one of those huts, but never chanced to pass one when the host was at home. I had not the temerity to invade one without invitation, although the latch-string invariably hung on the outside. We usually stopped only long enough to take a drink from the rusty cup that hung from a pail of water near the door.

One of the most wonderful sights on these desolate plains was the mirage. The first time this strange phenomenon appeared I was filled with astonishment. While riding one day along the monotonous level road and gazing ahead at the wide expanse of sand and sage brush, a peculiarly brilliant and dazzling light appeared like sunlight on the water. My first impression was that we were approaching a lake or some other large body of water. As I looked, this seemed to change, and a number of buildings came into view, but all upside down, and while still gazing at them they slowly faded from my vision, and the supposed water again came into view. I was so overcome with the wonderful vision that I could not wait for the others to overtake me, and turning my horse, rode rapidly back to the wagon to see if my husband and brother had witnessed the wonderful sight. They were as much surprised as myself, and though we had often read of the phenomena of mirages, this was our first sight of one. After that we saw them several times.

From Cottonwood after a tedious, long drive, we arrived one night at a place called Fremont springs, and here we found a fine spring of clear, cool, delicious water. For days we had climbed and descended hills and passed through a series of sand canyons. For many miles after leaving Cottonwood our road lay near the creeping, treacherous Platte. The Platte itself was not alkaline, but many times our trail was some distance from the river, and our cattle would become so thirsty before they could be driven to the river, that they would seek to satisfy their thirst in the many shallow lakelets that abounded near the stream, and these lakelets were in many instances almost saturated solutions of soda and potash.

We ourselves as well as our poor cattle enjoyed the delicious draughts from Fremont springs, which was considered the finest water between the Rocky Mountains and the Missouri River. We felt like falling down and worshipping this fountain, cooling the parched lips of man and beast whose fate had led them beside the stagnant pool and dull, creeping, muddy waters of the Platte.

Much of our journey after leaving Cottonwood was near and in sight of the South Platte River, but its proximity failed to moisten the stretches of sand along our gloomy pathway. It crawled along between low banks, and one day I ventured to take a bath in its waters, but on descending its banks, the oozy loam glided too swiftly beneath my feet and in a moment, I realised I was in its treacherous quicksands. I scrambled up the bank by main force, shuddering to think how soon I might have been engulfed in the muddy depths of its deceptive waters. On these desert wastes the wind blew at a rate of ten knots an hour and it was so filled with sand that it seemed like earth in motion instead of air.

Along this dreary route we walked day by day. Everything was grey. The few sickly weeds that grew upon its dry soil would crumble at the touch; here and there a single sunflower gave a touch of colour; a few sickly cacti bloomed. Flowers that had enlivened the landscape farther back had entirely disappeared. In their place the naked land swarmed with ant-hills and myriads of grasshoppers and huge brown crickets abounded. At night the wind blew even more violently, and the tempest of sand that came flying with it filled the air, and everything that lay untouched for a time was powdered half an inch deep with it.

Through one of these storms the overland stage from the East overtook and passed us. It surged along bearing about a dozen wearied, dusty, dejected looking passengers. I noticed that they seemed to be hanging on to life at the neck of sundry flat pocket flasks. As we came near Denver, the South Platte seemed to make its nearest approach to beauty, and in many places, it was studded with beautiful islands, picturesque indeed with their emerald green foliage of graceful willows. When we neared Beaver Creek a beautiful landscape began to unfold. The river seemed to widen out into a huge lagoon. I remember the rosy hues of a beautiful sunrise that unfolded to our view. The mirrored water was filled with wild ducks, the river swarming with teal and mallard, their beautiful green and blue plumage looking gay in the early sunlight as they glided through the water with exquisite grace.

The journey toward Denver might have been divided into four stages—the prairies, the less fertile plains, the desert, and then the Rocky Mountains. At this late day it is very easy to underrate the toilsome marches of many weeks—now that one can travel in forty-eight hours over an extent of country which forty or fifty years ago baffled the progress of the venturesome pioneer. I remember how joyfully we greeted the first scrubby pine trees, giving us hope that the desert was nearly past and the mountains were not far off. Their soft and tender green was soothing to our sunburnt vision, and when we halted at nightfall we found a numerous band, who had made the long journey through this woodless region, building huge fires with the dead pine branches, and taking solid comfort in the cheer and warmth of the ruddy, leaping blaze of which they had been so long deprived. Soon the foothills of the Rocky Mountains were in evidence.

Arriving at Bijou, Colorado, we encountered one of the severest storms I ever saw on the plains. We imagined we had seen severe storms in Kansas, but this one descended on us so suddenly and the rain and sleet came down in such torrents, that we had scarcely time to stow away the provisions made for our evening meal. While James and my brother were hurriedly chaining our oxen to the wagon to prevent them from stampeding before the pelting rain and sleet, and staking the wagon to the ground to keep it from being overturned by the fierce wind, I and my little son climbed into the wagon for shelter. The noise of the rain and hail on our canvas cover was deafening and seemed as if it would tear our frail shelter into tatters.

No warm supper for us that night. We crawled into our blankets damp, tired, and hungry, wondering how long it would continue. Not until after midnight was the wild fury of the storm somewhat abated. A drizzling rain succeeded which made the roads almost impassable for days, while the heavy grades became so steep and slippery that we were compelled to wait for help to pull us up their steep inclines. As we came nearer the foothills these high winds seemed to become more prevalent and swept over us at times with relentless force. Every night our wagon was securely staked to prevent an upset by the fury of the gale. These high winds no doubt accounted for the lack of timber, for the young trees were so rocked and wrenched that their roots were not firm enough to draw up what little nourishment the porous soil could give them.

But gradually a change was taking place. The pine trees which appeared at intervals, although stunted and dwarfed, gave variety and softness to the landscape which hitherto had been so monotonous and drear. The hills became more rolling, and the valleys deeper with water courses more frequent in their depths, and our thirsty stock could drink their fill without robbing those who came after us. The timberless plain ceased to be desert and was once more fertile. Our progress now was one of gradual ascent. In many instances our pathway was unlovely and unsatisfactory. Here and there a shady ridge forcibly reminded us of the drift of the many terrible sand storms we had so often passed through. When darkness came upon us, near some little mountain stream, where we made our lonely camp, our voices sounded singularly clear in the cool, clear air, and instinctively we drew nearer each other with the knowledge of our loneliness. This loudness of our voices was the first thing we noticed that gave evidence of a change of air from the plains. We could distinctly hear the sound of a human voice two or three hundred rods away.

Far out on the plains for miles before reaching Denver, we were told to keep a sharp lookout for a first view of Pike's Peak, and for many days we were straining our vision to the extreme limit. The first view I had of the mountain was in the form of a vaporous cloud. Gradually this began to form a sharper and more distinct outline, until at last, we could see clearly the glittering peak, covered with snow, rising to a height far above all other peaks, like a sentinel watching over the plain. As our gaze rested from time to time on this Monarch of the Mountains, so full of majesty and power, other less lofty peaks were presented to our view, until finally the whole majestic range of the Rocky Mountains was outlined before us. As our eyes were fixed upon the towering mountains looming up so grandly, we easily fancied that an ordinary swift pedestrian could reach them in a day's length.

At any rate our slow-moving team would bring us to them in a few short hours. But for days our course westward still lay along the plain and over additional rising foothills, while many weary miles intervened before we entered these mountain gorges and explored the strange and mysterious paths leading us up and down through those lofty ranges.

Chapter 7

The Parting with My Brother

At last, in the latter part of June, after three months' wearisome journey, we made our way down the mountains and over the lower range of the foothills into the then primitive village of Denver. Picture if you can an almost level plain surrounded on all sides by towering mountains, whose highest peaks were snow crowned even in midsummer. In the centre of this great plain stood Denver. I shall never forget our advent into that "City of the Mountain and Plain."

A few days previous we had fallen in with several wagons with their full complement of men, women, and children—a motley crowd, the men unshaven and unshorn, with long, sunburnt whiskers, their stained and weather-beaten garments begrimed with the dust and dirt of the plains—the women and children with their huge sun bonnets pulled over sunburnt brows, ragged, unkempt and dirty, their short, rough dresses in tatters from coming into too frequent contact with the camp fire, many of them bare footed from the rough roads and long travel which had played sad havoc with their only pair of shoes. I doubt whether any one of us would have been recognized, so changed was our exterior from the trim and nattily-attired trio that left home in the early spring, now wearied with urging contrary and tired cattle over miles of treeless and waterless wastes, barren deserts and alkali plains.

I had pictured Denver a thriving, bustling, busy city, but nearly fifty years ago it was an exceedingly primitive town, consisting of numerous tents and numbers of rude and illy constructed cabins, with nearly as many rum shops and low saloons as cabins, Horses, cows, and hogs roamed at will over the greater part of the village. Very few of the humble homes were enclosed with a fence. These inferior shanties, built of logs and rough boards, were clustered together near the banks of Cherry creek.

In the lower part of the town the vacant places were occupied by the Indian huts of a band of the Arapahoe tribe, who were at war with the Utes, and who trusted that the presence of the white man in their vicinity would afford protection to their families against attack, while their own braves were off fighting or stealing in the mountains beyond. The relations of the Arapahoes and the Ute Indians were not of the most cordial character, for hereditary feuds and occasional warlike sallies had from time to time disturbed that perfect mutual concord so important for neighbours to maintain. Each tribe prided itself on its superiority to the other, and it would be deemed a great disgrace for an Arapahoe maiden to marry a Ute, and *vice versa.*

Their poor, overworked squaws were busily engaged in the labours of the camp, cooking their vile compounds, and making the skins of wild animals into the garments that they wore. Loafing around in the sand and dirt were the indolent and unemployed braves, while their filthy offspring played naked in the sand. These so-called braves wore nothing but a narrow strip of cloth around their loins. While we were still camping in Denver, the warriors who had gone out to give battle to the Utes returned, bringing with them a number of horses captured from the enemy, and making both night and day hideous with their *pow-wows* and secret incantations. The dismal wailing and howling of the squaws, bringing back from the fight their dead and wounded, made the surroundings anything but cheerful.

Before our arrival, and imagining Denver to be a city with some pretensions to civilization, I had confided to my husband my intention of making a more prepossessing toilet before appearing on its streets. I carefully donned my best riding habit, and made myself as comely as circumstances would allow. Mounting my horse sidewise in the saddle, which I had hitherto ridden astride, I gaily rode through the one street of the town until we crossed a rude bridge, spanning Cherry creek. Here our wayward cattle balked. A loud crack from the swirling whip urging them on frightened my "Rosinante," who gave his accustomed squat, and I found myself ingloriously dismounted and lying at full length on the boards of the bridge.

I was quickly lifted up by a chivalrous miner. After this ignominious debut I was only too glad to retire from sight under the cover of our wagon until we found a place to locate. We drove across the stream and camped on the banks of the Cherry Creek opposite the village. We were very much discouraged by the outlook and the surroundings. The whole town seemed to be in a turmoil. In front of our camp on the other side of the creek we witnessed the hanging of two men by the Vigilance Committee. This filled me with horror and dismay, although doubtless they deserved it, for the town was overflowing with vile characters.

During our short stay in Denver, we removed the bed of the wagon from off the running gear, to make some necessary repairs, and placed it upon the ground. One morning James had gone into the town to purchase some needed supplies, leaving me and my little son alone in camp, although other campers were in our vicinity. I had baked my day's supply of bread and placed it in the back of the wagon to cool. Seating myself in the front of the wagon bed, for more privacy I had drawn my curtains while I sat busily mending and conversing with my child. Suddenly, without sound or warning, my curtain was rudely pulled aside and there before me stood a huge Indian demanding bread.

His tone and manner was so insolent and overbearing that it aroused my ire, and although frightened I assumed a brave front and quickly told him I had no bread to give him. He said, "You heap lie. Plenty bread," at the same time pointing to my cooling loaves, but I shook my head and gave him to understand that he could not have it. My brother's gun stood within the wagon close beside me. The Indian readied in as if to take it, but I anticipated his thoughts, and seizing the gun, placed it beyond his reach. While his gaze was fixed upon me in open-eyed wonder, I also had time to look him over and saw hanging at his belt a number of bleeding scalps taken in the last fight with the Utes.

These he loosened for my closer inspection and handing them to me, told or tried to tell in his broken jargon of English and Indian what a brave chieftain he was. Keeping up the show of courage I had assumed for the occasion, but inwardly quaking, I took the bunch of bloody scalps in my hands and counted them, taking care, however, that my hands should not come in contact with the blood. The Indian looked amazed and surprised at my temerity, and with the startled exclamation, "Humph, white squaw no fear," left me as suddenly as he came.

The people that inhabited the embryo city of Denver were a most diverse and varied lot. Every class of citizen was represented. Doctors, lawyers, merchants, stage drivers, gamblers and preachers, were all in evidence and from the general style of dress it was difficult to make a distinction. All alike wore the red flannel shirt of the miner and ox driver. The most prosperous lawyer or the most successful business man or merchant was as roughly garbed as the commonest labourer. Low drinking saloons were to be seen on every hand, and gambling dens of every kind abounded.

Many of the squalid adventurers lived in the crudest manner, with no law save that enacted by the Vigilance Committee. No wonder that so many coming into this dismal village, chafed and irritated with their long journey, were disheartened and discouraged and turned their faces homewards. Miners and laborers were constantly coming into Denver from the various mining districts with conflicting reports. We hardly knew whom or what to believe. Many of them were out of money and out of heart. Others who had been more fortunate told of the rich strikes they had made.

We met and talked with a number of these more optimistic prospectors who had recently come down for more supplies from a place that was then known as "Gregory's Diggings." Their encouraging reports of gold discovered re-kindled the ardour of my brother, who thus far on our journey had been satisfied to stay with us, but who now decided that he was tired of travel, and was persuaded to go back with the prospectors to the mines. Taking with him a few tools and a stock of provisions and with high hopes that he was to make his fortune in a little while and return home a rich man, he started for the mines. He was as sanguine and eager as if none had ever failed.

I dreaded to part with him and leave him in that wild country to battle with all the privations that must come to adventurous prospectors in their search for gold. All men were not fitted by nature for gold diggers, and this brother of mine—hitherto a pampered and petted darling, just from college, unused to hardships—what dangers menaced his footsteps. What trials lay in wait for him! But no pleadings of mine were of any avail, so I bade him God speed and we parted in Denver on the banks of Cherry Creek. Long afterwards I heard that after he had suffered untold privations and dangers, at last by weary stages of slow travel, sometimes on foot, he reached home, a sadder, poorer, but a wiser man.

I have mentioned our great disappointment in the village of Denver and its environment as we then found it in the summer of eighteen sixty. My husband said to me after bidding my brother farewell, "What are we going to do? Shall we remain here, return home, or push on to California?" My pride would not consent to turn my face homeward, although my heart yearned to do so, and I was so utterly disgusted with Denver and its squalid surroundings; with the Arapa-hoes who had made the last two or three nights indescribably hideous; with the combined drunkenness and rioting that existed everywhere in this society composed of the roughest classes of all states and nations; with this log city of maybe two hundred dwellings, not half of them completed, and the other half not fit to be inhabited by any self-respecting woman, that I felt life amid such surroundings would be to me unendurable. Without argument or hesitation, I said, "We will go on to California."

By this time, we had come nearly to the bottom of our very limited purse. We had our wagon loaded with plenty of provisions, enough and more to last us for a continued journey to California. Yet we could not think of going farther without ready money to pay for the numerous ferries and other incidentals that were likely to occur on the road. So here we had to consider ways and means to replenish our scanty hoard, and to see what we could spare from our scanty belongings that could be disposed of to the best advantage. The weather was growing colder as we advanced further into the mountains.

Hitherto we had travelled without a tent. We now found that we could no longer dispense with that comfort, and we must provide a camp stove for use in rainy weather. Among our stores we had packed two cases of thin, cutglass goblets and wine glasses, which were cumbersome and heavy, so we decided to lighten our load of them and strengthen our purse. James approached one of the best saloons that infested the town and told the proprietor of his wish to dispose of them to the best advantage. As freight of all kinds had to be brought overland, articles of that variety were in great demand and expensive as well. The saloon man at once offered him a very satisfactory price for all the glassware, enough to warrant us to make the necessary purchases for the comfort of our extended journey, and money sufficient to last, as we hoped, until we arrived at our destination in California.

After re-packing and re-adjusting our load, we two alone with our little son took up the lonely march through seemingly endless mountain chains, and over desert lands for more hundreds of weary miles toward the land of the setting sun. Our road led over what was then known as the "Cherokee Trail" which we had learned formed the shortest practical route from Denver to Salt Lake City.

CHAPTER 8

Celebrating the Fourth of July

We camped the first night out from Denver beside a small rippling stream, whose waters as they flowed over the pebbly bottom fell soothingly on the ear, while from its deeper pools I caught the most delicious fish I ever ate. The night was cool and breezy, but within our now comfortable tent, we set up our little camp stove and built our fire. We soon crawled in under our blankets, said our prayers to the stars that brightly twinkled through the trees overhead, and thought of home and the comfortable beds we had left so far behind us.

For several days we pushed on through a reasonably level country, though we encountered many deep, steep-banked, dry gullies, and some very rough roads, until we arrived at last at the banks of the Cache-la-Poudre River, seventy or eighty miles from Denver and by far the most formidable stream we had met. We had been told that a rope ferry was stationed here that would enable us to cross this stream with safety. Unluckily on our arrival we found that it had gone down the stream and nothing had since been heard of it. An old scout, whom we met here, assured us that there was no safe crossing for our team, as the current was very swift. If we were venturesome enough to try to ford it our wagon and cattle would be carried downstream.

Here was a dilemma. We dared to go no further without assistance, though anxious to pursue our journey with some degree of haste, prudence warned us that to cross an unknown stream alone was taking too many risks. We decided to wait and see what would turn up. A merciful providence had helped us before through many an obstacle. Why not trust once more? Here we prepared to camp for an indefinite period, as there were few people, if any, coming or going over this desolate road.

At the close of the second day of our waiting there appeared, mounted on powerful horses, a white man and two Indians, trappers, coming from their isolated cabin in the heart of the Rocky Mountains. They stayed with us an hour or more, sharing our evening meal. We begged their assistance in our perplexity, and they promised us if we would await their return the next day they would help us ford the uncertain stream. Of course, we waited for them, for we could not help ourselves, though we feared that they might not return for our relief.

However, our breakfast was scarcely over the next morning when our eyes were gladdened by the sight of them returning with their horses loaded with pelts. These they hastily unloaded, and mounting their horses, they plunged into the stream, swimming them up and down until they found a reasonably safe crossing and a secure landing place, where our team with their help could reach the opposite shore with safety. Then tying a rope to the heads of our two lead oxen, a man on each side on their strong horses, we went boldly down into the deep and turbid stream. Anxiously we watched each move of the fearless horsemen as they measured the depths of the foaming stream. The current was strong and swift, and should accident happen, fatal disaster seemed almost certain.

Committing our all into the hands of our Heavenly Father, we rode down into what might have been the chasm of death, where the rapid current, yawning: to receive us in its cold depths, seemed ready to bury us from sight. Owing to the steepness of the bank we came near upsetting the wagon as we entered the stream, but the second Indian rode by the wagon side and dexterously righted it. The water was deep for about fifty yards or more, the bottom broken and filled with huge boulders, and the current swift and strong. I crouched in the wagon with my little son trembling with fear, while my husband, riding the ox nearest the wheel, urged his swimming cattle on.

Luckily our wagon bed was not afloat, although the water came up into it. When the brave oxen pulled us up the steep banks safe once more, I uttered a prayer of thanksgiving and gladly helped unload and dry out some of our goods that had got wet in the crossing. With many and heartfelt thanks to the obliging trio, who refused any other remuneration, we bade *adieu* to them, as they again mounted their horses, re-crossed the stream and went on their way. Another day's delay waiting for our goods and wagon to dry out, and we resumed our interrupted journey.

The Cherokee trail, over which we were traveling, soon ran into the mountains near the Cache-la-Poudre, and henceforth for many weary miles we did not come across, neither were we overtaken by any emigrant or others moving westward. While in camp near this river I could not help but wonder at the beauty of the grand scenery surrounding us on all sides. Above us was the bright dome of a heaven so free from all earthly smoke and vapor, so clear and transparent, that the stars seemed closer and shone with an exceeding brilliancy. The air was filled with a balmy sweetness, and yet so limpid and clear that even in the starlight we could catch faint glimpses of the shimmering trees in the distant river.

Our camp fire leaped up and roared in great flames, as if it, too, tasted the unlimited oxygen in the atmosphere. Beyond its bright light, purple, black and grey bluffs towered up in the clear, dark sky. The silence was profound, broken only now and then by a yelp from a coyote as he sneaked warily beyond the gleam of our fire. The river flowed at our feet, hurrying on its way over rocks and boulders and bars of sandy debris, carrying its message of melody from Rocky Mountain snows to the Gulf and broad Atlantic. When at last our tired eye-lids were closed, we slept as profoundly as if we were in our own bedchamber.

On this part of our journey we encountered many bad roads. In fact they were only trails, crossing high and rugged hills, deep ravines with rough and jagged sides, dark and dismal canyons between towering mountains. Many times we forced our way over the rocks that had fallen during the heavy rains from their steep slopes, and had to cross streams filled with boulders and choked with brush and fallen timber. Frequently we chained and double-locked our wagon wheels to prevent them crashing down some long and steep incline, and often a fallen tree lay across our path that had to be hewn and lifted by main strength.

For days our progress would not average eight or ten miles. At times we came to a mountain up whose rugged slope it was almost impossible for our straining animals to pull the wagon. My husband would be at the oxen's heads urging and encouraging them in the fearful pull, while I followed closely behind the wagon carrying a big stone with which to block the wheels when the cattle stopped to blow and rest.

While travelling through the mountains between Denver and Laramie we had determined on keeping the Fourth of July as a grand holiday. I had taught my little son all the patriotic songs that I knew, brought forth from my goods and chattels our American flag and decorated our wagon and tent with the red, white and blue, regretting our lack of firecrackers or fireworks. From our limited larder I made preparations for a holiday dinner. We had camped the night before the Fourth in a little fertile valley, surrounded on all sides by high mountains. Many of the higher peaks were covered with snow, but down in this little valley the air was balmy and mild as a Fourth of July day should be. Here we picked our first wild strawberries, a luxury indeed to our appetites cloyed to satiety with salt bacon and beans.

Our bill of fare was constructed on very simple lines yet I do not think it would have been unacceptable even to a pampered epicure. A day or two previous we had bartered with an Indian a pound of sugar for a leg of antelope. For our first course we had antelope soup, then roast antelope, and a piece of boiled ham with a curry of rice and our last can of tomatoes. I also made some very palatable cookies, even without the eggs which were considered so very necessary in their make-up. Stewed dried fruit and the fresh strawberries formed our dessert, and with an excellent cup of coffee completed a meal that anyone might enjoy, notwithstanding that the cups and dishes were of tin, and our table a board over a humble and empty soap box.

We had hardly finished this bountiful repast when up the narrow defile that led into this little valley, we saw approaching us two white men on horseback, leading two horses. They informed us that they were prospectors on their way back to Denver, all they possessed being the few provisions and blankets that were packed on their extra horses. They requested our hospitality for the night, which we gladly gave them. It was often our good fortune to meet with a trapper or scout or some wandering prospector from whom we could get some useful information. I was glad I had such a good dinner for them. When they had finished eating there was not enough left to feed the birds. They very feelingly remarked that it was the best meal they had eaten since they had left their homes in the far East. We knew not whether they were friends or foes, but treated them as royally as we could. Next morning, they started over their lonely road for Denver.

The next night brought a change of spirit for our camp was pitched near a little village of Indians whom we had been warned were very hostile to emigrants, and we were truly at their mercy for they were a warlike band. While I was preparing our evening meal the chief and a number of his braves came and sat down in a semi-circle around our camp fire and asked in their broken way and by signs for coffee, sugar, and. "bishkit." I gave what I could from the quantity already cooked, and James gave them some tobacco to smoke. After sitting and smoking in silence one got up and went away followed at intervals by another, until finally we were left alone. How anxiously we spent that night none can ever know who have never been exposed to the dangers of savage life. Our fears proved groundless and the next morning we passed through their camp. They were making preparations to break up their own encampment. Having a large band of ponies, they were compelled to move farther on for newer and more abundant pasturage.

This was our first sight of a moving Indian village and a more novel, curious, animated scene I never witnessed. I was quite indignant while I watched the indifferent braves lounging carelessly around, unmindful of the labour of their poor, overworked squaws—the former too proud and disdainful to assist the squaws in their burden of taking down their lodges, dismantling their camp, and loading their various trappings upon their primitive means of transportation, drawn by ponies and dogs. A number of lodge poles were fastened to the sides of the ponies, the ends of which trailed on the ground and on these poles, behind the animal, was fastened a light frame work interlaced with slips of rawhide, which formed a sort of platform.

Over this strong trellis of rawhide and frame work were spread buffalo robes, the paraphernalia of their camp, and their most treasured clothing. On top of all were stowed their papooses and young puppies. The whole, camp with the exception of the stolid and lazy braves was in motion. Squaws, dogs, and ponies were all on the alert and moving, ready to leave the old camp for the new. The women trudged patiently along by the litter that carried their offspring. These youngsters, strapped to their straight boards with their uncovered eyes blinking in the sun, looked anything but comfortable, yet I do not remember of ever hearing an Indian baby cry or murmur. Occasionally a squaw, becoming weary with her long walk after her arduous labour of loading up the animals, would mount the litter to rest or nurse her papoose.

This method of riding was said to be very comfortable as the elasticity of the supporting poles made the motion easy. A number of these litters were prepared for the aged and infirm braves and others who had been crippled in their numerous combats, and this was their only mode of locomotion. They had to be assisted on and off by their ever-faithful squaws, who drove the animals as well. The numerous dogs that infested all Indian encampments were made to do duty on these occasions, and a similar equipment to that of the horses, but on a smaller scale, was attached to them, on which were loaded the lighter articles of the camp.

We followed on in the wake of these moving aborigines until our noon halt, while they continued on their way to their further abiding place. The chief remained behind with us, waiting, no doubt, for an invitation to our mid-day meal, to which we felt compelled to invite him, very much to his satisfaction. After filling his capacious stomach to repletion and eating as much as three men would take at a meal, he arose and tried to express his gratification by rubbing his stomach with great gusto. It was characteristic of the Indians, whenever an opportunity offered, to lay in a supply of food against any future fasts. Evidently our hospitality and courteous treatment won their hearts, for they showed no signs of hostility to us. In fact, from their general demeanour they rather inspired us with a confidence which seemed to sanction our presence in their midst.

CHAPTER 9

Arriving at Fort Laramie

I cannot now remember how many times we crossed that wonderful river, the North Platte and its tributaries. It seemed to roam hither and thither at its own sweet will. It appeared quite a torrent as it rushed out of some deep canyon, clear as crystal and cold as ice, and again it was a wide stream filled with small islands, and except at the melting of the snows in the spring, one could almost wade across it. The Indian name for this river was "Weeping Water," but tradition said that the name had been changed to Platte for a woman missionary who was very much beloved by a tribe of Pawnee Indians. During high water the crossing of this river was very dangerous, owing to the quicksands and the continual changing of the channel. Usually in the vicinity of the fords, men were stationed whose business it was to see emigrants and their cattle safely over, often at a tax of eight or ten dollars a wagon. Occasionally we would arrive at the banks of the stream and find the ferryman away from his post, and much against our will were compelled to wait his return. We made the welkin ring with our shouts and halloas to bring back the missing guide.

At one of these crossings of the Platte the ferryman advised us to take the trail leading more to the north than west, in order to more quickly reach the opening of Cheyenne Pass, thereby saving us several days' hard driving over a mountainous country. We arose at the dawning of day and with an early start, hoped to reach the entrance of the Pass by nightfall, but the drive proved as usual to be longer than we expected, and the miles lengthened out until we found ourselves at night in a barren, inhospitable spot, where the feed was not abundant. James here tied two yoke of our oxen together in pairs and let them roam in order to get sufficient sustenance on the scanty feeding ground. The remaining two oxen he had picketed with long ropes, thinking that the loose cattle would not wander far away from them.

Imagine our dismay when we woke the next morning to find no sign of the other stock. This was not an agreeable, prospect, as we could not hope to recover or replace our faithful animals. What were we to do? I was afraid to be left alone while my husband went in search of them, and I greatly feared for his safety in the uncertain chase. I watched him leave me with feelings of doubt and anguish, but we both knew there was no alternative as we could go no farther with only the one remaining yoke. So mounting the horse, he ascended the range of mountains beyond us, and there to his wonder, saw an Indian driving the loose stock towards our camp.

James halted until the Indian reached him, not knowing what was awaiting him, but the Indian on his near approach, by making signs and pointing backwards, implied that he had found the wandering cattle in the range beyond. James turned at once and came back to camp, the Indian following with the cattle. On reaching our camp the Indian, catching up the rope with which he had tied our cattle together, placed it in my husband's hands. We were overjoyed and surprised at the manner of their restoration and wondered greatly that the Indian, who had us completely in his power, had returned them in that way.

It truly seemed to us in our long journey traveling alone that the Indians watched over us. Perhaps our utter loneliness and unprotected position, showing them that we had the most implicit confidence in them awoke in their breasts a feeling of chivalrous protection. Our confidence and resolution in the face of overpowering numbers may have won their regard. Be that as it may, in our ignorant fearlessness we came through the many hostile tribes unmolested and unhurt, while we heard details of various raids against emigrants who had preceded us. I was led to believe that the tribes with whom we came in contact had some secret sign whereby they communicated with one another, for we frequently noticed the smoke of fires on different heights as we travelled or stopped at our numerous camps.

Sometimes the smoke would ascend straight up into the air in columns, at other times it would be diffused and wavering. By degrees learning then and long after that this was their method of communicating with each other at a distance, we at last came to the conclusion that in this or some other way the Indians had taken charge of us. With feeling of gratitude at the kindly action of the Indian, who had brought our wandering stock back to us, I prepared a bountiful breakfast, for I had learned that the way to a red man's heart lay in the same direction as that of his more civilized brother, and I have never found an appeal to the stomach in vain.

I even made extra efforts to whet his ever-ready appetite. I made my lightest flap-jacks, browned them; with the lovely hue that made them most inviting, sprinkled them with sugar so tempting to the Indians, and poured cup after cup of my aromatic coffee, which evidently from the number he drank, fully satisfied his critical tastes, while slice after slice of bacon and beans without stint went into his capacious stomach. I wondered if he had eaten anything for a month, so marvellous was the quantity that disappeared. He stayed with us until we left camp and started out on our day's travel. I gave him a loaf of the warm bread I had baked and a piece of bacon to take with him. He followed us for a while, then took his departure down the canyon and was lost to view.

As we proceeded northward toward the main line of overland travel, our route lay over a badly gullied region, and we crossed many streams emerging from the mountains. By one of these our trail ran for more than forty miles, and in its tortuous windings we crossed it many times. The Red Buttes were conspicuous all along this river. The earth which gave them their peculiar colour was said to be rich in iron. On the lower bottoms of this stream the grass was luxuriant, but the mosquitoes and gnats swarmed in such numbers that our stock could neither feed nor rest, while the annoyance to ourselves was more than tantalising.

Finding it impossible to sleep in this camp, we arose early and drove eight or ten miles before we could leave the persecuting horde of insects behind us. We drove until we came to a most excellent spring of clear, cold water, unimpregnated with any trace of alkali, and the best water we had drunk since leaving Clear creek west of Denver. Most of the many streams we had crossed were muddy and tasted more or less of the ever present alkali.

Finding it necessary to repair our wagon we stayed at this spring for two or three days. It was a most picturesque spot, lying between rows of magnificent buttes looking in the distance, like ruined castles, some of them perpendicular and circular in form. They presented a variegated and fantastic appearance when viewed from a distance. In spots they were brilliant vermillion, but when broken by the water courses passing over them, they presented uneven surfaces of white clay, which gave them their peculiar appearance. After leaving these larger buttes, our road gradually descended until we reached the banks of a ravine, where we had great difficulty in getting down to the bed of the stream.

Unyoking the forward oxen, leaving only the wheel oxen attached to the wagon, we chained and locked our wagon wheels, but even with all these precautions we came to grief, for the heavy wagon rushing down the steep incline, caused the oxen to swerve in such a manner that the wheels cramped and the wagon was thrown against a mound of earth and loose rock that partly held it from a complete upset. Here we were in a deep ravine with no help near. We could neither get out nor go on. Not a spot of ground was level enough to stand upon in any comfort. The wagon had to be unloaded before it could be righted, and as the noon hour had passed there was a prospect of spending the night in this gloomy cavern.

There was no other alternative but for both of us to go to work and unload as soon as possible. Even unloaded the wagon was too much for one man to lift. James rigged up a sort of lever and with the help of the oxen, managed to right it again and pull the half empty wagon to a place less steep, and more secure farther down the slope. By the time we had carried our goods down the hill to the wagon and reloaded it, it was near sundown. Hitching on all the oxen, we drove down into the narrow and deep stream. The opposite side was fully as steep and it required the combined strength of our cattle to pull us up the bank. This stream was called the Chugwater, where we spent the night, expecting in a few days to arrive at Laramie.

Before reaching Laramie, we drove one night into a little park at the base of a mountain. It was almost a semi-circle, rimmed with dark and forbidding mountains. A small stream winds its way along its timbered banks. There seemed to be a strange witchery in this place. The wind moaned and wailed most sadly. All through the night we imagined we heard strange sighs above and around us. We could hear stealthy trampings which seemed to come from other beasts than those that drew us on our journey. While we were stopping in Laramie, a soldier told us that this peculiar spot was called the "Haunted Hole of the Black Elk." Perhaps if we had known that this little park had such an uncanny reputation, we might have pushed farther on for our night's rest. However, nothing harmed us, and only the huge mountains that surrounded us so closely overpowered us with their immensity.

The next morning, long before the sun's rays could penetrate this little dell, we were prepared to push onward, but not with great speed, for we were to climb another mountain up whose steep ascent we were to lift ourselves over two thousand feet. In one place we wound around tall, ragged cliffs. The soil was loose and unstable, composed of pulverised debris and shaly rock, which kept constantly slipping, so that the oxen had great difficulty in keeping their footing. It had been a steep and tiresome climb. For a time, we had been riding in the wagon but the way seemed so rough and dangerous, that to assure our safety, we alighted, and very fortunately, for in less than twenty yards further, the rear wheels of the wagon began to slip over the shelving embankment, and it was with almost miraculous effort that our brave cattle pulled the wagon beyond the danger point.

Every moment I expected to see it topple over the precipice, pulling our valiant oxen with it. James plied his ox goad more furiously than our cattle had ever felt before, but it was the time for greater effort, and after the danger was past, he almost wept over the cruel blows he gave our gallant team. Weary from the excitement of this clay, probably more than the fatigue, we went into camp, I made great effort to be cheerful and happy and tried to laugh away the remembrance of the peril through which we had passed, but all through the night in my fitful slumbers I had visions of the towering cliff, and in my broken dreams felt the motion of the treacherous soil giving way over the sloping walls of the precipice.

While traversing this slope of the Rocky Mountains we climbed numberless ridges and penetrated many passes, descending one lofty plateau only to encounter another. One morning we struck an almost level plain which appeared several miles in extent. There was only a dim trail to follow, growing fainter as we proceeded, until we finally lost it altogether. The grass on this plain, though coarse, grew thick and close. The way had been little travelled that season and the heavy growth had obliterated all signs of the trail. We wandered over this plateau for hours, trying to keep our northerly course, growing more fearful every moment that we were lost. At last, we discovered afar off a fringe of trees, denoting a stream. On reaching it we drove up and down its timbered banks, when to our great relief we again struck our lost trail at the ford. We named this stream, "Lost Trail Creek," but it should have been "Box Elder," so thickly were its borders covered with a growth of those trees.

Crossing this stream we again ascended a high, rocky, barren plain, and for two or three days the trail led us over a most peculiar formation, composed of large pebbles, averaging the size of a goose egg. Our cattle became foot-sore traveling this rough roadway. Their hoofs were worn almost to the quick. They could no longer travel with any degree of haste, and it was truly pitiful to watch their limping efforts. We decided, to stop at the first water we came to and give them a chance to rest. It was almost dark that night before we came to a little spring near the roadside, and as soon as the poor brutes were unyoked, they immediately lay down in their tracks, and for several hours neither ate nor drank, so weary and footsore were they.

Next morning on looking down from our lofty camp into the small valley below us, we discovered a tiny cabin and a wreath of smoke issuing from its wide chimney. This cabin, though rough and primitive, denoted the presence of the white man. Our curiosity soon grew beyond bounds and the next day we yoked up our lame team and drove down to investigate. We found two grizzled, old mountaineers located in this fertile valley. They had a small herd of cattle with which they supplied the nearest forts with beef.

They informed us that they had lived in this lonely place for four or five years, seeing no one for months at a time, except the few emigrants who passed during the summer season, or when driving their stock to the forts. They had built a rude forge, where they shod their own horses and those of passing emigrants. From them we learned that we could have our lame cattle shod with heavy leather shoes. This detained us however for two or three days as each ox had to be tied and thrown during the shoeing process. But it enabled them to travel in comfort for many miles before it had to be repeated.

Perhaps I have tediously described this cross march from Denver, before we reached the high road that led to California. This part of our journey was the only portion not traversed by mail, stage or pony express. It lay through a region in which there were few white settlers but the providence which had been with us from the beginning, safely guided us through all the perils that might have beset our path. After many days we arrived at Fort Laramie from where we were to follow the regular overland road to California. We forded the swollen Laramie river in the early twilight and camped on its farther shore, feeling thankful that the loneliness which had hitherto oppressed us over the Cherokee trail and through Cheyenne Pass was removed.

Though young and inexperienced, I had learned to adapt myself to the rough life of an emigrant—crossing swollen streams, encountering terrific storms and dreading constantly an attack from hostile Indians. But an American woman well born and bred is endowed with the courage of her brave pioneer ancestors, and no matter what the environment she can adapt herself to all situations, even to the perilous trip across the western half of this great continent, ever ready to wander over paths which women reared in other countries would fear to follow.

CHAPTER 10

A Threatened Attack of Indians

While we were camping near Fort Laramie, the soldiers warned us of danger. A detachment had been sent out from the fort on a reconnoitring expedition and reported an attack of Indians on an emigrant company of eight men, whom they had killed or taken prisoners, burnt their wagons and taken their mules and horses. These soldiers also informed us of the approach of a train of emigrants of about sixty men with a large number of horses and wagons. The officer at the fort insisted on our remaining in its vicinity until the arrival of that company, as we were running recklessly into danger traveling alone. Deciding that it would perhaps be wiser to heed his counsel, we waited and in due time the large caravan made its appearance and we joined their company.

This proved to be the most unhappy part of our journey. Hitherto we had proceeded at our own sweet will. Accustomed to traveling alone, we stopped when and where we pleased, and started out in the same manner. Now all was changed. It was the custom for every large company of emigrants to select from their number a captain. His word was law. Every one belonging to that company was supposed to do and act as he ordered. We were obliged to keep our place in the moving caravan, travel as long and as fast as he thought best, and camp when and where he chose. Previous to this time we had made shorter drives and stopped before dark.

With this company, we frequently drove until after nightfall. This was to me an unaccustomed hardship. Cooking in camp by daylight, was no easy task, and darkness made it still more difficult. Our camp fires were often of sage brush which emitted only evanescent flames. Our lanterns dimly lighted with one small candle made only a glimmer in the darkness of the wilderness. My husband, too, had always been with me at night, but now had to take his turn as night watchman, and my little son and I would be left in our tent alone, while he was posted as sentinel on the outskirts of our encampment. Never before had I suffered with fear as I did while with that company. I could not rest or sleep while my husband was away from me, exposed to all the perils of the night and the treacherous foe. We might have been in the same danger before, but we were together.

My fears were not only of Indians. These people with whom we were traveling were the roughest, most uncouth and ignorant people that I had ever come in contact with. Perfectly lawless, fighting and quarrelling among themselves, using language terrible to hear, they were the champion swearers of the world. They swore at their wives, at their horses, at each other, at the wind that blew, at the stones in the road. The air was constantly filled with their curses. The women of the company were fitting mates for the men.

The whole company was made up of outlaws from Texas, Arkansas and Southwestern Missouri. They imagined that they were so strong in numbers that they could whip any band of Indians, and it was their usual custom whenever the Indians approached our camp or sat by our camp fires to tease and play various tricks upon them. I noticed on different occasions that the Indians looked on their manoeuvres with a resentful glare, and conversed with each other in low muttered tones, and I trembled with fear for what they might do in retaliation. Many times, I tried to expostulate with these men, but they laughed with scorn, saying they were not afraid of any band of Indians.

Very soon their bravado was put to the test. At the close of one day's long travel, we had barely set our camp for the night, when a lone, frightened pony express rider came galloping in haste into our camp, shouting to us that the Indians were near and would very soon attack us. While he was descending into a little canyon, they had suddenly come upon him from their ambush, pursued and shot at him several times, and only that his horse was fresh and faster had he been able to escape them. Every minute we were expecting to hear the blood-curdling yells of the approaching foe. For the first few moments after the report reached us, the men who had hitherto boasted of their fearlessness were palsied with fright; however, they soon rallied and made hasty preparations to meet and repel the attack. It was a night long to be remembered. Here indeed was a grave and perilous situation—overloaded wagons, tired horses and oxen, defenceless women and children. For what power was there in the hands of a few white men against a horde of Indians, bent on murder and robbery, and coming so suddenly on our far-away camp in the wilderness, most of whose numbers were defenceless women and children?

Our wagons had been arranged in the usual semicircle enclosing the camp. Our animals were brought within and picketed as closely as possible. The men hurriedly put their guns in order. The women held their children closely to their breasts not knowing how soon they would be ruthlessly torn from them and dashed to death or put to torture before their eyes. After hours of suspense, we began to hope that our fears were groundless, but this hope was soon dashed from our minds by the startling cry from another messenger, that an attack from the opposite side was momentarily expected. Every ear was listening for the sound of the fleet feet of their ponies, every heart throbbing with anxious fear, but every lip was silent.

At this hour a fearful storm of rain and hail with continued thunder and lightning fell upon us. The sharp hail and the continued peals of thunder so frightened our restless stock that there was imminent danger of a stampede. The pelting rain flowed into our frail tents, wetting our pillows and blankets. At any other time, this would have been considered a great misfortune. Now we hardly noticed it, while we sat through that terrible night, drenched to the skin, beaten upon by the gusts of wind and hail, deafened by the continuous peals of thunder, every moment expecting the attack of the lurking foe. The darkness was so complete that we might have been surrounded by hundreds of the demons and yet been none the wiser, and the uproar of the storm was so loud that hearing was as useless as sight. No one slept save the little children. The night which seemed interminably long at last passed away and morning showed no enemy in sight. My husband and I uttered a fervent prayer of thanksgiving. No doubt the fearful storm had caused the attack to be abandoned.

In the course of a few hours, we ventured on our way, hoping that we were not to be molested, our number of nearly sixty mien marched with loaded rifles each side of the wagons to guard the women and children who were huddled closely within. The day was long and anxious and nightfall brought us little relief, for our next halt was among the charred remains of an express station which had been burnt by the savage foe. Half our men stood guard, while the others slept with their ready guns at hand.

The now frightened emigrants with whom we were traveling were more civil and subdued in their manner. This lasted for a few days, but as the fear of an immediate attack from the Indians wore away, they resumed their usual tactics. They quarrelled among themselves and were brutal and domineering to their wives, never caring for their comfort or wellbeing. The captain of the company was a tyrannical, ignorant man, who ruled with an iron hand. His every effort was to impress all that he was paramount and everyone must obey. It was he that regulated the length of the day's travel, selected the camp, formed the corral at night, appointed the guards and arbitrated all disputes.

My hot Southern blood soon rebelled at his imperious and despotic rule. Every day about an hour before camping time he rode with two or three of his henchmen, a mile or two ahead of the wagon train and selected our camping place for the night. His selections were frequently very unwise and uncomfortable. Sometimes his choice was a side hill, and our beds would slope too much for comfort, or a rocky spot by the road when a few rods either side would be smoother or less rugged. But whatever the discomforts, where he decided, there we camped.

One night I felt it necessary to assert myself and renounce his petty authority. We had driven many miles that day over a long rough road and all were tired and hungry. When we came to the place where we were to pitch our tents, we found that it had been occupied the night before by emigrants who had preceded us from all appearances with a great number of stock. Within twenty rods of the place selected was a clear, grassy spot and just as near the water. A number of the women, although grumbling at the filth, prepared to make their lowly beds, while the men hurriedly raised the tents. My husband drove his team into the wagon stockade as usual. I said to him in an undertone, "You need not unhitch your oxen in this place. I will not camp here."

He replied "If we do not obey the rules of the company we will have to leave it."

"All right," I said, "The sooner the better it will suit me. I would rather trust myself to the mercy of the Indians than to travel another day with these ruffians and their ignorant captain. If you do not drive me to a cleaner place to camp and sleep tonight I will take my blankets and go alone."

He knew full well that I meant to do as I said. So without another word he turned his team and drove to the place I selected. The other women looked on my daring insubordination with wondering eyes, and, envious of my cleanly quarters, at last plucked up courage to follow my example, and with much profanity the camp was moved. That night James and I held council together and we decided to withdraw from the company, feeling that we were safer and more comfortable travelling alone.

The next morning when the order was given to break camp and all were busy preparing to move onward except ourselves, we remained quiet in camp. Some of the more friendly women offered me their assistance, thinking I was not well. I thanked them kindly and assured them I was well, but felt tired and needed a longer rest, and that it was our intention to remain in camp until we were thoroughly rested. The men jeered at us and said by nightfall our scalps would hang at the belt of some wild Indian. We paid but little heed to their remarks. Finally perceiving that we were indeed going to stay behind, the captain gave the command and the big caravan drove on leaving us alone in the wilderness. We remained in camp two days, giving them an opportunity to get so far ahead that we might never overtake them or see them again. Alone in the wilderness, we felt more secure and far happier than when travelling with this uncongenial band. Afterwards we heard repeated rumours that they had been attacked and almost annihilated.

From Laramie for some distance, we encountered no one save Indians. It was a barren and desolate region. Off to our left were the Black Hills, so called because they were covered with a dense growth of pine, cedar and hemlock trees which gave them a dark and forbidding appearance. Farther to the south, at a distance of thirty miles or more arose Laramie Peak, towering up to a height said to be over six thousand feet. The milky streams in the neighbourhood of Laramie, running through the peculiar white clay soil, formed numerous buttes and bluffs, and by some strange alchemy of nature the most singular formations would crop out here and there, like ruined towers, castles and battlements. Over the facades of the numerous cliffs, strange forms and faces would stand out in bold relief.

In a few days after leaving Laramie, we came to the Sweetwater River, near which we travelled for a week or ten days and owing to its tortuous course we crossed it many times before leaving it near the South Pass. I must not forget to mention a famous land mark in the valley of this river and near our road, Independence rock, so named by a party of emigrants who made their camp there on a Fourth of July in the earlier emigration of 1849 and had held a grand patriotic celebration. Many of their names had been painted on the face of the huge rock, but time and long exposure to the elements had nearly obliterated them. This rock stood out on almost a level plain and was entirely detached from the mountains near it. In this fertile valley of the Sweetwater the grass was luxuriant, and our cattle regained the flesh and loss of strength that befell them on the rocky trails that lamed them so terribly. But soon again we struck another sixteen-mile desert and a mountain beyond, and after toiling up its long ascent and down into the little park on its further slope, we came upon a camp of weary Mormon emigrants.

These recruits of the Mormons were mostly Swedes and Norwegians and were accompanied by several Mormons who had been sent to Norway and Sweden for them and who had induced them by alluring promises to take this long and perilous trip. There were young women with them with hand carts which they had trundled all the long distance from the Missouri River. They were a most unprepossessing lot, sunburned and weather-beaten and stolid. They were dressed in their old country costume of stout woollen material. They wore heavy striped yarn stockings that barely reached to the knee. Kerchiefs that had once been bright were carelessly knotted under their chins and formed their only head covering but were no protection for their faces, which were nearly as brown as the Indians', in spite of their original fair complexions.

The Mormon missionary never attempted to proselyte among the rich or educated, or even among those in moderate circumstances, but always among the poorest and most ignorant, who had been born in utter misery and who had nothing to lose. These missionaries drew the most glowing pictures to the ignorant of what their lives would be in the City of the Saints—of the independence and ease that awaited them, of the freedom from privations, and of the marvellous profits to be derived from their labours. No wonder the heads of these poor creatures were turned by such proselyting, and that converts to Mormonism were continually arriving.

For several days we travelled along in sight of them and camped near them at night It gave me the heartache to see those poor girls take up their burdens every day, load up their hand carts and push them over those rugged mountains, stopping at intervals to rest their weary backs and wipe the perspiration from their dripping brows. Our conversation with them was necessarily very limited as they spoke but little English, and the Mormon men who accompanied the outfit rather discouraged any intimacy with gentiles. After a few days we passed them on the road and saw them no more.

One night somewhere between Laramie and Green River we halted at the foot of a mountain over which we had travelled laboriously all day. Early in the afternoon we discovered a spring of water and fairly good grass for our cattle. While it was too soon to make a camp on that long summer day, yet our stock seemed weary and footsore, and we ourselves were willing to take the good thus provided and go no farther. While we were pitching our tent and making preparations for camp, a team of mules and several men came in sight. They proved to be French Canadians, who like ourselves were bound for California.

On reaching our camp they told us that the tribe of Indians roaming over that region was hostile, and that we were incurring great danger by remaining there alone. They insisted that we join them and go on over the next mountain. But we were tired and so were our cattle. Their proposal meant a long heavy pull probably until midnight. We had encountered no troubles with the Indians so far, why should we fear now? We advised them to tarry with us. But no, they were in a mad, wild rush to push on and bidding us farewell, went on their way.

Next morning after a refreshing and good night's rest, we were up bright and early on the road. It took us several hours before we reached the summit of the next mountain, with its remote view of the canyon below. After a while we discovered what in the distance looked like the wagon of the Canadians, but as we came nearer, we could discover no sign of life or movement in their camp. No mules were browsing in sight and not a man visible. When we came within hailing distance no one greeted us.

We found the wagon rifled of everything. The ground bore traces of a struggle. The mules had evidently been stampeded and the men taken prisoners to the camp of the Indians to be tortured to death. We traced the tracks of the mules and ponies for some distance in an opposite direction to the one we were traveling; but as we had met no Indians, we concluded that discretion was the better part of valour, and did not extend our search, feeling only too thankful that a merciful providence had been with us. Had we taken the advice of the men I am afraid we should never have lived to tell the tale.

After leaving the Sweetwater River our road gradually led us to the beginning of the South Pass, which I imagined to be a narrow, difficult, winding gorge between towering mountains. In this I was happily mistaken, and for a few days we travelled over a road as smooth and as hard as a well-kept country thoroughfare. On reaching the summit of the South Pass one could hardly believe that we were crossing the backbone of the Rocky Mountains. The gradual ascent was not laborious. And here we found the dividing line between the Atlantic and the Pacific, for as we traversed several miles of rolling land two low mounds, called Twin Buttes, marked the point where all the little streams and rivers flowed toward the Pacific. I could see but little difference in the taste of the waters, the alkali flavour still predominated. In the course of a few days in our gradual descent we struck a springy marsh of fifteen or twenty acres where the ground seemed to shake as we went over it, and in the centre of this morass we found the so-called Pacific springs. The water was cold and clear, but so obnoxious to the taste that I could not drink it.

Not far from the Pacific springs we struck the Oregon trail where the road branched off further to the north, while our route led us in a more southerly direction. We were now out of the South Pass, and camped one night on the treeless banks of the little Sandy River. A band of Snake Indians were in our vicinity, and according to my usual custom I prepared for company. Strange to relate not one of them approached us. This alarmed us somewhat because we had been ac-customed to have them drop in upon us on all occasions, and in this seeming indifference we feared a sinister motive.

The fear of hostile Indians was not our only worry, for once again our little hoard of money was running low. The numerous ferries over the Platte and its tributaries made heavy inroads into our slender purse. On one or two occasions it had been replenished by sales of flour and bacon to emigrants who had not laid in so large a store as we, but even with that help we were at our last extremity for money. Food we had in abundance, but only coin would pay our way over a formidable stream that must be crossed by ferry and was impossible to ford.

My husband, worried beyond measure at our predicament, had fretted himself almost sick. I, probably owing to my nature of blissful ignorance, took a more optimistic view of the situation and urged him not to worry. We had been told that it would cost twenty dollars to cross the Green River by ferry. I fondly hoped that the amount had been exaggerated or that some way would be provided. My trust was not in vain, for a few days before reaching that stream, we were overtaken by a solitary horseman who rode by our wagon side until our noon halt. He asked my husband if he could share our noon meal with us, and said he would gladly pay for it.

He was a Frenchman by the name of Philip. We never knew any other name for him. After dinner he took my husband aside and explained why he was alone in the heart of the continent. He had fallen out with the company with which he was traveling, and taking his guns and blankets, left them, depending for food solely on the wild game he could shoot. He begged my husband to board him for a week or two until he reached his destination beyond the Green River. James felt some qualms about taking in a stranger and came to me for advice. At once I replied "Tell him we will take him for twenty dollars."

I have often thought since if we had asked a hundred, he would have just as gladly have paid it, as he seemed well provided with money. He proved to be a very kindly gentleman while with us for the few days before reaching his destination, and his twenty dollars carried us well along on our journey and tided us over a precarious time. For years afterwards when the hour looked darkest and both of us were discouraged, I would say "Don't worry, maybe Philip will turn up." The name was a synonym of good luck for us.

CHAPTER 11

The Pony Express

In due time we arrived at Green River, which we had been told was a dangerous and difficult river to ford, and that to transport our stock and wagon over its depths would take all our little hoard of money. Instead, we hailed it as an oasis in the desert, for it furnished us with clear sweet water to drink, and our thirsty stock revelled in it to their hearts' content. The Green River no longer held any terrors for us. The huge flat-bottomed boat, drawn by ropes suspended from either side across the deep stream and at a price much less than we expected, safely landed us on the farther side of the stream that had been such a great bug-bear to us. Here we rested a few days. The river flowed through a narrow valley. The grass, though coarse, proved to be good feed for our cattle, and the rest put new courage and endurance in their weary frames. Here, too, were green trees on which to set our tired eyes. They were only willows and cottonwoods yet we enjoyed a camp under their grateful shade.

A trading post had been established at this ferry for the few mountaineers who owned large herds of cattle. Other emigrants besides ourselves were camping here. Their broken down teams forced them to trade their worn-out oxen for fresher ones on almost any terms. The mountain stockmen did a lively business with unfortunate emigrants, taking a woeful advantage of their necessity. My sympathy was strongly aroused by their distress. Two or three families had been delayed there for two weeks waiting for their cattle to get strong enough to resume their journey. Their own provisions were getting short and the season growing late, they gravely feared that they would not get through their long journey before the snow fell again on the mountains.

We became acquainted at this place with an old trader who in his earlier life had been a man of considerable polish and intelligence, but owing to some unfortunate circumstances in his youth had drifted thus far over the continent in the early forties. Homeless, penniless and an outcast, he managed in some way to establish himself here at the Green River, and by slow degrees had acquired several hundred head of cattle and a considerable band of horses. With true Mormon spirit he also annexed several squaws for wives, and had any number of half-breed children, who swarmed around the filthy quarters that he called home. The rude huts they occupied were in the most squalid surroundings.

For many years this had been his home, yet not the slightest effort had been made to improve his mode of living. With all that fertile land surrounding him there was neither garden nor orchard. Fresh fruit and vegetables were unknown to him and his half breed family. He was said to be worth seventy-five or one hundred thousand dollars, and yet appeared to be perfectly satisfied with these most wretched conditions. Somewhere I had read that it would take only a few years for the white man to return to the aboriginal condition, and it certainly proved true in this man's case.

Most of the men who inhabited these trading posts had squaws for wives. It was quite the ordinary thing for the Indians to bring their most attractive and winsome daughters and offer them for sale to the white men. Those not quite so comely would bring thirty or forty dollars, while others more pleasing would bring sixty or seventy according to their charms. The women thus bought and sold were no truer to their masters than their more civilized sisters of the same caste in other countries and were ever ready to decamp with any soldier or other man who offered sufficient inducements in the way of beads, blankets, or other gaudy paraphernalia.

After leaving Green River at many points, we would come across the discarded belongings of the emigrants who preceded us. We were enabled to form an idea of the condition of their stock, whether horses or cattle, by the goods and chattels they were continually discarding in their endeavour to lighten the burden of their overworked and worn-out teams. Once by the roadside, we came across a heavy old-fashioned cook stove which some emigrant had hauled all those weary miles of mountain and desert, only to discard it at last. No doubt some poor forlorn woman was now compelled to do her cooking by the primitive camp fire, perhaps much against her will. I could imagine the heated arguments when day after day that heavy stove had to be loaded and unloaded.

No doubt the air was blue many times with the volley of emphatic and profane words, hurled against that inoffensive but cumbersome article. A little wooden cradle nearby looked pathetic in its loneliness; and the tiny new made grave that we had passed a few days previous told too truly the cause of its desertion. It was no unusual sight to see wagon boxes, log chains, tires and other heavy articles abandoned to lighten the loads, and the most astonishing thing to me was that these things would lie there without attracting the notice of either Indians or herdsmen. They proved to have no value to these denizens of the wilderness.

The hills west of Green River were thinly covered with straggling groves of pines and cedars. Grass was more abundant in the little valleys, and the streams of water had lost the milky look which they acquired from the clay wash lying near the desert lands. We were still in the midst of sage brush, even in these fertile valleys, but it was no longer universal and alone. The wild currant and other shrubs became more abundant.

Occasionally we came upon a little patch of land cultivated by some progressive Mormon. It was a matter of astonishment to us that the herdsmen of these fertile districts, with their cattle roaming over a thousand hills, had never experimented with cultivating the soil. They never knew the taste of cabbage or tomato. A potato was considered the greatest luxury, and was brought to the trading posts from miles away. As for cultivated fruit of any description they knew it not. We found in the canyons a wild and sour gooseberry which proved to be fairly palatable, and at intervals near the streams grew a wild grass whose succulent roots gave out the flavour of the cucumber.

We had watched the Indians eating this grass, and testing it ourselves, thought it very good, but it was found rarely. I had grown very tired of bacon day after day. The very smell of beans cooking nauseates me to this day. I have never overcome my antipathy to rice in any form, while stewed prunes are still an abomination in my sight. Our diet was confined mainly to these articles. It was impossible to buy fresh vegetables on our route, and our canned fruit and vegetables had long given out. We had grown so weary of the sameness of our daily diet that the intense longing for something different grew upon us, and we looked forward anxiously to Fort Bridger where we hoped in a few days to find fresh meat and vegetables.

From Laramie westward we were in the line of the celebrated pony express, which was established in April, 1860, to carry important mail more rapidly than was possible in the overland stage. Our daily excitement was in watching for its fearless riders as they flew by us on their swift ponies. It was nearly ten years in advance of the first overland telegraph, which could not be maintained until there was a line of railroad parallel to it. The pony express was an attempt to carry letters by private service from St. Joseph, Missouri, to Sacramento, California in ten days. It was a daring enterprise to attempt to cover nearly two thousand miles of prairie, desert and mountain by solitary riders from station to station.

These stations were at intervals of about thirty miles. In a year's time it proved more than human endurance could stand. The stations consisted of a rude hut for the keeper, enclosed in a high stockade where the relief ponies were corralled. The certainty of always finding water at these stations induced us to make extra efforts to camp near them at night fall. Once it became our sad duty to bury the partially burned and mutilated body of the man in charge of the station to prevent the wolves and coyotes from devouring his remains. The Indians had been there before us, killed and scalped the keeper, run off with the ponies, and left the stockade in flames. Alarming as this was, we were obliged to camp near the smouldering ruins.

One morning while we lingered near one of these stations, a rider who looked like a mere boy came flying into the post, the man whose place he filled having been killed by the Indians. The pony had made his way to the next station alone. This youth had ridden hard through the darkness of the night trying to cover both his own ground and that of the man who had been shot. He quickly changed horses, took his package of letters, and was off again on his perilous way. These brief stops at the stations were all that broke the monotony of untold hardships and danger. While the riders were young, sturdy and robust men, one of the essential requirements was that they must be of light weight, as the ponies were not expected to carry more than one hundred and fifty pounds. The superior endurance of those ponies saved many a fearless man in his race for life with roaming bands of Indians.

For some time after we had separated ourselves from our unpleasant travelling companions, we travelled without adventure of any kind, and saw nothing of the Indians that were supposed to be on the war-path. We flattered ourselves that we were too near Fort Bridger to have any fears. One evening, however, as we drove into a little fertile valley, we came in sight of an encampment of the supposed foe, with a large band of ponies feeding on the rich grass. Their rude *tepees* were clustered near the stream within a mile of the road. Uncertain of the reception awaiting us, we made camp as usual. In a little while first one Indian then another came around our fire, until I had an audience of several watching me prepare our evening meal. I was careful to bake an extra quantity of biscuit that night, for we were so completely at their mercy I thought it wise to conciliate them in every way possible. I found it no easy task, as it required several skillets full before I had enough. James generously handed out his precious tobacco for them to smoke with him around our camp fire.

Next morning, we drove away from our camp, leaving a number of them who still hung around for the last cup of coffee. As we waved our farewells to them, we noticed one of them mount his pony and follow us, not closely, but keeping us well in sight. When we stopped for our noonday rest he soon joined us, and of course we invited him to partake of our frugal luncheon, hoping that he would return to band. But he continued to follow us until nightfall. When we prepared to camp, he did likewise.

Staking out his pony with the long rope of braided leather which he carried, and approaching my box of cooking utensils, he took from it the large knife I used in cooking, and pointing to some coarse grass that grew near the water he proceeded to cut and gather an armful, which he placed under our wagon and prepared his bed for the night. While alarmed and anxious we were powerless and made the best of our novel situation. I prepared a more bountiful meal when I found we were to entertain this most unwelcome guest. After eating a hearty meal, which he seemed to enjoy, he smoked a while with my husband. All this time there was no word of conversation, as neither he nor we could communicate except by signs. Finally, he rolled himself beneath the wagon, and we went to rest in our little tent, but slept fitfully with one eye open the balance of the night.

This continued for three days and we concluded that he had adopted us and intended to remain with us for the balance of our pilgrimage. On the evening of the third day, after replenishing his inner man with a hearty supper, he arose, caught his pony which was feeding a short distance from the camp, and, pointing backward, tried to make us understand that he was going to return to his tribe. As soon as we divined that he was about to leave us, I tied up a loaf of bread, some bacon, a cup full of sugar, and gave it to him, and we saw him depart, wondering why he came and why he went.

Not for several days was the mystery explained. Meeting an old scout at a watering place where we stopped one night, we related the circumstance to him. He told us that the country through which we were going at that time was filled with Indians who were unfriendly to emigrants, and this Indian was sent with us to show that we were under their special care and not to be molested. If that were true, it went to prove that there was honour among these savage tribes of the wilderness. Our lonely and unprotected situation must have appealed to them, and our uniform kindness was rewarded in many ways perhaps when we knew it not. At any rate we could truthfully say we never received any ill at their hands, and came through the various tribes without the loss of anything save one bright new tin tea kettle that I had bought in Denver. Its brightness proved too much of a temptation to an elderly squaw who came to visit us, and carefully seated herself beside it. It disappeared when she did under the folds of her soiled and tattered blanket.

Another circumstance I think worth mentioning here. Once in passing a group of Indians I noticed that one sat wrapped in his blanket the image of despair. The expression on his countenance showed that he was suffering great pain. My husband spoke to his squaw who was standing near and said to her, "Brave, heap sick." She shook her head but at the same time opened her mouth and pointed to her teeth, and then to the suffering brave. James approached the Indian and by signs coaxed him to open his mouth. He found the molar had a large cavity which was the cause of his suffering. I had brought with me several vials of toothache drops, for my little son had frequent attacks of toothache. Bringing forth one of the bottles containing the soothing drops and a piece of cotton, with the aid of a sharp splinter I inserted some of the remedy into the aching tooth.

The effect was magical, and I was surprised to watch the change that came over the sufferer's expressive countenance. He raised his eyes that had been sternly fixed on the ground, rubbed his face slowly, then turned towards his squaw who was standing behind him watching the effect of the remedy the white squaw was employing, and in a low tone communicated to her that the pain was relieved. Then turning to the other Indians who were grouped around, he spoke in a louder voice. In a moment we were surrounded by them eager to see the little vial that contained the magical drops. It was critically examined and passed from one to another, and although we could not understand a word, yet their expressions of gratitude were perfectly intelligible. I left the bottle and the piece of raw cotton with the Indian sufferer, for I well knew that the toothache would again return.

Another time while waiting in camp over Sunday, I had been re-pairing some of my husband's red flannel shirts. One was too far worn to be of any service further, and I had relegated it to the rag-bag. A number of Indian children stood around watching me at my work, and my sewing utensils seemed very curious to them. The idea came to me to fashion for them a rag doll and see what the effect would be on these stolid children of the wilderness. With a portion of white cloth taken from my work-bag, and the remains of the discarded red shirt, I made a rag baby, marking the features of the doll with coloured thread. My efforts were closely watched by the curious children, and when I finished the doll I handed it to the smallest girl. At first the child did not seem to realise that she was to keep it.

After each one of the children had examined it thoroughly, they gave it back to me. Finally, I made the little one understand that she was to keep it, and when one of the larger children attempted to take it from her, she uttered a weird cry and started off on a swift run with the rag baby hugged closely to her breast. In a little while two or three squaws came into our camp with the child and doll, and by signs asked for another. I soon discovered I would be very busy if I attempted to supply them with rag babies. But I made another for them, showing them how to do it, gave them the remains of the red flannel shirt and other pieces of cloth that I could spare, and sent them off rejoicing. This was my last effort, however, in trying either to instruct or amuse the Indians. Only on Sundays did we linger in camp long enough to have any extra time on our hands, and our inability to make ourselves understood made the effort tiresome.

CHAPTER 12

An Old Acquaintance

At last, we reached Fort Bridger, so named for a trader who first settled there. Later on it was used as an outpost and relief station for the great rush of Mormons to Salt Lake, and afterwards as a fort of the United States Government. We were told that Fort Bridger was the terminus of the Great American desert, and we fondly hoped to get a supply of fresh vegetables within its borders. But the few potatoes were held at such a price that we could not afford to buy them, and they proved to be the only vegetable we found cultivated until we reached Salt Lake City.

As soon as we arrived at Fort Bridger James went immediately to buy some fresh meat and vegetables, never dreaming for a moment that there would be any difficulty in getting them. On approaching the sutler of the fort he was informed that the government did not allow the sale of meat or other provisions to outside parties. No persuasion was of any avail. James tried to explain that his wife was not well and needed fresh meat sorely, but the man turned a deaf ear to all his entreaties. Very much disappointed James turned to go without it, when a private soldier who overheard the conversation said, "Stay, pilgrim, no sick woman shall go without a bite of fresh meat while I'm around. We can't sell any, but I can give her my ration and not go hungry either." In this manner was the meat procured. In return for the kind thoughtfulness of the soldier I sent to him my beloved Ivanhoe.

Most of our journey between Denver and Salt Lake, when not desert, was through and over the interminable ranges of the Rocky Mountains. For many weary days we were continually ascending and descending. We no sooner arrived at the top of one rugged mountain, when as far as the eye could reach, other ranges just as steep loomed up before us, and it seemed an endless time before we struck the long gradual slope or plain and arrived at the summit of these grand old mountains through the South Pass, and thence through Bridger and down Echo canyon, where our shouts and songs reverberated from the mountain side.

We followed its little stream until we reached that plain which we knew to be the centre of Mormondom. Ever since we had crossed Green River, we had been told that we were now in the country of the Mormons, and we had been warned, if we desired their good will, we should be careful in what manner we expressed ourselves about their peculiar institutions to the cattlemen or settler whom we might meet on the road. Especially had we been warned not to admit that we had emigrated from Missouri, as the people of that state had incurred the most bitter hatred of the Mormons.

It was the Missourians who had ousted them from their first stronghold in Nauvoo, Illinois, and caused them to take the long perilous journey to this distant land, where they could not only preach but practice their religion without molestation. Fearful tales had been told us of how whole trains emigrating from Missouri were surrounded and captured by Mormons disguised as Indians, the women and children kept in bondage, and the men put to death.

It was at the end of a long, hot summer day. We had been winding down through narrow ravines and over the abominable roads still used by all the heavy merchant teams that bore goods and other provisions to the City of the Saints. Emerging from the hills we came out on the broad plateau that overlooked the valley of the Great Salt Lake. The city was still several miles from us, and although we had two or three hours of daylight before us, we had to curb our desire to enjoy the comforts and luxuries that we had hoped to find within its boundaries.

Not until towards noon of the following day, did we descend, weary, dusty and browned with over a thousand miles of jolting, fording and camping, into the veritable city that so long had seemed a myth. To us poor emigrants it bore a most delightful aspect. It was regularly and handsomely laid out on a level plain. Little irrigating canals flowed on either side of the streets, whose clear cold waters were led into the orchards and gardens surrounding every home. The houses of that time were generally small, one storey buildings of *adobe*, and every householder had an acre of ground to cultivate around his home. The gardens diffused an air of freshness and coolness that all could appreciate, but none more than the traveller who had just crossed the great desert. At that day the City of Salt Lake boasted of only one business street on which were the post office and principal stores.

Since leaving Denver we had had no opportunity to get letters, and I did not allow any time to escape after reaching Salt Lake City before going to the post office. How eagerly I clasped the precious missives to my breast when they were in my possession. I was almost afraid to open them for fear that they might contain sorrowful news. Driving that thought from my mind I hastily read one after the other, and when I had been assured that all were well and happy as I had left them, then more at my leisure did I read over and over every word they contained. Letters from home! What a comforting sound to wanderers like ourselves, cut off from the world and beyond the pale of civilized life.

We camped for several days in the outskirts of the city, and enjoyed to our heart's content the green fruit and fresh vegetables that we were able to buy or trade from the Mormon women. These women thronged into our camp with everything in the way of produce, which they were glad to exchange for any articles the emigrants desired to part with. At that period when every pound of freight had to be brought overland by wagons, the tariff was fabulously high, and if these Mormon women could acquire anything by trading their fruits, vegetables, butter and cheese, they were that much ahead. So here I parted with my comfortable feather bed. Every Mormon who came into camp wanted to buy it.

At first, I steadily refused to part with it, but finally I was offered an amount which in our pressing need for money I thought it unwise to refuse. So great was the demand for feather beds and pillows that I might have sold it for even a larger sum. Through all the journey I had held on to my three flat irons, but for some time I had ceased to use them, as the clothing we wore required only cleanliness. These flat irons I bartered with a woman for a tub of fresh butter which I hoped would last us through to California. And I exchanged a much-battered brass handled shovel and tongs for a pair of cowhide shoes for myself, which in a few days grew rough, red and rusty, although they lasted until the end of the journey. I was only too glad to trade them many articles, which I could dispense with in exchange for their fresh fruit and vegetables, butter, eggs and cheese of which I laid in as liberal a supply as would keep for the rest of our trip.

While we camped in the outskirts of the city, we found it necessary to buy hay for our stock. This was brought to us each day by a Mormon woman, the hay tied in a huge bundle and carried on her back and shoulders. This required several trips before a sufficient quantity could be brought in this manner, and when we expressed our surprise that a woman should bear such a burden, she replied morosely "Mormon women are only beasts of burden." A man came into camp one day to sell us some grain. While dickering with my husband over the price and quantity, he kept his eyes fastened on me as I stood preparing our dinner. Suddenly he came over and reached out his hand to shake hands with me. I gazed at him in amazement, and I suppose my countenance showed my surprise. He said, "You do not know me."

"No," I replied, "I do not."

"Well," he said, "I know you and you are the daughter of Robert Honeyman," calling my father's name. He then said that he had worked for my father when I was a little girl, and telling me his own name brought to my recollection the time, place and circumstances. I could not deny to him that while we were not Missourians yet we had emigrated from Missouri. I felt somewhat startled and annoyed to meet him in Salt Lake City. However, I assumed a smiling face and said, "O, yes, I now remember you well," and made him welcome to our humble camp. He informed me that he had embraced the Mormon faith, marrying a mother and two daughters, and invited us very cordially to visit him in his home. I replied that, if his wives would care to see me, it would give me great pleasure to accept his invitation.

In the evening he returned bringing his wives to call upon me. They were plain, common-place people on a par with most of the women I had seen there, except that they were Americans, while the majority of the women were foreigners. They insisted that we should dine with them the next day. To gratify my curiosity to see how a Mormon household was conducted, I accepted their kind invitation, and we enjoyed their hospitality exceedingly.

There was no reference to the difference in our opinions, and from all I observed each wife was treated alike. The mother, who was also the third wife, entertained us, while the daughters, who were the first and second wives prepared a very excellent dinner. They seemed perfectly contented with the existing order of things. But many of the Mormon women with whom we conversed, were dissatisfied and unhappy. They worked hard and looked worn and dejected. They performed the most menial labour, many of them working in the fields all day in the broiling sun. But I must say that I never saw a community wherein existed so much industry and thrift, combined with so much ignorance and such implicit faith in their fanatical leaders.

We lingered for several days in Salt Lake City and cleaned house so to speak. That is we unloaded and rearranged our stores, repacked our depleted boxes, aired and cleaned our bedding, which was impossible when we travelled every day, brushed out the accumulated sand and alkali dust, repaired the wagon which the constant wear over the bad roads made necessary, and had our faithful old horse newly shod. We were soon to find that we had overstocked ourselves with fresh fruit and vegetables. We hoped that they might last us at least a month, but had not counted on the hot sun across the Utah desert, which so wilted and shrivelled them that they were no longer appetising and we threw them away.

The tub of fresh butter, which looked so hard and firm when stowed away in our wagon, was soon turned by the hot sun of the desert into liquid oil by day, though it hardened a little at night. For a while we used it even in its liquid state, but eventually it became so rancid that it, too, was left by the wayside.

We had been told by fellow travellers before reaching Salt Lake that the Mormons never allowed a young woman to leave their borders, and I must confess to a feeling of trepidation as we drove out of the city of Salt Lake. Even when we were several miles beyond its borders, my fears were not wholly allayed. We had heard rumours of emigrants pursued and overtaken, after they had thought they had gotten safely away. The women and female children were torn from husbands and fathers and taken back to the city to be held as wives to some noted elder of the Church, while the husbands were tortured and killed if they offered the least resistance. But happily, I found that I had been harbouring unnecessary fears, and in a few days, I had acquired my usual serenity.

(For more on Mormon life and their women see *Wife No. 19* by Ann Eliza Young and '*Tell it All*' by Fanny Stenhouse: Leonaur 2010.)

CHAPTER 13

The Deserts

Leaving Salt Lake City, our road crossed the River Jordan. We did not get a view of the Great Salt Lake as it lay some twenty miles and a good day's travel beyond our direct route. We left the green and fertile land around the near neighbourhood of the city, and again came on a desert as barren as the great Sahara. Here we encountered sixty miles of almost pure sand. Seas of water would not have produced verdure on its barren soil. The drought was intense and there was no cultivation or industry of any sort. The scanty vegetation was the everlasting sage brush and grease wood which I am tired of mentioning. The mountains and plains seemed to divide the ground equally. The valleys were from ten to fifteen miles across, though in the clear air of Utah they seemed only half that distance.

I remember clearly the beautiful sunsets. In this rainless climate the mountains in the full sunlight took on the hues of ruby and carnelian, and at sunset and twilight assumed tints of opal and amethyst. No artist, however skilfully he might handle his brush, could do justice to the brilliant stretches of rare and roseate colourings of these indescribable sunrises and sunsets.

But the arid soil produced little food for our stock. Here and there grew the bunch grass on which depended the life and sustenance of our cattle. Only at rare intervals would we reach a stream whose banks afforded forage for our stock and rest and refreshment for weary and thirsty travellers. Springs were most infrequent and often we had to dig to a considerable depth in the shallow, dry bed of the streams for water, finding barely enough to partially slack the thirst of our cattle. And oh, the suffering from the scorching, burning alkali dust. It filled the air, penetrated through everything, covered our bodies, found its dusty way into our food boxes, bedding, and clothing. All the water we drank was tainted with its soapy flavour. It choked up the pores of our skin, eating its way into the nostrils and lips. Our faces were continually cracked and sore from its action.

Dreary and monotonous as this country seems now as you travel over it in a comfortable Pullman, it was indescribably more so in the days of the slow-moving ox team. It was over six hundred miles from Salt Lake to the base of the Sierras, but the roundabout way that sometimes we had to travel in order to find food and water for our stock made the distance much longer. The best time we could possibly make would not average over a hundred miles a week. At that period for miles over these inhospitable plains there was not a habitation visible. Now on the line of the railways thriving towns and villages abound and the iron horse bellows forth his deep-throated song almost hourly. The thousands speeding over this unfriendly soil little realise the discomforts impeding our slow journey.

We occasionally met some strange characters while traveling on the plains and through the mountains of Utah and Nevada—men who had drifted over these tractless wilds, isolating themselves from the companionship of their kind, and becoming partial savages. The monotony of our journey was sometimes dispelled by one of these men dropping into our camp, and we became much interested in the strange stories of their wonderful adventures. It appeared that every hour in their roving lives had its dangers and hairbreadth escapes. Some were trappers and scouts, others stockmen and herdsmen. Many apparently had no other desire than to live close to nature and remote from civilization.

We encouraged them to tell of the remarkable episodes of their venturesome lives, and it seemed to give them as much pleasure to relate as it did us to sit alternately thrilling or trembling at the wonderful stories. None of the many tales we had read of Western adventure could so have moved us, not even the famous Fennimore Cooper, over whose stories we had burned the midnight oil. Two of these frontiersmen met us on the road one day. They had been alone in the wilderness for weeks, hunting and prospecting. They turned back and went on with us for the balance of the day. We were informed that one of these men was the greatest Indian exterminator on the frontier. His whole family had been massacred by the Indians and his greatest pleasure was in shooting Indians whenever opportunity offered.

We looked forward to Saturday night in camp as a welcome rest and relaxation. Six days' travel was enough for man and beast. We needed the quiet and repose of Sunday. It was not always a complete rest for me, for there was the usual laundering and baking. Still, it was a change from the continual moving on. It also gave us the opportunity to indulge in two extra hours of sleep in the morning which proved a blessing to me. Early rising was my *"bête noir."* The extra time gave me a chance to cook a better Sunday morning breakfast.

A yearning filled our souls, or rather our stomachs, for a broiled chicken, fried oysters, or an omelette. Hot rolls we had always for breakfast, but Sunday morning's flap-jacks were our greatest treat. These were made from the sour milk I had carefully saved a day or two. Our milk supply was gradually failing as our little cow could no longer give us a sufficient quantity on the dry and scanty grazing. In place of butter the ever-ready bacon gravy thickened with flour and milk was used. We had both become adept in tossing the flap-jacks up into the air, turning them over and back into the frying pan, and these had to satisfy us in lieu of all the good things that we had in our imagination. We were happy if we had decent water to make our coffee palatable. Travellers on these desert wastes found scant provision for sensitive stomachs. Fortunately, our outdoor life and exercise found us with appetites whetted for bacon and beans.

By this time my condition became apparent to the most casual observer. Frequently the squaws approached me and patting me on the bosom, would say, "By and by *papoose."* The urgent need of some new maternity gowns appealed to me every day. But where was I to procure them, hundreds of miles from any dry goods emporium? Necessity, that stern mother of invention, came to my aid. Before starting on our journey, I had made, to protect it from the dust of travel, a stout covering of blue plaid gingham for my feather bed. This outer covering, I had removed when I sold the bed in Salt Lake. Ripping open the plain straight seams, I cut and fashioned without guide or pattern a comfortable and serviceable, if not a stylish, garment, making it by hand at odd moments in camp or as I rode along on my way. From a big flowered dressing gown that my husband had discarded as being too effeminate to be worn on the plains, changing its lines from its too masculine contour, I made another suitable and befitting dress, although the colouring was almost too bright and gay for that style of garment.

Time hung heavily on our hands as we plodded along over the barren stretches of Utah. We became almost as lifeless as the country over which we were traveling. Even by day there was an all-pervading silence. No chirp of bird, no hum of insect. Far ahead of us a white line marked our road. It seemed to ever beckon us on over more arid stretches of desert, sand and sage brush. This part of our journey was one perpetual search for water, and when we were fortunate enough to find it, we did nothing but condemn and criticize it all night, grumbling at its quality and lack of quantity. Yet we left it in the morning with fear that we might not again find any so good. The nights were unbearable with the unutterable stillness. The unbroken silence seemed to overpower us with its subdued indifference. It struck a chill to our hearts, and we sought our lowly beds with dread, and timidly slept under the distant and unfamiliar stars.

Just before reaching Fish Springs, we passed one of the salt wells that were common to this part of the country. Its depth was unknown, but the water contained therein was so strongly impregnated with salt that it was like a strong brine. This well was six or eight feet in diameter, and all around it the vegetation was covered with a white incrustation. The suction of this strange well was so great that it would draw in anything used in attempting to explore its depths. A rude fence had been thrown around it to guard the unwary traveller.

Fish Springs was a large pool of water lying at the base of a low mountain. For three or four miles it sent out a large and copious stream, but the thirsty sands soon absorbed it. The water, while brackish, was said to abound in fish.

We threw in our line and tried to coax a bite from the finny denizens, but the only bite we got was from the swarming mosquitoes, immense in size and venomous as starved creatures. They stung our cattle to the verge of madness, and at early dawn we were glad to get beyond their onslaughts. A rude stage station was established at Fish Springs, and the solitary keeper greeted us warmly. The sight of travellers to pass the night brought some variety into his isolated life, which had no companionship save the horses and his dogs and cats. We filled his heart with gratitude by leaving with him some of our tattered and torn literature. From this man we learned that the nearest water to be found was over thirty miles away, and he urged us, if possible, to make the drive in one day.

Next morning, long before the sun was up, we were traveling our way through a dusty, sandy pass. The sky was overcast with heavy leaden clouds. The heat was intense. Peal after peal of thunder shook the air, but only a slight shower overtook us. However, we hailed it with delight, for while there was more thunder than shower, we were gratified for any moisture. This unusual rain served to cool the air, and we hurried along with renewed zeal, hoping to reach by nightfall, the point already described to us as Pleasant Valley. Darkness overtook us long before we reached its precious locality.

We knew, however, that it could not be far off by the way our thirsty cattle snuffed the air, and by their increased gait, which required no urging. A little later we drove into the valley, where the pure and sparkling water of Willow Springs greeted us with its refreshing coolness. How we revelled in its pure, sweet depths. Our thirsty cattle drank again and again, stopped to graze a while, then returned to dip their brown muzzles into its leaping waters. The vegetation around Willow Springs was the most luxurious we had seen since we left Salt Lake, and as we had overdriven our stock, we stayed there for two or three days.

We were told by the keeper of this station that we were now over the Utah desert, that is the northeast corner of it, though it extended some two or three hundred miles south of us. For a time after leaving Pleasant Valley, our road lay over the mountains of Utah, which brought us some relief from the everlasting sage brush and sand of the desert. These mountains were fairly wooded. A few cedars raised their gnarled and stunted bodies from the ground to a height of ten or fifteen feet. There were also pine of equally scrubby character. But in the canyons grew large balsam firs. My little son engaged himself in gathering large quantities of the gum that exuded from these trees. The flavouring and chewing qualities very much resembled that of the spruce gum of the East.

Our route through these Utah mountains led us over innumerable ranges. We seldom lacked for water there, but the way was devious and wild. One afternoon, leaving the higher ranges behind us, we struck a level plain, and saw ahead of us a drove of five or six hundred cattle which their drivers were urging over a low, marshy piece of ground over which had been built a rough pole bridge. Such a large number crossing at one time had torn the frail structure to pieces. As the ground was too miry and uncertain for us to attempt the crossing, we were compelled to wait over a day, until James with the help of the herdsman repaired the bridge, over which our timid oxen reluctantly trod. Our horse for a time utterly refused to trust his precious bones on the uncertain structure.

When we arrived at Ruby valley, we were told that we were in Nevada Territory. I looked in vain for the precious stones that I supposed had given name to the little station. On reaching Diamond

Springs, I found them also lacking in the sparkling gems whose name they bore.

Finally, we arrived at the banks of the Humboldt River. I say banks, for most of the way along its course was little else but banks. I had heard tales of the Humboldt since I was a child. I had studied its devious wanderings through sandy deserts in my geography at school. Mythical stories had been repeated by different people we met on our journey, and yet I was wholly unprepared for the sight of that river which appeared such an insignificant stream. In many places there was scarcely enough water to dignify it by the name of a stream, although it was said to be three hundred miles long.

In the fullest part that I saw, it was never larger than an ordinary brooklet. Its narrow bottom at intervals produced a coarse grass, but so strongly impregnated with alkali, that no man who had any regard for the life of his stock would allow them to eat it, if there was any alternative. In some places they had to eat or die and many of them did eat and die, as the numerous whitened bones that covered its banks and borders testified. James turned his stock away from it if possible, preferring to let them browse on the bullberry or the buffalo bush, which grew here and there among the willows. Or if it was imperative that they should feed on this coarse grass in lieu of something better, he would take his sickle and cut the grass for them, as by so doing the stock would not get at the roots, which contained much more of the alkali.

Along its ugly, sandy borders no tree worthy of the name was seen. But there were innumerable droves of gadflies, mosquitoes, and gnats, countless and bloodthirsty. There was no comfort to be found either night or day along its borders. During the day the heat was intense, and the thick dust permeated the atmosphere. We thought we had driven over many barren lands, but our pathway along the Humboldt discounted anything with which we had come in contact.

Our pilgrimage through these scorching deserts of Nevada was one long to be remembered. Each morning as the blazing sun arose above the horizon, our tired and sunburned eyes looked in vain for some green spot in all that burning sand, and as we slowly and wearily plodded along its glowing surface, overcome with heat and consumed with thirst, we suffered almost beyond endurance. Unless one has travelled by our slow method, they can have only the slightest conception of these blistering, waterless wastes. Many emigrants whose stock was in no condition to stand this long-continued travel without water, found their stock dying and leaving them with no means of transportation. Often, they were compelled to abandon their wagons, pack a few provisions on a single ox or mule, and toil on afoot.

The bones of hundreds of cattle lay bleaching in the sun. Graves without number were dug by the wayside. It was pitiful and heart rending to see them in such numbers. Scarcely a day passed that we did not observe the lowly burial place of some poor sufferer, who had at last succumbed to the hardships of this long journey. These rude graves were sometimes covered with a pile of stones. Others bore a headboard on which was rudely cut the name of him who lay beneath. For them no weeping willow sighed a sad requiem nor enfolded their lowly mounds with its tender, swaying branches. No marble shaft praised their deeds or told their fame. No flowers rare and sweet rested on the unconsecrated soil. But the horned toad and lizard glided beneath the growth of scanty weeds. Those lying here were lonely now, deserted by the loved ones whose bleeding hearts had been forced to leave them at rest beneath the bitter soil.

Fortunately, at this late day the horrors of this region have been overcome. In numerous instances wells have been dug and water led into the arid desert. Railroads have been built, and in this age of fierce and furious competition men and money have overcome many difficulties. And now a trip Westward to the Pacific Coast in a comfortable car is sought for by all, and considered a delightful and entertaining journey of a few days. Since our long hazardous journey of eighteen hundred and sixty, I have travelled back and forth a number of times over much of the route we slowly toiled over so long ago. It has been a constant source of wonder to me how we were able to endure it.

CHAPTER 14

Climbing the Sierras.

We had been in the Humboldt region only a few days, when one night we drove into a camp of emigrants who had preceded us all the way from Salt Lake. Their teams, which consisted of mules and horses, kept a day or two ahead of us. But owing to the sickness of a valuable horse, they had been delayed on the road. The company consisted of a white-haired, and rugged old patriarch from the State of Michigan, with his aged wife and two daughters, girls near my own age. A son and a nephew, together with three hired men who had charge of the fine horses the old gentleman was driving through to California, completed the company.

Their traveling outfit consisted of a substantial carriage fitted up with every comfort and convenience for the tedious journey, and drawn by four large mules, two huge prairie schooners carrying their camp equipage and tents, and another wagon conveying grain and provisions for the family and horses, The camp wagon held every comfort that could be devised for a family tenting on the plains. An immense cook stove was loaded and unloaded every day, for it required a great amount of cooking to feed so many. A dining table of rough boards, strong hickory bottomed chairs, and any number of minor comforts that were unknown to us with only our single team to carry all our possessions.

The old gentleman whose name was Brookfield, was a grand-looking specimen of a Western farmer. He was stout, rather short, with snow-white hair and beard, and a ruddy countenance beaming with genial good nature, and still vigorous in spite of advancing years. His wife was just the opposite, painfully angular, and inclined to be somewhat shrewish, a perfect paragon of neatness, and just as much a stickler for order and cleanliness on the plains as she doubtless was in her well-ordered home in Michigan. The daughters were comely girls of eighteen and twenty with long, beautiful, naturally curling hair that hung in ringlets to their waists, and which curled so tightly that no amount of pulling could straighten it. These curls were a source of great curiosity to the Indians. Their own hair hung so straight they could not understand the difference, and watched the girls most intently. Sometimes an Indian, more curious than the others, would venture to examine the curls. Drawing one out to its extreme length and releasing it, he would look so surprised to see it quickly renew its original curl. The girls became uneasy at the sensation their hair produced and wore their bonnets whenever the Indians invaded the camp.

The son of Mr. Brookfield was a capable and attractive young man much like the father. The nephew was the cook, and also the wag of the party, witty and quick at repartee, and a great practical joker. His name was Bert Brookfield. He called the old lady Aunt Debby and he truly was a thorn in Aunt Debby's side. For morning, noon and night he was ever racking his brains for some joke to play upon his nervous old aunt. To me it was an amusing sight to watch Bert, as he gaily donned his cook's cap and apron preparatory to cooking what he called "an elaborate coarse dinner." Aunt Debby hovered around to see that he washed his hands before mixing the bread. He now and then pretended to wipe his floured hands on the seat of his pants or his nose on the dish towel, or carelessly caught up the corner of a horse blanket to wipe the dust from the frying pan, much to the disgust of his fastidious aunt, who continually scolded and fretted until the meal was served.

The meeting with this congenial company was a source of great pleasure to us, for after leaving Salt Lake I had not even seen a white woman. James and I had gradually grown silent and taciturn, and had unwittingly partaken of the gloom and sombreness of the dreary landscape. We no longer gaily sang or joked as we kept step beside our slow cattle, we were tired and jaded to absolute silence and to passive endurance by the monotony of the desert. This lively company of young people near our own ages brought new life and interest to us two lonely travellers. They were all musical. The girls had well-trained voices and sang sweetly, while the young men played on different instruments that they had brought with them. For the few weeks that we travelled together, the time passed pleasantly and harmoniously. Our camp at night was a season of mirth and good-fellowship. And no matter how long and tiresome was the day's drive, or how many vicissitudes we encountered, we each managed at nightfall to furnish our quota of amusement.

One morning at breakfast we heard Aunt Debby berating Bert because the coffee was not up to the usual standard. He insisted that he had prepared the coffee as usual, only the alkali water gave it a disagreeable flavour. I had finished up my camp work and was spending a few moments in visiting them in their camp. Aunt Debby was looking after Bert, keeping up her usual careful scrutiny over his pots and pans to see they were properly cleansed. I observed Bert taking up the coffee pot, and from its cavernous depths draw out a long and loathsome worm which he held up to Aunt Debby's view. With a cry of horror, she made a dash for his curly head. He nimbly eluded her clutches, but did not escape her tongue, lashing. He informed me afterwards that he had dug two or three feet into the banks of the stream for that worm with which to electrify his squeamish aunt and had put it into the pot after the breakfast was over.

Another morning Bert arose from his slumbers, making a great hue and cry over the loss of one of his *moccasins*, and went limping around the camp with one bare and unshod foot. As I watched him beating up his huge pan of batter for the hot cakes that he cooked every morning, he turned and gave me a sly wink denoting mischief on his part. Our drive for the day was to be one of unusual length. Everyone was hurrying his or her work, in order to get an early start before the sun grew so intolerably hot. Aunt Debby was busily engaged in helping Bert stow away his cooking utensils. Her tongue in the meanwhile was running over with his many derelictions, while he drolly parried her sharp thrusts at his lack of order and neatness. Picking up his half-emptied batter bowl, he looked into it a moment with apparent surprise and consternation. Then drawing forth the huge *moccasin* that he claimed had either been lost or stolen, held it up before the horrified eyes of Aunt Debby, all dripping with the remnants of the batter. These and similar harmless jokes he was constantly playing on the irascible old lady.

The few weeks spent with this company were the most enjoyable part of our journey. While their males and horses made faster time than our oxen, yet at the end of the day, by driving a little later we managed to camp together. Owing to the lameness of their fine bay stallion, they, too, made shorter drives. But after the animal had almost entirely recovered, Mr. Brookfield was anxious to make up his lost time and get his fine stock into California as soon as possible. He decided to still follow the Humboldt to its sink, and from there to take the road to California, where his final destination was to be Marysville. We had learned that the route by way of Carson Valley, led us through more fertile lands with better forage for our cattle, a very important matter to us, though it was a longer and more indirect route.

Very reluctantly we parted company with these good people, promising each other at some future day we should meet in California. But alas for promises, we never saw or heard of them again, although we wrote to them and made enquiries concerning them from people of Marysville. Whether they changed their minds, like ourselves, and never went to their intended destination, we knew not. To this day I have never forgotten their pleasant companionship on the desolate plains of Nevada.

As we turned our faces in the direction of Carson River a feeling of thankfulness took possession of our hearts. We were leaving the alkali soil of the Humboldt desert behind us, and though the Carson River was absorbed by the same desert, yet a glance at even its worst features was enough to convince us that it watered a far more hopeful region. Large cottonwoods dotted the banks, here and there were willows, and the wild rose in full bloom occasionally cropped out on its sandy banks. Still the prevalence of drought was everywhere visible, and long before we reached Carson City we travelled over miles of land doomed to sterility. As we neared the town there appeared to be a great rush of miners and prospectors headed for some new mines opened up in that vicinity. Some of these men were so enthusiastic over the prospect that they urged us to go no further, but to locate in the new mines. Our faces, however, were set for California and we would not be persuaded. This embryo town was so small and scattered that we hardly knew when we entered it. Yet it aspired to be the emporium of the new gold region.

The features of the country had notably changed. From the dry and thirsty sagebrush land we gradually drove into soft meadows, with numberless rivulets flowing down from the Sierras. Owing to the shallowness of their beds they were easily controlled, and had been made to irrigate a large portion of the land. Small farms and gardens occasionally came in view, and for our stock we found the sweetest and most nutritious grass in abundance. The village of Genoa was a most picturesque little spot. It stood on a bench between the mountains and the valley, with rivulets flowing through and around it to give fertility to its soil and fructify its gardens and green fields.

I was charmed with its quiet beauty and seclusion, the brightness of its innumerable streams, and the grandeur of the neighbouring mountains whose emerald verdure impressed my mind with a vividness which only those who have passed long months on a shadeless desert can fully realise. From Carson to the pretty little village of Genoa was a drive of nearly twenty miles. After a night spent in those charming surroundings we began the ascent of the Sierra Nevadas, the last range of mountains we would have to climb before we viewed the land we had travelled so long and far to see.

There were still two weeks of mountain travel ahead of us, and we proceeded slowly owing in a great measure to my condition. The continual jolting of the wagon over the uneven roadway was exceedingly trying to me, so much so in fact that I finally gave up ridings altogether, taking my slow way up the mountain on foot. Day after day for the next two weeks I trudged slowly and painfully through the red dust of the Sierras, from Genoa, at the eastern base, to the foothills of California. I had always boasted of my pedestrian powers, but when I surveyed that road winding up and still up, my pride in being a great walker vanished, and like the old bishop who was so fond of worldly comfort, I said, "All, all is vanity except a carriage." I could no longer mount my horse, and only by slow degrees made my way on foot, stopping frequently to rest the weary muscles. Then upward again, every nerve as tense as steel and every faculty alert, I climbed with painful toil.

After leaving Genoa, we wound around the curved border of a narrow roadway excavated on the mountain side, and only a little wider than the wagon's tracks. So frequent and sharp were these curves that the forward yoke of oxen would be out of sight as I followed the wagon. Looking down the precipice on which we were traveling I shuddered at the thought of what might happen if our sturdy cattle made a misstep on the narrow roadway that seemed to hang' on the mountain side. My little son had been suffering for several days with a sprained ankle and was compelled to ride, so on his account I was extremely anxious as I watched the wagon lurch around the sharp and narrow curves.

The scenery along these winding roads was magnificent. The tall pines grew straight as arrows and clinging to their sturdy trunks were beautiful variegated yellow and green lichens. The smaller trees of these immense forests were here in richest profusion. Hemlocks, balsam, pines, and fir trees filled up the intervening spaces. The whole forest seemed gay with life and motion. Squirrels frolicked and scampered from tree to tree. The agile and graceful chipmunk darted hither and thither in the low hazel bushes, chattering noisily as he ran, as if scolding us for disturbing him on his own domain, his bright eyes twinkling as they peered up at us from some leafy bough. The blue jay, with his towering crest and noisy discordant call, flew swiftly through the dark foliage of the evergreen trees. Here and there a dusty lupine lifted up its blue-tipped stem, all strangely beautiful when compared with the alkaline deserts over which we had so recently toiled.

This first day's climb into the Sierras was a novel experience to me. These mountains were so different in aspect from the bare bald Rockies. Ever and *anon* a little spring by the roadside gave the thirsty climbers a chance to quench their thirst. As I plodded slowly up the mountain side, I had ample time to observe all the beauties of its ever-changing scenery. Winding around some steep cliff new surprises would burst upon my vision, here a transient view of still more towering summits covered with snow, there a glimpse of a stream flowing between or at the base of some deep and dark ravine. These beautiful mountains which rose like castellated towers astonished me with the immensity of their huge pines attaining heights that seemed wonderful.

The enormous cones were often a foot long and the rich, green foliage, like long needles, swayed with the passing breeze. Lying prone by the wayside, and crossing each other at every imaginable angle were hundreds of these monarchs of the forest laid low by the woodman's axe. It seemed a sacrilege to gaze upon them in their prostrate grandeur. On every side were huge stumps at whose bases lay the fallen trunks of the once noble trees. Civilization made roadways a necessity, and these grand old trees were the victims of the march of improvement. The Rocky Mountains failed to compare with the Sierra range in the variety and grandeur of this great forest growth.

Bewitched by the beauty of the surroundings I hardly realised that I had grown weary and footsore, until the setting sun began to cast its shadows over the pine-hung slopes of these mountain gorges. Looking down this slope far below us lay the hamlet of Genoa that we had left so early in the morning, still in sight although we had climbed steadily above it all that long September day. Under a huge pine tree we placed our tent, cooked our humble supper, and prepared to sleep our first night in the vastness of the great Sierras, breathing that balmy air balsam-tinctured from the fragrant pines. Through the open door of our little tent, we watched the moon as it shone down upon us through the interlacing boughs. I was too weary to sleep, and traced the movements of the bright and radiant sphere until it passed beyond my vision. At last, I must have fallen asleep, for I was awakened long before dawn by the most unearthly shrieks ringing through the forest and coming back again in plaintive echoes from the hills beyond. These fearful wails were caused by a death in a camp of Indians who were located in our near vicinity, but of whose presence we had been totally ignorant.

CHAPTER 15

The Journey's End

We imagined when we had progressed so near our journey's end that we had bid a final *adieu* to "Lo, the poor Indian." But we were yet to see a more degraded specimen of the red man than had been our privilege hitherto. Certainly, the Indians we met in the Sierra mountains were more degraded and more filthy than any tribe we had met in our wanderings. These Indians migrated from the valleys to the mountains in the fall to harvest the pine nuts growing so plentifully in these forests, and on which depended their food for the winter months. We came upon them frequently everywhere through these mountains. The lazy braves mounted, leading the way unhampered and free, were followed by troops of obedient and slavish squaws on foot, laden with huge baskets in which the harvest of nuts was loaded.

These Indians were inferior in size and stature. The largest brave rarely exceeded in height a little over five feet. They were extremely homely and had wide mouths and flat noses. Their hair, black as jet, cut straight over their low foreheads, hung at the back and sides in long, straggling strands. The squaws wore their hair thickly plastered with pitch, and a broad band of pitch was smeared across noses and cheeks. They were horribly filthy and covered with vermin, and their dirty offspring were strapped as usual to a board, and carried on their backs.

While this band of Indians was busy harvesting their annual crop of pine nuts, one of the young squaws was taken suddenly ill and died. She was the wife of the chief and great was the commotion among them at her untimely taking off. It was the custom among these Indians, when a death occurred in their tribe, for the superannuated squaws to become professional mourners. They would immediately proceed to stain their already tarred heads and faces with a more ample supply of pitch, and then burst forth into the most dismal wails indeed. The forest and mountains reverberated with their unearthly shrieks for the dead. This weeping and wailing was continued through the long hours of the first night and all the following day until near sunset.

It was our privilege to witness the strange funeral ceremonies over the body of this squaw. It was carefully rolled in her soiled red blanket, then a huge pile of dried pine branches was erected, on which was placed her dead body. Her nearest relatives grouped themselves about the funeral pyre, while the others stood around the outside of the circle. For an interval of ten moments or more perfect silence reigned. The loud wailing of the aged squaws had ceased and just as the setting sun was about to sink below the horizon, one of these ancient mourners, an old squaw whose head was literally covered with tar, raised her arms heavenward and gazed long and steadily at the sun as it slowly sank from sight.

At intervals she muttered some low incantation, her bronze countenance lit up with a strange intensity. For a short space of time, she stood in this position. Then, suddenly with a blood-curdling shriek, she sprang forward and seizing a brand from the camp fire lighted the funeral heap. The flames shot high in the darkened forest. The aged squaws, whose bent bodies rocked to and fro in rhythmic time, renewed their plaintive wailing and all the other Indians of both sexes joined in a pathetic chorus, and chanted a funeral dirge sounding to our listening ears like, "*Emaylaya, emaylaja*." All swiftly turned their faces toward the setting sun, then back again upon the funeral pyre. It was a strange weird sight to us, that circle of bronzed Indians around the burning corpse. While the song or chant was being sung each one swayed mechanically to the measure of the dirge, but their stolid countenances hid any expression of grief or woe.

For several days before reaching the summit of the Sierras I toiled slowly up and over the narrow winding trails, stopping frequently to rest and catch my breath, on and on and always higher and higher, frequently meeting the mule pack trains carrying freight and merchandise from California over to the deserts of Nevada. These mules were burdened with every variety of merchandise, furniture, flour and freight of all kinds, securely fastened on to huge pack saddles. Around their necks was strung a string of bells which warned teamsters and pedestrians of their approach. These mules never gave the right of way to anyone.

In many places the road was so narrow and the mountain so steep above and below us, that I was obliged to squeeze myself as closely to the cliff as possible, hunting if I had time, some place that had been excavated a little deeper in the side of the cliff than usual, and standing there perfectly still until they passed me by. Their burdened sides pressed close against me as they crowded along. It was rather trying to the nerves to have from sixty to a hundred pack-mules rushing past one with scarcely room for one's body.

As we continued to ascend, I found that I could no longer keep up with the team and the slow-moving oxen would out-walk me. In the early part of our journey, I could without effort out-walk them, but not so now. My husband frequently halted the team to wait for me. Oh, how glad was I to catch a sight of the waiting wagon in which I could lie down for a brief respite. At last, we reached the summit in the early days of October and camped a day and rested in Strawberry valley. The atmosphere at this altitude began to grow shivery at nightfall. A keen, frosty air permeated everywhere. Our camp was in the neighbourhood of a lumber, or rather a shake settlement.

Four or five young and vigorous men from the New England states had located a timber claim in the heart of these immense pine forests, and were busily employed in getting out lumber and making the shakes that were in demand for building purposes all down through the Sacramento valley. With true California hospitality they visited our camp, and as the nights were cold insisted on our sharing the comforts of their cabin for the night. James turned to me to see what I thought of the proposition. I could easily see that he wanted to accept the invitation and have a talk and smoke with these hospitable mountaineers. I, too, longed to be under a roof and sit by a warm fireside. Needless to say, we accepted. Before we reached their cabin, I heard strains of music from a favourite opera which I was surprised to hear in this mountain wilderness. When the cabin door was opened, we found a young man who played the violin with the skill of a virtuoso.

The bright light from within the cabin showed us a most cheerful interior. There was an immense room with a roughly boarded floor. The spaces between the logs of which the cabin was built were unchinked and let in volumes of fresh mountain ozone. In a rough stone fire-place huge logs were burning. A square home-made pine table occupied the centre of the room. It held a few books, interspersed with pipes and tobacco. At one side of this room was a rough couch covered with the skins of wild animals and very comfortable. There was a rocking-chair that one of the men had made, the seat and back formed of skins like the couch.

This was immediately whirled in front of the fire for my benefit, and it was a great luxury to be seated once more in a real rocking-chair, as for the last six months I had either sat upon the ground, or on a humble soap box with neither arms nor back for support. Indeed, the smallest suggestion of home or home comfort was very grateful. The rough walls of the cabin were decorated with the various trophies of the forest, antlers, skins of wild animals, Indian bows and arrows, and guns of various kinds were stacked in the corners or hung on the rough walls. The huge fire place took nearly one side of this room. Around the other sides were bunks built into the walls which served for beds. The mattresses, made from flour sacks and filled with hay, were fairly comfortable when covered with their grey and blue blankets. They whole interior presented an inviting and homelike look to us belated emigrants, and for a mountain cabin occupied solely by men it was cleaner and more neatly kept than would be expected.

Our little son greatly amused these men with his childish prattle, and continually questioned them about the various trophies decorating the walls of the cabin, demanding the history of each one and the manner of acquisition. His infantile opinions, given without the least reserve and with a seriousness beyond his years, caused many a covert smile and frequently a hearty laugh from them. Such a long time had elapsed since they had seen or conversed with a child that they pronounced it a great treat, and he was handed around from one to another until the Sandman caused his weary eyelids to hang most heavily, and he called loudly for bed.

One of the larger bunks was assigned to us for the night. Then the men lit their pipes and stole forth into the night, giving me ample time to undress and get to bed. At early dawn they made themselves just as scarce until my morning toilet was completed. A knock at the door was answered by my husband and there stood one of our hosts with a freshly-scrubbed tin wash basin filled with warm water, and a clean flour sack for a towel, politely apologizing because he could do no better for us. The hearty breakfast was prepared in the rough shed adjoining the cabin and I greatly enjoyed a meal that I had not cooked myself. And I found the biscuit made from sour dough and soda most excellent.

While eating our breakfast the men insisted that we should tarry with them another day. They appeared to take unusually kindly interest in us and complimented my husband on the pluck and energy he had exhibited in so successfully engineering his way across the plains alone and unaided. We were both inspired with hope and confidence, by hearing that such enterprise and courage as we had shown was bound to succeed in a new country. Taking James around part of their claim, they showed him their primitive workshop and told him of different sections of good timber land waiting for someone to pre-empt and open up. They told him also much of their own prospects and the already successful business they had acquired.

Finally, they wound up the conference of the forenoon with an offer to James to stay and go into the lumber business with them, asking for no money in the transaction. Of course, we had our good three yoke of oxen which were very much needed in a logging camp. As a farther inducement for us to stay, they offered to build another cabin near their own for us. A family in their camp would add so much pleasure and company to their isolated lives, particularly as the long winter was approaching.

James felt almost persuaded. Here was a business and a means of living opened to us who were strangers in a strange land with little or no capital except that vested in our traveling outfit. I think were it not for my approaching confinement he would have consented to remain with them. He finally told them that he would abide by my decision. I was weary enough from my long journey to stay and rest, and under other circumstances would have given the kind and opportune offer a grateful acquiescence. But I was young and inexperienced and dreaded going through my coming ordeal so far from nurse or doctor. I have since learned that pioneer women in a new country can do without the services of either one and fare just as well. We enjoyed our stay with these people and reluctantly bade them farewell, promising them if we found no location or business suited to our wants, that in the coming spring we would return to their cabin among the pines of the Sierras.

As we began the descent of the western slope, the wayside houses grew more frequent and we met numerous vans carrying freight over the mountains into Nevada. Occasionally a fruit wagon appeared, with pears, apples and other fruit from the fertile Sacramento valley. This was the first fruit we had seen since we had left Salt Lake. The huckster kindly consented to sell me two pears for fifty cents and I think the price made them more enjoyable.

While we were descending what was then called the Hangtown grade, we stopped to water our stock at a wayside inn. The proprietor noticing that we were emigrants came out to our wagon and said to my husband, "Stranger, have you got any sugar to spare in your outfit? We're clean out. The freighter who was to bring our groceries from Sacramento is way behind time. There's nary a pound of that sweet stuff in the house, and the women folks are all clamouring for it." Fortunately, we were able to oblige him with several pounds, and as it was near dinner time, he insisted on our coming into dinner with them.

I demurred at making my appearance at dinner, even in a country hotel, as my blue plaid gingham gown was much soiled with the red dust of the road, and I had neither time nor opportunity to make a fresh toilet. But all my excuses were overruled, and we were ushered into the rough dining room. I found the other guests were as unkempt looking as myself. While enjoying the luxury of a meal with fresh meat well cooked, and plenty of vegetables with good mountain butter and cream, I forgot I was not dressed for dinner. Never was there a meal more thoroughly enjoyed. The potatoes were soggy and the saleratus biscuit golden-hued. But oh, I such a welcome change from bacon and beans.

As we continued down the western slope of the Sierras, we found besides the towering pine other trees with a strange and beautiful foliage; such a wonderful variety of oaks and the picturesque madrona with its bright and shining leaves. The peculiar bark was very curious to Robert, my little son, who discovered when he cut a branch that the red bark peeled off smooth and clean. The handsome manzanita with its brown berries furnished food to birds and bears and to the roving Indian as well. On the down grades as we more rapidly approached the foothills, we felt that at last our feet were planted on the soil of California, the far-famed land of gold, where we thought to pick up the precious metal by the wayside.

How we searched the dust and rocks as we passed along for traces of the golden ore. We observed ditches running here and there filled with yellow water which in our ignorance we imagined was coloured by the particles of gold running through them. Along the ravines and near the brooks were men prospecting and washing the dirt and gravel in a queer arrangement called a rocker, in the hopes of finding what they called pay dirt. Many of the water courses had been deeply and widely cut for miles, bringing the water to miners in their different locations.

Little cabins serving to shelter the busy miners dotted the hills which were honeycombed and tunnelled in every direction, in the eagerness to find the precious metal. We were greatly interested and enthused as we lingered and talked with some of the more fortunate miners who had struck a rich find of pay dirt in the surface diggings. But the beauty of the surrounding country was much disfigured with all manner of ungainly heaps and ridges. Prospecting perhaps was necessary but it did not tend to beautify the face of nature. Beautiful little natural springs abounded, bright and clear, as crystal; but every rill leading from them was turned to liquid mud by some devastating prospector or gold seeker. California in yielding up her wealth of hoarded gold surrendered much of her charm and beauty.

Near a branch of the American River, we saw our first Chinamen. These strange looking men were then a source of wonder to us with their queer habits, style of dress, and their long, braided queues hanging down their backs or else tightly wound around their shaven heads, that were covered with a most peculiar hat looking like inverted wash bowls made of straw. In groups of five or six they were digging the dry gravel and washing it with a sort of Hume and wheel arrangement that brought the water down into the rocker. Several times we stopped to listen to the curious intonation of their voices.

Once we made enquiries of a group of these strange men about the road we should follow, as we had arrived at a point where it forked in two different directions. But they stupidly looked at us and said, "*No sabby.*"

Getting no information from the Chinamen, fate took us in hand and decided our direction. We took the road that appeared to be the most travelled, and thought we were on our way to Placerville, expecting by nightfall to camp within its outskirts. The sun was getting low and still no town in sight. A prospector carrying his pick and shovel and a bundle of blankets met us in the road. From him we learned that we were miles off our road to Placerville, but on the direct route to the town of Folsom. It had been our intention to drive to Sacramento via Placerville as we had been directed and make that city the terminus of our long pilgrimage. We felt chagrined that we were so far off the road. But the prospector, who seemed to be well-informed about the country, told us that we were even nearer to Sacramento than if we had taken the road to Placerville.

Next day at noon we drew near a thrifty-looking farm house, and finding no place for our stock to graze, as all the land was fenced in, we drove up to the barnyard gate and sought permission of the rancher to drive within his enclosure, and asked him to sell us some hay to feed our stock. To this he readily consented, allowed us to make a fire in his barnyard to boil our coffee, and seemed very accommodating. All the time he was walking around our cattle and appeared to be very much interested in them. They, in spite of their long journey, were in excellent condition, looking sleek and well-kept. James was a careful and prudent driver. He was always solicitous for the welfare of his stock and kept them curried and groomed until their hides shone like satin.

The rancher looked them over and over again, pleased at their gentleness and docility. He examined our wagon also, and asked numberless questions in regard to our journey, the length of time we had been on our way, and to what place were we going. Finally, he ended his interrogatory conversation with an offer to buy our whole outfit for the sum of four hundred dollars. This offer coming upon us so suddenly caused us both to hesitate for a moment before replying. Noticing our hesitation, he added, "I will give you and your family a week's board in the bargain, and that will give you time to locate yourselves." This almost took our breath away, coming upon us in such an unlooked-for manner. We could not in reason refuse such a satisfactory offer. It was a much larger sum than we had even hoped to get although we had been told that horned cattle were very high at that time in California.

Within less than an hour's notice, our trunks and personal belongings were removed and our wagon, oxen, horse, tent and camp equipage were turned over to the rancher. Imagine my consternation when he insisted on our going at once to his house. I had no opportunity or time to make a change in my dress, and attired as I was in my soiled and tattered gown, dusty and dirty from the strain of travel and camp; my husband clad in his worn and begrimed red flannel shirt, his rough corduroys stuffed in his rougher boots; my little son in his worn outing garb, we presented anything but a prepossessing appearance.

I dreaded woefully to face the wife who knew nothing of the strangers her husband was ushering thus unceremoniously into her well-ordered household. We met with a more civil reception than I expected, although she looked somewhat askance at our worn garb. We were at once shown into a very plain but clean bed room adjoining the kitchen. My trunks were brought in and I unpacked some clean, fresh garments and after the luxury of a good bath and having removed the red dust of the road we gladly donned the garb of civilized society, and looked and felt fit to be once more within the pale of civilization.

When the bell rang calling us out to supper, I was pleased to note the change in the demeanour of our hostess, who gazed upon us with ill-concealed surprise. Such is the power of good clothes, for the unkempt and soiled emigrants had blossomed out into really good-looking people. My husband, although browned by six months' exposure to the sun and wind, was wonderfully improved when shaved and dressed in a "biled" shirt and collar and well-fitting clothes. I felt proud of him when I compared him with the somewhat slovenly rancher. As for myself I had worn my shaker sun bonnet so closely and was always so vain of my white hands, never allowing myself to go ungloved save when cooking, that I bore no marks of the emigrant, when I discarded my emigrant garb. My fair-haired little son, Robert, looked exceedingly picturesque in his natty suit of blue. I could easily perceive that we were making a new and more favourable impression.

Our bedroom for the night was in such near proximity to the kitchen that I could overhear every word that was spoken there. The next morning I was awakened by a conversation between our hostess and the hired man who had come in with his pail of milk. "Has the boss been buying any emigrant cattle lately," he asked.

"Yes," she replied, "He bought out an emigrant family yesterday, and they are to stay a week with us."

"Well," replied the man, "There are two dead oxen and one cow laying in the corral."

Nothing was said to us at breakfast about any dead animals. But after breakfast was over James went out to the corral to see for himself, and there lay stretched out dead and cold our beautiful black Jill and Buck, our favourite lead oxen, and our gentle little cow. Each of them had apparently been well and sound the day before. Feeding that last day in the open foothills, they had eaten of the poison parsnip which grew there so profusely. At the time of the sale, they had shown no signs of illness, either to us or to the rancher, James insisted on returning some of the money that had been paid to him but the man would not take it. He insisted that it was his loss under the circumstances of the trade.

Our hostess the next morning gave us a large airy room upstairs. During the day, the elderly lady, mother of the rancher, said to me, "We have a piano in the parlour that we brought around the horn with us but no one here can play upon it. Perhaps you play?" I replied that before we left the States, I had been considered quite a musician,

115

but had had no practice for the last six months. At once I was ushered into the unused parlour and the piano unlocked and divested of its rubber covering, and I revelled once more in the touch of the familiar keys, playing over and over my long-neglected music.

I soon had an audience from all the household, including the hired man and the Chinaman. My effort seemed to captivate them all, not that it was excellent, but because they were hungry for music. After discovering that I had this accomplishment, nothing was too good for us. Each vied with the other to make our stay delightful and begged of us to remain until the end of the month. But James was anxious to look about for business, and I felt the need of getting settled before my fast-approaching confinement.

At the end of the week, we left the home of these good people, to whom we became very much attached. We found in the neighbouring town of Folsom, and five or six miles from our new-found friends, a little cottage of two or three rooms exceedingly small and primitive, but roomy enough for our needs, larger than we cared to furnish under the circumstances. We had not fully decided where we were going to locate permanently, and only provided ourselves with the bare necessities that we must have for comfort.

At last, we were settled down for a rest from our long and perilous journey. How I enjoyed the quiet of this humble little home, the cessation from the continual moving on—my morning's peaceful sleep without having to arise at the first peep of day and get ready to travel onward. And here, after an interval of two short weeks the stork put in his appearance and our babe came to us, the mother of the grandsons for whom I pen these lines.

My dear husband was worried beyond all measure for fear that the long and tiresome journey would prove disastrous for me, but I came bravely through the trying ordeal.

I have now finished my narrative of my six month journey overland to California. Many things have been omitted owing to forgetfulness, or lack of skill in selecting what to many would have been more interesting. Some things have been included which, perhaps, it would have been wiser to omit. I have tried to relate all faithfully as I remember it. While striving with my refractory memories, I realised that they were sometimes unsatisfactory to myself and probably would be to others, and, while I have forgotten much of the less interesting parts of the journey, yet, in the main I have kept close to the most striking incidents of our long trip. As we congratulated ourselves that all was well that ended well, we could happily say with California's own poet, Joaquin Miller, in his *Pioneer:*

> *That rest, sweet rest is reckoned best,*
> *For we were worn as worn with years.*
> *Two thousand miles of thirst, and tears,*
> *Two thousand miles of bated breath*
> *Two thousand miles of dust and death.*

Days on the Road: Crossing the Plains
in 1865

SARAH RAYMOND HERNDON

Contents

Preface

I do not expect to gain fame or fortune by the publication of this little book. I have prepared it for publication, because a number of the pioneers who read my journal twenty years ago, when published in *The Husbandman*, have asked me to.

At that time, I was a busy wife, mother and housekeeper, and could only write when my baby boy was taking his daily nap, to supply the copy for each week. No one knows better than I how very imperfect it was, yet many seemed to enjoy it, and the press that noticed it at all spoke very kindly of it.

S. R. H.

Reminiscences of the Plains

By Dr. Howard

Editor *Husbandman.*—Through your kindness to Mrs. Howard, we are a reader of your excellent journal. Hence a few months ago our eyes fell upon "Reminisences of Pilgrimage Across the Plains in 1865," by S. R. H., and at once recognised the writer as the "lady who rode the gallant bay." And now, sir, as we were a humble member of the gallant McMahan train, frequently referred to in her interesting journal, permit me through the columns of your paper to tender her the thanks and gratitude, not only of ourselves, but every surviving member of that train, for affording us the pleasure of again traveling that eventful road without the fatigue and hardships of a long and tiresome journey.

And even now, after the lapse of fifteen years, to be so pleasantly reminded of our "Gallant Bearing" and the confidence reposed in us for protection, while passing through the Indian country, we almost regret that the Indians did not give us a striking opportunity of displaying our prowess. It was our pleasure to form the acquaintance of the writer, as correctly stated, on the north bank of the South Platte, near the foot of Fremont's Orchard. The present editor of the *Husbandman*, then a beardless youth, had been suffering with typho-malarial fever from the time we left Nebraska City, and we visited her camp (ostensibly) begging bread, and obtained as good as was ever baked upon the plains.

From this time on, at least for some hundreds of miles, it was our pleasure to meet her on the road and in camp. We were in different trains, but camped near each other every night for protection from the Indians. Very soon, somehow or other, when our trains were preparing to drive out every morning, and Miss R. was mounting Dick, we were in the act of mounting our pony Jo, and even at this day, in thinking over the matter, I am induced to believe that our ponies be-

127

came somewhat attached to each other, as they would instinctively fall into each other's company. This was the state of affairs existing at Elk Mountain, where the bouquet was gathered and presented, and where, it is frankly admitted, we became somewhat partial.

Well do we recollect the crossing of North Platte, that turbulent stream on the Fort Halleck route. Train after train was crossing all day long. We were standing on the bank, with Captain McMahan, when the Hardinbrooke train, the one in which she was traveling, approached the crossing, and we discovered Miss Raymond on the front seat of the wagon, with lines in hand, in the attitude of driving. We remarked, "Good gracious, look yonder, is it possible Miss Raymond is going to drive that team across this terrible stream alone?"

"Now," said Captain McMahan, "is the time to show your gallantry."

And before we could think twice, she drove bravely in. Of course, we mounted Jo and followed after her, and here on a little island in the middle of the river is where we rode up and congratulated her on her skill as a driver. As we approached the place of our destination our trains became separated. Miss R. preceded us a few days to the Golden City. It was our pleasure, however, to visit her in the little domicile mentioned in her narrative, and

Talk our troubles over, our journey through at last,
And in her happy presence we forgot the gloomy past.

We sojourned in Virginia City but a short time, then crossed a tributary of the Missouri near their confluence, and wintered at Diamond City Confederate Gulch. The June following we returned to our native State.

A year after our return Captain McMahan and myself received cards announcing the nuptials of Miss Raymond and Mr. Herndon, which cards now occupy receivers on our centre tables, for which we were ever thankful, and at which time, of course, the bouquet crumbled to dust. And now wishing the "lady who rode the gallant bay" and the lucky gentleman whose home she makes happy, long life and the enjoyment of a Montana home; I am,

Truly yours,

W. Howard.

Press Notices

"Crossing the Plains in 1865," is the title under which a lady in the *Rocky Mountain Husbandman*, is publishing a series of letters. The story of everyday life on the plains is so prettily written, that these papers repay perusal. We have been charmed by the native grace of the author, and we send her our compliments whoever she may be. We crossed the plains the same year, also, six years before, and we can fully appreciate the experience of our unknown friend who writes so charmingly—*Stock, Farm and Home Weekly*.

In this issue we close our narrative of pleasure, trials, etc., of a trip across the great American plains in 1865. It has been a plain, simple story and true to life and full of interest to Montana's old-timers, and all who made the journey of the plains in wagons. To the editor of this paper, it has been a story of particular interest, for he, a beardless boy then, crossed the plains, was a member of the McMahan train, the sick man for whom Dr. Howard often went foraging for bread—*Rocky Mountain Husbandman*.

"Crossing the Plains in 1865," is the title of a story which was written by a well-known lady of Virginia City, for the *Rocky Mountain Husbandman*, and came to a conclusion in the last number of that paper.

It was a plain, unvarnished recital of the experiences of the journey across the plains when ox-trains were the favourite conveyances, and the voyagers were subjected to many vicissitudes, unknown to travellers of the present day (1902). Though quite unpretentious as to literary merit, it has been interesting in recalling to the minds of the pioneers, who have read it, the eventful scenes of their own pilgrimage, and to them, it has been pleasant reading—*Madisonian*.

"I have felt a deep interest in S. R. H.'s, 'Crossing the Plains in 1865,' all through these long series of letters, and many a familiar spot has been brought back to me that had long been forgotten. And as some of the actors in the play live in Challis. I will say to S. R. H., that Mrs. Hardinbrooke is still loved by a large circle of friends, and that little Annie is now a blooming young lady, and ever worthy the goodbye kiss; that the captain has never disgraced the title bestowed in 1865.

"I am, Mr. Editor, respectfully yours,

"O. E. Penwell."

Days on the Road

May 1.

As I sit here in the shade of our prairie-schooner, with this blank book ready to record the events of this our first day on the road, the thought comes to me:

"Why are we here? Why have we left home, friends, relatives, associates, and loved ones, who have made so large a part of our lives and added so much to our happiness?"

"Echo answers 'Why?'"

"The chief aim in life is the pursuit of life, liberty, and happiness." Are we not taking great risks, in thus venturing into the wilderness? When devoted men and women leave home, friends and the enjoyments of life to go to some far heathen land, obeying the command: "Go, preach my Gospel, to every creature," we look on and applaud and desire to emulate them. There is something so sublime, so noble in the act that elevates the missionary above the common order of human beings that we are not surprised that they make the sacrifice, and we silently wish that we, too, had been called to do missionary work.

But when people who are comfortably and pleasantly situated pull up stakes and leave all, or nearly all, that makes life worth the living, start on a long, tedious, and perhaps dangerous journey, to seek a home in a strange land among strangers, with no other motive than that of bettering their circumstances, by gaining wealth, and heaping together riches, that perish with the using, it does seem strange that so many people do it.

The motive does not seem to justify the inconvenience, the anxiety, the suspense that must be endured. Yet how would the great West be peopled were it not so? God knows best. It is, without doubt, this spirit of restlessness, and unsatisfied longing, or ambition—if you please—which is implanted in our nature by an all-wise Creator that has peopled the whole earth.

This has been a glorious May-day. The sky most beautifully blue, the atmosphere delightfully pure, the birds twittering joyously, the earth seems filled with joy and gladness. God has given us this auspicious day to inspire our hearts with hope and joyful anticipation, this our first day's journey on the road across the plains and mountains.

It was hard to say goodbye to our loved and loving friends, knowing that we were not at all likely to meet again in this life. I felt very much like indulging in a good cry, but refrained, and Dick and I were soon speeding over the beautiful prairie, overtaking Cash, who had lingered behind the others, waiting for me.

"A penny for your thoughts, Cash?"

"I was wondering if we will ever tread Missouri soil again?"

"Quite likely we shall, we are young in years, with a long life before us, no doubt we will come on a visit to Missouri when we get rich."

We were passing a very comfortable looking farmhouse, men, women, and children were in the yard, gazing after us, as we cantered past.

"Don't you believe they envy us and wish they were going, too?"

"No, why should they?"

"Oh, because it is so jolly to be going across the continent; it is like a picnic every day for months; I was always sorry picnic days were so short, and now it will be an all Summer picnic."

"I wish I felt that way; aren't you sorry to leave your friends?"

"Of course, I am, but then I shall write long letters to them, and they will write to me, and I will make new friends wherever I go, and somehow I am glad I am going."

After we came within sight of our caravan we walked our ponies, and talked of many things, past, present, and future. When within a mile or two of Memphis our first camp was made. Our six wagons, with their snow-white covers, and Mr. Kerfoot's big tent, make a very respectable looking camp.

OUR FIRST CAMP.

As we were provided with fresh bread, cake, cold chicken, boiled ham, pickles, preserves, etc., supper was quickly prepared for our small family of four, and we enjoyed it immensely. Then comes my time to write, as I have promised friends that I will keep a journal on this trip. Mr. Kerfoot thinks the Government is going to smash and greenbacks will not be worth one cent on the dollar, so he has turned all his money into gold coin, and stowed it into a small leather satchel—it seems quite heavy to lift or carry.

As Mrs. Kerfoot was sitting on a camp-chair near our wagons, Mr. Kerfoot came toward her, saying, "Here, mother, I want you to take care of this satchel, it is all we will ask you to do, the girls will cook and wash dishes, the boys take care of the stock, and I will oversee things generally, and we will do nicely." She accepted the responsibility without a word, and as he walked away, she turned to me, and said, "I wish it was in some good bank, I expect nothing else but that it will be stolen, and then what will become of us?"

While I have been writing Neelie (Cornelia) and Sittie (Henrietta) have been getting supper for a family of twelve, no small undertaking for them, as they have been used to servants and know very little about cooking.

When everything was ready, Neelie came to her mother exclaiming, "Come, mamma, to supper, the first ever prepared by your own little girl, but not the last I hope, see how nicely the table looks, Emma and Delia picked those wild flowers for you, how brightly the new tinware shines, let us imagine it is silver and it will answer the same purpose as if it were."

Her mother smiles cheerfully, as she takes her arm, Cash sneers at Neelie's nonsense—as she calls it. Mr. Kerfoot nods approval, as Neelie escorts her mother to the table. When all are seated Mr. Kerfoot bows his head and asks God's blessing on the meal.

Everyone seems to enjoy this picnic style of taking supper out of doors, and linger so long at the table, that Neelie has to hint that other work will have to be done before dark. When at last the table is cleared, she says to Emma and Delia, "Don't you want to help me wash these nice, bright dishes and put them away?"

They are always ready to help Neelie, and the work is soon done. Amid laughter and fun, they hardly realise they have been at work. Mr. Kerfoot insists that we women and the children must sleep in houses as long as there are houses to sleep in. Mother and I would greatly prefer sleeping in our spring-wagon, to making a bed on the floor in a room with so many, but as he has hired the room, we do not want to seem contrary, so have offered no objection. The boys have carried the mattresses and bedding into the house, and Neelie has come for me to go with her to arrange our sleeping-room. So, goodnight.

May 2.

We were up with the sun this morning after a night of refreshing and restful sleep. Neelie and I commenced folding the bedclothes, ready to be sent to the wagons, when she startled me with a merry peal of laughter, "Look here. Miss Sallie, see ma's treasure, she has left it on the floor under the head of her bed. Don't say anything, and I will put it in the bottom of a trunk, where it ought to be, and we will see how long it will be before she misses it."

She thought of it while at breakfast, and started up excitedly, "Neelie daughter, did you see that precious satchel?"

"Yes, ma, I have taken care of it, and put it where it will not be left lying around loose any more."

"Thank you, my dear, I am glad you have taken care of it."

"Why, mother, I did not expect you to carry that burden around on your arm by day, and sleep with it at night. I only intend for you to have entire charge of it, and put it where the rest of us do not know the hiding place, so that when we are obliged to have some, we will have to come to you to get it. And then give it sparingly, for much, very much depends upon what is in that satchel."

I Meet an Acquaintance.

We came to Memphis about nine a.m. Court is in session, several friends and acquaintances, who are attending court, came to the wagons to say goodbye. Mother's brother, Uncle Zack, was among them, he said, "Remember, when you wish yourselves back here, that *I* told you not to go."

"Yes, we will when that time comes and send you a vote of thanks for your good advice," I replied.

Cash, Neelie and I have been riding our ponies all day. We are stopping in a beautiful place for camping, near the farmhouse of a Mr. and Mrs. Fifer. They are very pleasant elderly people, who have raised a family of six children, who are all married, and gone to homes of their own. It is a delightfully homey home, yet it seems sad that they should be left alone in their old age. We will sleep in the house again tonight, I shall be glad when we get to where there are no houses to sleep in, for it does not seem like camping out when we sleep in houses. Cash and Neelie want to sleep in the tent, but their father says no, and his word is law in this camp.

Wednesday, May 3.

Brother Hillhouse discovered very early this morning that the tyre on one of the wheels of the ox-wagon was broken. He started off ahead of the rest of the wagons to find a blacksmith shop and get it mended by the time we would overtake him. It was ten o'clock when we came to the shop, near a flour-mill. There was a very bad piece of road before we crossed the creek, a deep ditch had been washed out by the Spring rains. I waited to see the wagons safely over, when someone came beside my pony with outstretched hand saying, "Good-morning, Miss Raymond, I see you are in earnest about crossing the plains."

"Why, how do you do, Mr. Smith? Am glad to see you, of course I am in earnest about crossing the plains, but where did you come from? I supposed you would be at the Missouri River before this time, have you turned back?"

"Oh, no, we are waiting for better roads and good company."

"Come, go with us, I will promise you good company, and the roads will improve."

"Where are Cash and Neelie? I have not seen them."

"They did not stop, when I waited to see the wagons over the difficulties."

"Then I have missed seeing them; was in the mill when they passed. Remember me to them. We will start again tomorrow, and will overtake you in a few days, perhaps."

"Hope you will, goodbye until we meet again."

"Farewell, may you enjoy as pleasant a trip as you anticipate."

"Thank you," and waving him goodbye,

I spoke to Dick, and he cantered up the hill past the mill and the wagons. I soon caught up with Cash and Neelie.

"Guess who I saw at the mill?"

"Did you see any one we know?"

"Yes, an especial friend of yours. Cash, Bob Smith, of Liberty."

"Oh, dear, I wish I had seen him. Was Thad Harper with him? Are they going back home?"

"No; they are waiting for better roads and good company. I did not see Thad Harper. Bob said they will overtake us in a few days."

"I hope they will, they would be quite an addition to our party."

AN ADDITION TO OUR PARTY.

"Yes, but they won't; do you suppose they are going to let us see them cooking and washing dishes? Not if they know themselves. Then they would have to play the agreeable once in a while, and that is what they are not going to do on a trip of this kind. I do not expect to see them, they would rather stay where they are another week than join our party."

"I believe you are right, Neelie, for he did not say goodbye as if he expected to see me very soon."

When it was time to stop for lunch, we found a very nice place and waited for the wagons. While at lunch we saw an emigrant wagon, drawn by three yoke of oxen, coming up the road, and were somewhat surprised to see it turn from the road and come toward our camp. It proved to be Mr. John Milburn, of Etna, and his sister Augusta. They have travelled in one day and a half the distance we have been two and a half days coming.

Miss Milburn is a very intelligent, well-educated young lady, some two or three years my senior. We are not very well acquainted with her, but have met her frequently, and have known of her several years. She is an active member of the Presbyterian Church at Etna. She has her little nephew, Ernest Talbot, with her. He is seven years old, her sister's dying gift, a very bright child and considerably spoiled, but dear to his auntie's heart as her own life. They have started to Montana to get rich in the gold mines. Mr. Milburn leaves a wife and two small children with his widowed mother, to watch, and wait, and pray for his success and safe return home.

We crossed the dividing line—though we did not see it—between Missouri and Iowa soon after noon, and it is very probable some of us will never tread Missouri soil again. As we were coming through Stilesville, a small town this side the line, there were several loafers in front of a saloon who acted very rudely, to say the least.

We distinctly heard such remarks as the following, "Whew, what pretty girls, and how well they ride—Missourians I'll bet."

"Say, boys, let's try our luck; maybe we can each hook a pony to-night?"

Mr. Milburn's team is so tired out with such fast driving that we have stopped earlier than usual, and I have had more time to write. We are only two or three miles from Stilesville. The weather is perfect; we will sleep in the wagons tonight. Mr. Kerfoot thinks it necessary to guard the camp. I believe it an unnecessary precaution, for if those loafers at Stilesville had meant mischief they would not have expressed themselves so freely. However, Ezra and Frank Kerfoot (Mr. Kerfoot's nephews), Sim Buford, and Brother Hillhouse, will take turns standing guard, each one for two hours.

Thursday, May 4.

Oh, how we did sleep last night, dreamless and sound. Our first night in the wagons was undisturbed and sweet. We were up with the birds making ready for an early start. Mother prepares breakfast, while I roll up the beds and cover closely to protect them from the dust; one of the boys milks the cows, while I assist mother, and when breakfast of hot biscuit, ham and eggs, apple-sauce, coffee, and breakfast food (which I should have mentioned first), is over, I strain the milk into an old-fashioned churn that is big at the bottom and little at the top, cover closely and fix it in the front of the freight wagon, where it will be churned by the motion of the wagon, and we have a pat of the sweetest, most delicious butter when we stop in the evening that anyone ever tasted.

Mother washes the dishes, we prepare lunch for our noon meal, I stow it in the grub-box under the seat in the spring-wagon, the boys take the pipe off the little sheet-iron stove, empty the fire out and leave it to cool, while I am putting things away in the places where they belong. It is wonderful how soon we have learned to live in a wagon, and we seem to have an abundance of room.

When horses are harnessed, oxen yoked—and everything ready to start, we girls proceed to saddle our ponies; some of the boys usually come and offer assistance, which is politely declined, as we are going to wait upon ourselves on this trip.

The wagons start, leaving us to follow at our leisure. We don our riding-habits, made of dark-brown denim, that completely cover, and protect us from mud and dust, tie on our sun-bonnets, mount our ponies unassisted, and soon overtake and pass the wagons.

We started this morning at seven o'clock. It is delightful riding horseback in the early morning.

BLOOMFIELD, IOWA.

We were on the lookout for Bloomfield, about ten o'clock we could see the spires and steeples glittering in the sunshine. When we reached the suburbs, we stopped to wait for the wagons.

When we reached the business part of the city, I dismounted and made ready to do some shopping, as a few necessary articles had been forgotten when purchasing our outfit.

"Aren't you going with me, girls?"

"Oh, dear, no; not in these togs, short dresses, thick shoes, sun-bonnets, etc."

"I think we appear much better in our short dresses, thick shoes, and sun-bonnets than we would in trailing skirts, French kid shoes, and hats of the latest style, especially as we are emigrants, and not ladies at home. However, I do not wish you to suffer mortification on my account, some one of the boys will go with me."

"May I go. Miss Sallie?" Ezra asked.

"Certainly, and thank you to."

We called at two drug stores, one grocery and several dry-goods establishments, and made several small purchases. The clerks seemed quite interested, and asked numerous questions. Some wished they were going, too; others thought we had a long, hard journey before us.

When we came back, they were waiting for us. I gave the satchel containing the purchases into mother's care, mounted Dick, and we were soon on the way. About a mile from Bloomfield, we stopped for lunch of sandwiches, ginger-bread, cheese, fruit and milk.

We all have such ravenous appetites, the plainest food is relished and enjoyed, as we never enjoyed food before. If anyone suffering from loss of appetite, or insomnia, would take a trip of this kind, they would soon find their appetite, and sleep the night through without waking.

Brother Winthrop wanted to ride Dick this afternoon, so I took passage with mother and drove the horses until I began to nod, when I gave the lines to her and climbed back into the wagon for an afternoon nap. I waked up as we were driving into Drakesville, a small but very pretty town. Mother and I talked the rest of the afternoon, she enjoys this life as much as I do; we built air-castles for our future habitation; I trust there was not enough selfishness in the building material to hurt us if they tumble about our ears.

Mother seems happier than she has since the war commenced, and our eldest brother, Mac, went into the army. We stopped for the night earlier than usual, about five o'clock. We are camping in a lane near a farmhouse.

Our little sheet-iron stove is taken down from its place on a shelf at the back of the freight wagon. Mother gets dinner and prepares something for lunch tomorrow, at the same time. The boys buy feed from the farmers, as the grass is not long enough to satisfy the horses and cattle. I write as long as it is light enough to see.

The young people complain about my taking so much time to

write, but since I have commenced, I cannot stop. I am thinking all the time about what things are worth recording.

(A call to dinner.)

BEAUTIFUL APPLES.

After dinner mother washes the dishes and makes all the arrangements she can for an early breakfast. She thinks I am another "Harriet Beecher Stowe," so she is perfectly willing to do the work in the evening and let me write. Oh, the unselfishness of mothers. I do my share, of course, mornings, and at noon, but evenings I only make the beds in both wagons.

We have white sheets and pillow-cases, with a pair of blankets, and light comforts on both beds, just the same as at home, and they do not soil any more or any quicker, as we have them carefully protected from dust.

I had been writing a little while after dinner, when Frank stepped up with a basket of beautiful red-cheeked apples in his hand, not a wilted one among them.

"Where shall I put them?"

"Oh, Frank, how lovely they are. Where did you get them? Thank you so much; they are not *all* for me?"—as he emptied the last one into the pan. "Are all the others supplied? This seems more than my share."

"Yes; they are for you, we bought the farmer's entire stock; the others are supplied, or will be without you giving them yours."

He had just gone, when Sim Buford came and threw half a dozen especially beautiful ones into my lap.

"Thank you, Sim, but I am bountifully supplied, don't you see?"

"So you are, but keep mine, too; I can guess who it was that forestalled me." Laughing as he walked off.

So, we are feasting on luscious apples this evening, thanks to the generosity of our young gentlemen.

Friday, May 5.

We came through Unionville and Moravia today. Have travelled farther and later than any day yet. It was almost dark when we stopped, and raining, too; to make a bad matter worse, we are camping in a disagreeable muddy place, and have to use lanterns to cook by.

We were obliged to come so far to get a lot large enough to hold the stock. We will be glad to sleep in the house tonight.

Mrs. Kerfoot is homesick, blue and despondent this evening; she has always had such an easy life that anything disagreeable discourages her. Perhaps when the sun shines again, she will feel all right.

Saturday, May 6.

This morning dawned clear and bright; all nature seemed refreshed by yesterday's rain, and we started joyfully on our journey once more. We came through Iconium early in the day, are camping in Lucas County, near a beautiful farmhouse. We expect to stay here until Monday, as we do not intend to travel on Sundays.

It is a beautiful moonlight night, someone proposes a walk. As Cash is giving Winthrop his first lessons in flirtation, they, of course, go together; Sim and Neelie, Miss Milburn and Ezra are the next to start, and Frank is waiting to go with me. Hill stays in camp, in conversation with Mr. Kerfoot and Mr. Milburn.

He is more like an old man than the boy that he is, not twenty yet. After we had gone a short distance. Miss Milburn asked to be excused, and returned to camp; Ezra, of course, going with her.

We walked on for a mile or more, enjoying the beautiful moonlight, and having lots of fun, as happy young people will have. When we returned and I had said goodnight to the others, I climbed into the wagon to finish my writing for the day by the light of the lantern.

The front of Mr. Milburn's wagon almost touches the back of ours, forming an angle. I had been writing a few moments when I heard sobbing. I was out in a jiffy, and had gone to the front of their wagon without stopping to think whether I was intruding. "May I come in?" I asked, as I stepped upon the wagon-tongue.

"Oh, yes, come in, Miss Sallie, but I am ashamed to let you see me crying, somehow I could not help it. I felt so lonely and homesick."

"I am sorry you feel lonely and homesick. Did any of us say, or do anything this evening that could have hurt you?"

"Oh, no; not at all, only I always feel that I am one too many, when I am with you all; you seem so light-hearted and happy, so free from care, so full of life and fun, that I feel that I am a damper to your joyousness, for I cannot get over feeling homesick and sad, especially when night comes."

"How sweetly Ernest sleeps, and how much he seems to enjoy this manner of life."

"Yes; he is a great comfort to me, as well as a great care. He is dearer to me than to any one else in the world; his father seems to be weaned from him, since they have been separated so long. He has not seen him more than half a dozen times since his mother died. I feel that he is altogether mine. May God help me to train him for Heaven. He will never know what I have sacrificed for him. I have a mind to tell you, if you care to hear, why I am here, and why I am not happy."

"It may perhaps relieve you, and lighten the burden, to share it."

And then she told me what I will record tomorrow, for it is almost midnight, and mother has been asleep for two hours, and I must hie me to bed.

MISS MILBURN'S LOVE STORY.

"Of course, you have heard about my engagement to Jim Miller. I know it has been talked about."

"Yes; I have heard the matter discussed."

"We have been engaged two years, and were to be married next month. He insisted that I must give up Ernest to mother. I felt that I would be violating a sacred trust, and that mother is too old to have the care of such a child, and I told him so. We quarrelled, and while I was feeling hurt and indignant, I told Brother John I would go with him to Montana. He gladly accepted my offer, and his wife was so glad John would have someone to take care of him if he got sick. So here I am and I know I ought not to have come, for Jim Miller is dearer to me than my own life."

"I am so sorry for you, yet I believe that in some way it will be for the best, you know the promise, 'All things work together for good, to those who love the Lord.'"

"I will try to believe it. You have done me good, Miss Sallie. I am glad you came. Come again."

Sunday, May 7.

"*Remember the Sabbath Day to keep it holy.*" Have we obeyed this command today? I fear not. We are all, or very nearly all, professing Christians, yet we have had no public worship in our camp today, but we have all, to some extent, desecrated the day by work.

Deeds of mercy and necessity may be done on the Sabbath Day without sin, and mother says, "It is very necessary that our soiled clothes, sheets and pillowcases should be washed, and that cleanliness is next to godliness."

The question comes to me. Why is it that Christians are so loath to talk of the things that pertain to their spiritual life, and eternal welfare? Why so backward about introducing a service of worship, when so well aware it would meet with the approval of all?

I felt that Mr. Kerfoot was the one to suggest a service of prayer and praise, and reading the Scriptures. Perhaps he thought some of the ladies would mention it, so all were silent, and it is numbered with the lost opportunities for doing something for our Lord and Master. May he pardon our sins of omission, and may we be permitted to atone for the manner in which we spent our first Sabbath on this trip.

We have not travelled, so our teams have rested and done no labour, if we have violated the commandment ourselves.

The weather is perfect; this is another beautiful moonlight night. The young ladies and gentlemen have gone for another walk in the same order as last night, except Frank went with Miss Milburn, and Ezra is waiting for me.

A Letter to Brother Mac.

Monday, May 8.

I left camp very early, and walked on alone, that I may write to Brother Mac before the wagons overtake me. I am seated in a comfortable fence corner, and here goes for my letter:

Lucas County, Iowa,
May 8, 1865.

Dear Brother: We were delayed several days after the time set for starting, when we wrote you to meet us at Council Bluffs by the 10th. We thought I would better write, that you may know we are on the way, and hope to meet you by the 15th or the 16th. You must possess your soul with patience, if you get there before we do, and have to wait. I could write a long letter, I have so much to tell you, but will wait until we meet. Mother seems in better health and spirits than she has since you went into the army. We are enjoying the trip very much, and I find myself feeling sorry for the people that have to stay at home, and cannot travel and camp out. Goodbye until next week.

With sincerest love,
Your sister,

Sarah.

The wagons are coming in sight, just as my letter is finished and addressed, and ready to mail at the next post-office. My pony is in harness today, as one of the work horses is a little lame, so I will have to ride in the wagon or walk. As the morning is so fine, I will walk until I begin to tire.

Evening.

Cash joined me in my walk, and we walked until noon. How wisely planned are these physical bodies of ours, how easily inured to the burdens they must bear. Before we started on this trip, such a walk as we took this morning would have completely prostrated us; now, we did not feel any inconvenience from the unusual exercise.

Frank invited us, Cash and I, to ride in his wagon this afternoon. We accepted the invitation, and made an emigrant visit. He had arranged his wagon for our convenience and comfort, and we spent a very pleasant afternoon. Frank mailed my letter at Charaton, and on his way back bought candy and nuts for a treat for his visitors, which we, of course, enjoyed exceedingly.

I should not care to ride in an ox-wagon all the way across the plains, but for half a day, once in a while, it is a pleasant change, especially when so delightfully entertained. The afternoon passed quickly. We are camping near a large party of emigrants, some of the men came to our camp. They look tough; they are from Pike County, Missouri, on their way to Oregon.

Tuesday, May 9.

A beautiful day for horseback riding, until late this afternoon, when it commenced blowing a perfect gale, too severe to travel, so we drove into camp early. We came through Ottawa and Osceola, are camping in Clark County.

Wednesday, May 10.

A very cold day for this time of year, too cold to think of riding horseback, so we all took passage in the wagons. As we have plenty to read, and lots of visiting to do, it is no hardship to ride in the wagon for a day.

The boys have made a splendid camp-fire, and we are getting thawed out, cheered, and ready for a jolly evening. There was just one stunted oak left standing, away out here in this great expanse of prairie—for our especial benefit, it seems. The boys cut it down, and taking the trunk for a back-log, the top and branches to build the fire, we have a glorious camp-fire away out here in Union County, Iowa. It is surprising to find Iowa so sparsely settled, we travel sometimes half a day and do not see a home. There are always a few farms near the towns. The settlements are the only breaks in the monotonous landscape.

Oh, the tedious, tiresome monotony of these vast extended prairies: To look out and away, over these seemingly endless levels, as far as the eye can reach, and see only grass, grass everywhere, with beautiful prairie flowers, of course, but the flowers cannot be seen in the distance. No earthly consideration would induce me to make a home on any of these immense prairie levels. How my eyes long for a sight of beautiful trees, and running streams of water; how delightful to stroll in the woods once more.

Thursday, May 11. The wish expressed last evening is realised in a manner. We are camping in a strip of timber along the banks of a creek—or branch, rather. But then it is such a slow-going stream, not at all limpid, clear, or sparkling as a brook ought to be. It can hardly be called a running stream, for it goes too slowly. I think creeping or crawling would be more appropriate. We came through Afton today.

THE ICARIAN COMMUNITY.

Friday, May 12.

Brother Hillhouse's birthday. He is twenty years old. We made a birthday cake for him last night. We divided it into twenty pieces at lunch today, and there was just enough to go around and leave two pieces for himself. The girls say we must have some kind of a jollification tonight. I hope they will leave me out, for I want to write about the "Icarian Community." We came through Queen City this morning, and this afternoon came to a town of French people, called "The Icarian Community."

(Call to dinner.)

Later.

They have excused me.

But why Icarian? I cannot understand, for certainly they did not impress me as high flyers, neither as flyers at all. They seemed the most humdrum, slow-going, even-tenor, all-dressed-alike folks I have ever seen. Every dwelling is exactly alike, log-cabins of one room, with one door, one window, a fireplace with stick chimney. I rode close by the open doors of some of the houses, and tried to talk with the women, but we could not understand each other at all. The floors, windows and everything in the houses were scrupulously clean, but not one bit of brightness or colour, not a thread of carpet, or a rug, and all the women's and girls' dresses made of heavy blue denim, with white kerchiefs around the shoulders and pinned across the front of the waist, the skirt above the ankles, and very narrow and heavy thick-soled shoes. The men and boys all looked alike too, but I did not observe

144

them closely enough to describe them.

There are several large, long buildings, one with a large bell in belfry on top of building. They are dining-hall, town-hall, school-house and two others. I did not learn what they are used for. All the buildings are one story, of the plainest architecture, for the one purpose of shelter from sun and storm. There is not a thing to ornament or beautify, not a shade-tree or flower, yet everything—men, women, children, houses, yards and streets—are as clean as they can be made.

They are peaceable, law-abiding citizens, live entirely independent of the people of adjoining neighbourhoods. They are supposed to be wealthy; the town is the centre of well-cultivated and well-stocked farms.

The principle upon which the community is founded is "Brotherly Love," a sort of cooperative communism, in which all things are the common property of all. They live upon what their farms produce, have vast herds of cattle and sheep, a fine site for their town, and seem the picture of contentment, which is better than riches.

We stopped within sight of Quincy, and another camping outfit. We soon learned they are Mr. Harding and Mr. Morrison and family, from Lewis County. We are acquainted with Mr. Harding and have often heard of the Morrisons.

Mr. Morrison and Mr. Harding came over, and the men have had a sociable, gossiping time this evening; the men can surpass the women gossiping any time, notwithstanding the general belief to the contrary. The young folks have been playing games to celebrate Hillhouse's birthday. They had hard work to get him to join them.

A Swing Among the Trees.

Saturday, May 13.

We drove only until noon, and stopped to stay over Sunday, so that we can do our washing and baking, without violating the Sabbath. We do not have collars and cuffs, and fine starched things to do up, but we have a great many pocket handkerchiefs aprons, stockings, etc. We have pretty bead collars made of black and white beads, tied with a ribbon, that always look nice and do not get soiled. We are in a beautiful grove of trees. The boys have put up a swing. There is nothing in the way of play that I enjoy as I do a good high swing. There are plenty of boys to swing us as high as we want to go. I fear the Sabbath will be desecrated with play tomorrow, if not with work, for the temptation to swing will be hard to resist.

Sunday, May 14.

The horses went off two or three miles last night, the men were all off bright and early this morning hunting them. Mr. Kerfoot found them, and came back about nine o'clock. By the time they were all here the morning's work was finished and we were ready—for what?

A day to spend in rest and service for the Master? Oh, no. A day spent in swinging, frivolous conversation, and fun. I am ashamed to tell it, but it is nevertheless true, and I believe we all thought less about a service of worship than we did last Sunday. It is so hard to get right, if we do not start right.

We have visitors in camp tonight, two gentlemen from Clark County, neighbours of the Kerfoots—Mr. Suitor and Mr. Rain. They started for the gold mines in Montana two or three weeks ago. After reaching the Missouri River they heard such frightful stories of Indian depredations being committed on the plains that they sold their outfit for what they could get, and are returning home on horseback. Poor fellows, how I pity any man that has so little grit. I should think they would be ashamed to show their faces to their neighbours, and say, "We were afraid, so we came back home."

I believe Mrs. Kerfoot is the only one of our party who would be willing to turn back, and perhaps she would not if it were put to the test. We would not like to be scalped and butchered by the Indians, but it does seem so cowardly to run away from a possible danger. "The everlasting arms are underneath." God can, and will, take care of us as well on the plains as anywhere. He is leading us through unknown paths. We can trust Him. Heaven is as near one place as another.

Our second Sunday has not been much of an improvement on our first. The first we worked, today we have played. The boys swung us all morning, until we were ready to "holler nuff." We had Sunday dinner between two and three o'clock, then we wrote letters to friends at home, read until sleepy, took a nap of an hour, then Mr. Suitor and Mr. Rain came, and we listened to their frightful stories of what the Indians are doing to emigrants.

I left them in disgust, to come and record our misdoings of this, our second, Sunday on the road. It is almost bedtime, and I must make the beds, for we are early to bed and early to rise while on this trip.

A FATAL ACCIDENT.

Monday, May 15.

Alas, alas! How can I write the disastrous happenings of this day?

My hand trembles and my pencil refuses to write intelligibly when I attempt to record the sad, oh, so sad, accident that has befallen us. We parted from our visitors this morning, and started on our way, feeling rested and glad to be journeying on again. How little we knew of what a day would bring forth. We stopped for lunch at noon in a little vale, or depression, on the prairie, but where there was no water. Just as we had finished our lunch, Neelie came, she said, to see if we could make an exchange for the afternoon, her mother riding with mine, and I with the young folks in the family wagon.

Of course, it was soon arranged, and I told her I would come as soon as I helped mother put things away. (We sometimes visit in this way.) Mrs. Kerfoot soon came around, and when everything was ready, I started to go to their wagon. It was the last one in the train. As I was passing Mr. Milburn's wagon he called to me to "Come and get a drink of water." He had taken a long walk, and found clear, pure water, not very cold, but much better than none at all. I gratefully accepted a cup. He and his sister then invited me to ride with them. I told them of my engagement with Neelie, and, of course, they excused me.

Oh, that I had accepted their invitation; just such a little thing as that might have prevented this dreadful accident. Such great events turn on such little hinges sometimes. About three o'clock in the afternoon, as we were plodding along after the fashion of emigrant teams, we young people in the last wagon, having a jolly sociable time, with song and laughter, fun and merriment, the front wagons stopped. Ezra, who was driving, turned out of the road and passed some of the wagons to see what the trouble was. Mr. Kerfoot came running toward us, calling to Neelie, "Get the camphor, daughter, Mr. Milburn has shot himself somehow, and has fainted."

Ezra got out to go with him and Neelie asked, "Shall we come, too, papa?"

"No, my daughter, you girls would better stay here, your ma and Mrs. Raymond are with Gus, and they will know what to do."

Before he had finished what he was saying they were running to the place of the accident. We could only wait, hoping and praying, oh, so earnestly, that it might not prove so serious as Mr. Kerfoot's manner and tone caused us to fear. Afterward, Winthrop came to us; he was pale, with compressed lips, and sad eyes; he came up close, leaned upon the wagon wheel, and said in a low tone, "He is dead." Oh, how dreadful. We all left the wagon and went to the front as fast as we could.

I have gathered from witnesses the following account of how it happened. There was a flock of prairie chickens ahead of the wagons to the left of the road. Mr. Milburn and several of the boys took their guns and were going to try to thin their number. The wagons had not halted, but were moving slowly on, the hunters had gone on a little in advance of the wagons, they tried to fire all together, one of the boys snapped two caps on his gun, it failed to go off, so he threw the gun into the front wagon, and took his whip, in disgust. The wagon had moved on to where Mr. Milburn was standing with his gun raised; there was a shot, Mr. Milburn dropped to his knees, turned and looked at his sister, saying, "Gus. I am shot." And fell forward on his face. She was in the next wagon.

BEREAVEMENT.

Gus screamed, jumped from the wagon, ran to her brother, and raised his head in her arms. All who were near enough to hear her scream ran to them and she said, "John has hurt himself with his gun and has fainted, bring restoratives quick."

In a few seconds, there were half a dozen bottles, with brandy, camphor, ammonia there, and every effort was made to restore him, but all in vain. He died instantly and without a struggle.

When Mr. Kerfoot knew he was dead, he looked for the wound and found a bullet-hole between his shoulders. Just then one of the boys picked up his gun where he had dropped it and exclaimed, "It was not this gun that did the mischief, for it is cold, and the load is in it."

On looking around to find where the deadly shot had come from, someone took hold of the gun in the front wagon. "Why, this gun is warm. It must have been this gun went off."

"Oh, no; it could not have been that gun, for there was no cap on it," said the boy who had thrown the gun there.

Circumstances proved that it was the gun without a cap that did the fatal shooting. I would have supposed, as the boy did, that it was perfectly harmless without a cap. I have heard it said, "It is the un-loaded gun, or the one that is supposed to be unloaded, that gen-erally does the mischief." No doubt the hammer was thrown back when he threw it in the wagon. On investigating we found a rut in the wheel-track just where he fell. It is possible that when the front wheel dropped into the rut with a jolt the hammer fell, igniting the powder, either by the combustible matter that stuck, or by the flash

148

occasioned by the metal striking together. Mr. Milburn was not opposite the wagon when he raised his gun to shoot, but the wagons were moving slowly and the front one came up with him as he was taking aim, and that was why Gus thought it was his own gun. She saw the smoke rise, he stumbled and fell to his knees, she called to him. "Why, John, what made you fall?"

He looked around at her and said, "Oh, Gus, I am shot." The last words he spoke.

How hard to be reconciled to such a dispensation when such a little thing could have prevented it, only one step in either direction, or the gun pointed the other way. Why, oh, why, has this awful thing happened?

The poor boy seems to be as heart-stricken as Gus. In her unselfish grief she has been trying to comfort him.

I have read of a minister of the Gospel "who dreamed that he died; after entering the gates of Heaven he was led into a large empty room, on the walls of which his whole life was spread out as a panorama. He saw all the events of his life, and many that had been hard to understand in his lifetime were here made clear, and through it all the guiding, protecting hand of God had been over him." Perhaps Mr. Milburn is saved from a worse fate.

We were about three miles from Frankfort when the accident happened. We came on here as soon as possible—a sorrowing, and oh, so sorrowful, procession now. It does not seem that we can ever be the merry party that we have been. Winthrop had been riding Dick; he stood there, ready, saddled and bridled when Mr. Milburn fell; Frank mounted my pony and rode as fast as he could go to Frankfort to get a doctor. Mr. Milburn was dead before he was out of sight. We met them as we came. A room has been rented and Mr. Milburn prepared for his last long sleep. The people of Frankfort are very kind, and sympathetic.

A Funeral.

Tuesday, May 16.

The boys sat up with the corpse last night. I stayed with Gus. We had only just shut ourselves in when a terrific storm came upon us; the wind blew, and the rain fell in torrents. Before eleven o'clock it had passed; soon after Gus slept heavily. It seemed hours before I slept. Very early this morning Gus awakened me praying. How surely do the sorrows of this life drive us to the mercy-seat for comfort, refuge

149

and strength.

> *Had earth no thorns among its flowers,*
> *And life no fount of tears,*
> *We might forget our better home*
> *Beyond this vale of tears.*

What a precious, what a comforting, satisfying faith the Presbyterian faith must be, if one can really and conscientiously accept it. According to their belief one never dies, nothing ever happens without God's providence, approval, and foreknowledge that it will happen in just that way.

I wish I could accept such a faith, and believe it, but I cannot. I do not believe it was ordained that Mr. Milburn should die in that way and at that time. I believe it was an accident that might have been prevented by the most trivial circumstance. The laws of nature are inexorable. If a bullet is shot into a vital part of the body it kills. Yet God is able to bring good out of this seemingly great and grievous evil. I do not know which suffers most—the poor boy whose gun did the deed or Gus. They seem to take comfort in each other's society, and are together the most of the time today. I am so sorry for both of them.

The funeral services of the Presbyterian Church were held at two o'clock this afternoon, a resident minister officiating. Mr. Milburn was very nicely laid away, and his grave marked and enclosed with a neat, strong fence before Gus and I left the cemetery. The people have been so very kind. The funeral was largely attended for a stranger in a strange place. There is no telegraph office here, so we have had to write letters instead of sending telegrams.

I believe Gus's plans are to go on with us to the Missouri River, sell her outfit, and return home by steamboat down the Missouri River, up the Mississippi to Canton, where friends will meet her and go with her to Etna.

Wednesday, May 17.

Another night with Gus. She wakes in the morning to weep. We started once more on our now sad journey. I have ridden with Gus all day. We do not hear the sound of song and laughter as we did last week; we all seem to be under a pall. We came through Redoak this morning, are camping in a beautiful place, near a pleasant, homelike farmhouse. The weather is perfect.

Thursday, May 18.

The friends that stayed with us Sunday night told us that the authorities are not allowing emigrants to take the northern route, because of the Indian depredations that have been committed on that route. That if we went to Council Bluffs, we would have to come down the river to Platsmouth to get on the southern route. So, we changed our course accordingly.

We came through Whitecloud, Glenwood and Pacific City today. At Whitecloud I made a few purchases, traded with a little German merchant who crossed the plains a year ago; he says we have a delightful trip before us. He expects to go again to the Rocky Mountains, and make his home there, as soon as he can sell out and settle up his business here.

Just before we came to Glenwood, as the girls passed on their ponies, Gus said to me, "Sallie, go ride your pony, too; you have not had a ride for several days. Pardon me if I have been selfish in my great sorrow."

"No, Gus, I would rather stay with you than to ride Dick, as long as you need me."

"Thank you, dear; your company has been very grateful to me, but now I would really enjoy seeing you ride through Glenwood."

To please her, and myself, too, I soon had saddled and mounted Dick and overtaken the girls. As we were riding through Glenwood a photographer sent a messenger to request us to "Please stop five minutes and let him take our picture." We rode to the position indicated, doffed our sun-bonnets, and looked as pleasant as we could. We did not wait to see the proof, and I expect he was disappointed.

Pacific City is on the Missouri bottom, or lowlands. Above the town are the highest bluffs I have ever seen. We hitched our ponies and climbed to the top. The view was magnificently grand, the sun sinking in the west, the river could be seen in the distance, with large trees on the banks, the lowland between the bluffs and the trees was dotted with cattle and horses grazing, here and there a pond or small lake with its waters shining and sparkling in the glimmering sunset, the city below us in the shadow of the bluffs. Everything was so sweet and peaceful, we were more than paid for our climb. The wagons had passed before we came down, so we mounted and hastened to overtake them before driving into camp.

ON THE BANKS OF THE BIG MUDDY.

Our journey across Iowa at an end, we are on the banks of the Big Muddy, opposite Platsmouth. We will stay here until Gus's things are sold, and we have seen her off on the steamboat. I stay with her nights, and this afternoon is the first time I have left her since the 15th.

Friday, May 19.

I went over to Platsmouth on the ferryboat this morning with some friends that are camping near us, to do some shopping for Gus. I bought a black bonnet, crepe veil and collar, and material for black suit, which we will make up in camp, as there is a dressmaker with us. I was away about five hours and came back tired and hungry. The weather is perfect. We have a very pleasant place to camp, and pleasant people camping near us. We are surrounded on all sides by emigrants' camps, and still they come. It seems like a young town, only the houses are built of canvas instead of lumber, brick or stone. The boys have put up a swing, but I have no time for swinging today.

Saturday, May 20.

We have had a very, very busy day. Mr. Kerfoot has sold Gus's wagon and team (three yoke of oxen) for $550, a good price everyone says. More than they cost them, I believe. The freight will be sold at auction. We have all helped with Gus's suit and it is almost finished. Hillhouse went up to Council Bluffs this morning, expecting to bring Brother Mac back with him. Instead of finding him he got a letter— also the one I wrote a week ago—saying he was not coming. He has decided to study medicine and will come west when he is an M.D. We are disappointed, of course, yet perhaps it is for the best—we must try and believe so anyway. Most perfect weather.

The Morrison and Harding outfit have come, also several other families from Lewis and Clark counties. The Kerfoots are acquainted with some of them. They had heard of the sad accident. Some of them were friends of Mr. Milburn.

OUR LAST DAY WITH MISS MILBURN.

Sunday, May 21.

Mr. Thatcher and his wife came to call upon Gus this afternoon, and invited her to their home in Platsmouth to stay until she takes the steamboat for home. Mr. Thatcher and Mr. Milburn have been friends for years. She accepted their invitation and will go there tomorrow.

As the people from different camps were sitting around an immense camp-fire, not far from our wagons, someone proposed music. Some of the men in Mr. Clark's camp are fine musicians, they brought their violin and flute, and gave several instrumental pieces, then some

152

familiar songs were sung and someone started "Just Before the Battle, Mother." They had sung two verses when I heard a shriek from Gus's wagon. I hastened to see what was the matter. "Oh, Sallie, tell them to please not sing that, I cannot bear it. Dear Brother John used to sing it so much. It breaks my heart to hear it now."

I sent Winthrop, who had followed me, to ask them to stop singing. Poor Gus, she was more overcome than I have seen her since her bereavement.

Monday, May 22.
Mr. Kerfoot, Cash, Neelie, Ezra and I came with Gus to Platsmouth. She said goodbye to mother, Mrs. Kerfoot and the others this morning. All were sorry to part with her. She has become very dear to us all. Gus's freight was brought over in the wagon and sold at public auction and brought good figures, thanks to Mr. Thatcher, who, when he saw anything going below its real value, bid it in himself. He has a grocery store. He and Mr. Kerfoot have attended to all business transactions for Gus, so that she has not been bothered at all, and have done better for her than they could have done for themselves.

We have had a quiet, pleasant day with Gus at Mrs. Thatcher's home. She is very kind, and has invited us girls to stay with Gus until she takes the boat for home, and Gus begged us to stay with her as long as possible; so, Cash and I are staying all night, and will see her on board the boat tomorrow morning. Neelie has returned to camp with her father and Ezra.

Ernest is a great care and worries his auntie. He will not stay in the house, and she cannot bear to have him out of her sight for fear something will happen to him; she has just now undressed him, heard his little prayer, and put him to bed in the next room. So, I hope we can have uninterrupted quiet for a while.

Tuesday, May 23.
Mr. and Mrs. Thatcher, Cash and I came with Gus and Ernest to the steamboat. We parted with them about nine o'clock on board the *Sioux City*. Dear friend, I have become greatly attached to her, in the three weeks we have been so intimately associated. May God grant her a quick and safe journey home. We cannot hope it will be a happy one.

(Note.—*Miss Milburn and her lover were married about six months after her return, and have lived happily, etc.*)

Cash and I came directly to camp, after saying goodbye to Gus; found everyone busy getting ready for an early start tomorrow. We have been here almost a week, yet I have not had time to try the fine swing the boys put up the next day after we came here until this afternoon. The camps that were here over Sunday are all gone except those that will travel with us. It is probable there will be half a dozen more camps here before night. It is surprising to see what a great number of people are going west this Spring.

We hope to start very early tomorrow morning. I trust our party will not be so much like a funeral procession as it has been since the 15th. Vain regrets cannot remedy the past, and I believe it is our duty to be as cheerful and happy as possible in this life.

WE HAVE OUR PICTURES TAKEN.

Wednesday, May 24.

We were up with the earliest dawn, and our own individual outfit ready for a very early start, yet it was the middle of the forenoon before all the wagons were landed on the west bank of the Missouri. It takes a long while to ferry fifteen wagons across the river. We girls rode our ponies onto the ferryboat. They behaved as if they had been used to ferryboats all their lives. As we were waiting near the landing a stranger came, apologised for speaking to us, and asked, "Are you going to Montana?"

(*This man is mentioned here because of what happened him before he reached his journey's end.*)

"No, sir, our destination is California, or Oregon; we are not fully decided which."

"Oh, you ought to go to Montana; that is the place to get rich."

He told of his marvellous success in that country since 1863; the Indians were mentioned. He spoke of them with such contempt; said he would rather kill an Indian than a good dog. Says he left a wife and six children in Iowa, the oldest boy about fourteen who wanted very much to go with his father, but his mother needed him. Last night he came into his father's camp. He had run away from home; says he is going to Montana, too. His father told it as if he thought it smart, and a good joke. What sorrow and anxiety his poor mother is no doubt suffering.

Cash, Neelie, Sim Buford, Ezra, Frank, Winthrop and I while waiting in Platsmouth went to a photographer's and had our pictures taken; tintype, of course, all in one group, then each one alone, then Sim and Neelie together and Cash and I on our ponies. We only came five miles after our rush to get an early start. There are nine families and fifteen wagons in our train now. Miss Mary Gatewood has a pony for her especial use, so there will be four of us to ride horseback. There are enough wagons now to make quite a respectable corral. I did suppose, as we had been resting so long, we would make a long drive. Feed for the stock is very good here, and as it is fifteen miles to the next good camping place, where there is plenty of water and feed, it has been decided that we stay here until tomorrow. The boys have put up the inevitable swing, and we have concluded "that what cannot be cured must be endured." So, we will make the best of it, but certainly at this rate we will not reach our destination before it is cold weather.

Thursday, May 25.

Oh, dear; here we are yet, only five miles from Platsmouth. Morrison and Harding have lost two fine cows, half a dozen men have been hunting them all day, but without success. There is not a doubt but that they have been stolen. Our stock will have to be herded, hereafter, to guard against thieves. We have spent the day reading, writing, sleeping, swinging, and getting acquainted with our neighbours. The Morrison family wagon is just in front of us, and the Kerfoot's just behind, so we are to have the most pleasant neighbours possible to camp next to us. Mrs. Morrison is almost as pretty as Cash, although the mother of four children; she is so bright and cheerful, so full of life and fun, she will be great on a trip like this.

Mr. Morrison has an impediment in his speech, and when he is excited—like he is this evening, because they cannot find their cows—he stutters dreadfully, and will say, "Or sir, or sir, or sir," until it is hard to keep from laughing. In ordinary conversation and when not excited, he talks as straight as anyone. He seems so fond and proud of his wife and children I like him. Neelie and Sim, and Frank and I took a stroll this afternoon in search of wild flowers. They are few and far between, yet we enjoyed the walk through the woods in this lovely springtime weather.

A Yankee Homestead.

Friday, May 26.

We came fifteen miles, are camping on a high rolling prairie, not a tree or shrub within sight; we are near a neat white farmhouse. Everything seems to be very new, but does not have that "lick and a promise" appearance that so many farmhouses in Nebraska have. Things seem to be shipshape, the house completed and nicely painted, a new picket-fence, and everything on the place—barns, hen-house, etc., all

155

seem well built, as if the owners are expecting to make a permanent home. I would prefer a home not quite so isolated and far away from anywhere. There do not seem to be any women about the place, perhaps they are coming when everything is ready for their comfort.

Saturday, May 27.

We came to Ashland, on Salt River, only a fifteen-mile drive, got here soon after noon and will stay over Sunday. Several of us young folks went fishing this afternoon. I have often gone fishing but do not remember ever catching anything of any consequence, or having any luck, as the boys say, so imagine my excitement and surprise when the fish began to bite, and I drew them out almost as fast as I could get my hook baited. Frank baited my hook and strung the fish on a forked willow switch. After I had caught six or eight, they seem so dry and miserable I thought they would feel better in the water, so stuck the willow in the bank, so that the fish were in shallow water. I caught another fish and went to put it with the others, when lo, they were all gone. I could have cried, and the rest all laughed—well, I shall try again.

After securing the one I had—and leaving it on dry ground, I threw in my hook, and almost immediately I had caught something so large and heavy I could not draw it out and had to call for assistance. I was fearful it was a mud-turtle or something else than a fish, but it proved to be a fine, large fish, larger than all the small fish I had lost put together. When Frank had taken it from the hook, and strung it with the little one, I said, "Now I am going, before this fish gets away." All had fairly good catches, but none that compared with my big fish. There are about twenty corrals within sight, each of from twelve to twenty wagons. Ashland is a miserable looking place, the houses log-cabins with dirt roofs. One store, where dry-goods, groceries, and whiskey are sold, and a blacksmith shop are all the business houses. I do not see anything that would pass muster as a hotel.

Sunday, May 28.

All the trains that camped near us last night, except one, have gone on their way, Sunday though it is. I am glad there are some people going West who regard the Sabbath day. Some of our young people went fishing, and some went rowing on the river in a canoe or small boat the boys hired. It has been a day of sweet rest, a quiet peaceful Sabbath.

Monday, May 29.

Travelled all day, and made a long drive without meeting anyone or passing a single habitation. We are camping near—what the people west of the Missouri River call—a ranch. There is a long, low log-cabin, with dirt roof, a corral, or enclosure for stock, with very high fence, and two or three wells of water in the vicinity, and that is all. No vegetable garden, no fields of grain, nor anything to make it look like farming. I think it is a stage-station, and the people who occupy do not expect to stay very long.

There are three other camps near, the people of the other trains are having an emigrant ball, or dance, in a room they have hired. They sent a committee with a polite invitation to our camp for us to join them, which was as politely declined. They are strangers, and the conduct of some of the women is not ladylike, to say the least.

We Meet a Friend.

Tuesday, May 30.

We girls were riding in advance of the wagons when we saw a long freight train coming. We stopped to let our ponies graze until they would pass. I glanced at the driver on the second wagon and recognized an acquaintance. "Why, girls, that is Kid Short," I exclaimed.

He looked at me so funny, and began to scramble down from his high perch.

"Why, Miss Sallie, I could not believe my eyes at first. Where did you drop from?" shaking hands with each of us.

"Didn't drop from anywhere; have been thirty days getting here by the slow pace of an ox-train. Sim Buford and some more boys that you know are with the train you see coming."

He soon said goodbye to us, spoke to a man on horseback, who dismounted, gave him his horse and climbed to the seat Mr. Short had vacated in the front of the freight wagon, drawn by eight mules, while Kid hurried off to see the boys. He and Sim have been neighbours, schoolmates, and intimate friends all their lives. Sim says Kid is homesick and expects to go home as soon as he can after reaching Omaha. He has been freighting from Omaha to Kearney, and has been away from home since last Fall. We are camping near another station, with the same trains we camped near last night not far off.

Wednesday, May 31.

We are camping in the valley of the Platte. We are obliged to stop at the stage-stations to get water for ourselves and the stock from the wells. The water is very good, clear and cold. The same trains that have been camping near us since we left Ashland are here again tonight. Two of the women called upon us a while ago. We were not favour-

157

ably impressed. They are loud, boisterous and unladylike; they speak to strange gentlemen with all the familiarity of old acquaintances. According to Thackeray, they are "Becky Sharp" kind of women.

Thursday, June 1.

Our little village on wheels has stopped near a large two-storey log-house that was built in the early fifties for a wayside tavern; there are fifteen rooms; there are frightful stories told of dark deeds having been committed under that roof, of unwary travellers homeward bound from California that never reached home, but whether true or not I cannot say. The people of the other trains are having a dance in the large dining-room of the old house.

Friday, June 2.

As Ezra and I were riding in front of the train we came to where a man was sitting on the ground hugging his knees, two men were standing near trying to talk to him, seemingly. As we rode up one of them came toward us, saying, "That is an Indian, over there." We rode close to him, and Ezra said, "How;" but he did not even grunt. He was very disappointing as the "Noble Red Man" we read about. He wore an old ragged federal suit, cap and all. There were no feathers, beads nor blankets. He was not black like a negro, more of a brown, and a different shade from the *mulatto*.

On The Banks of the Platte.

Saturday, June 3.

Here we are on the Platte with about two hundred wagons in sight. We are now on what is known as "The Plains." My idea of the plains has been very erroneous, for I thought they were one continuous level or plain as far as the eye could reach, no hills nor hollows, but it is nothing else than the Platte River Valley with high bluffs on either side.

There is some timber on the banks, but the timber of any consequence is on the islands in the middle of the river, out of reach of the axe of the emigrant.

This is the junction of the roads from St. Joe and Plattsmouth, and that is why there are so many wagons here tonight. Surely, among all these people there must be a minister of the Gospel, so perhaps we will have public worship tomorrow. Our trip grows more interesting, even Mrs. Kerfoot seems interested, as so many people are going West, it must be the thing to do.

Sunday, June 4.

We are organised into a company of forty-five wagons, a captain and orderly sergeant have been elected, and hereafter we will travel by system. Mr. Hardinbrooke is our captain. He has gone on this trip before; he is taking his wife and little girl with him to Montana. A Mr. Davis is our orderly sergeant.

We are now coming into a country infested with Indians, so it is required by Government officials that all emigrants must organize into companies of from forty to sixty wagons, elect captains and try to camp near each other for mutual protection. The grass for stock is unlimited. About twenty of the wagons in our train are freight wagons, belonging to the Walker Brothers, Joe and Milt. Joe has his wife with him. Milt is a bachelor; their sister, Miss Lyde, and a younger brother, De, are with them. They are going to Montana. We have been introduced to Mr. and Mrs. Hardinbrooke, and to the Walkers and their ladies. They are pleasant, intelligent people, and will add much to the pleasure of our party, no doubt. Frank and I went horseback riding this afternoon to the station to get some good water from the well. I cannot drink the river water.

No public worship today, although there were so many of us here.

Monday, June 5.

We were awakened at an early hour this morning with a bugle call. Three companies were organised yesterday; there were about twenty wagons that were not asked to join either party, so they pulled up stakes and left while Frank and I were away. The strange women were of the party; they must be some miles ahead by this time, and I hope they will stay ahead. When our long train of wagons are stretched out upon the road, we make a formidable looking outfit for the Indians to attack. As far as the eye can reach, before us and behind us, there are wagons, wagons, wagons; some drawn by oxen, some by mules, and some by horses. All fall into the slow, sure gait of the oxen.

There are whole freight trains drawn by oxen; there are more ox teams than all others.

After our evening meal, a number of us started for a stroll along the bank of the river. Before we reached the river, we were met by a perfect cloud of mosquitoes that literally drove us back. I never came so near being eaten up. There is a strong breeze blowing toward the river, which keeps them from invading the camps, for which I am thankful, otherwise there would be little rest or sleep for us tonight. They are the first mosquitoes we have seen on the road.

Tuesday, June 6.

It is sweet to be awakened with music, if it is only a bugle. Our bugle certainly makes sweet music. The road is becoming very dry and dusty, which makes riding in the wagon rather disagreeable sometimes. Mother and I take turns driving the horses and riding Dick. Rather the most of the time I ride Dick. One of our boys goes out with the herders at night, so one of them is generally sleepy, and sleeps during the day, while the other drives the ox-team.

THE ORDER OF OUR GOING.

Wednesday, June 7.

There is such a sameness in our surroundings that we seem to be stopping in the same place every night, with the same neighbours in front and back of us, and across the corral. When we organized, Mr. Kerfoot's wagons were driven just in front of ours and Mr. Morrison's just behind ours, so we have the same next-door neighbours, only they have changed places. We are in the central part of the left-hand side of the corral. The wagons occupied by the Walkers and Hardinbrookes are just opposite in the right-hand side of the corral.

We always stop in just this way, if only for an hour at noon—which we do every day for lunch, and to water the stock.

When we halted today, the rain began to pour, the stock scattered in every direction. When it stopped raining, the cattle could not all be found in time to start again this afternoon, so we only made half a day's drive. It has commenced raining again, and promises a rainy night. It is not very pleasant camping when it rains, yet it would be much more unpleasant if it did not rain—to lay the dust, refresh the atmosphere, and make the grass grow.

When the captain finds a place for the corral, he rides out where all can see him, and gives the signal, the first and central wagons leave the road; the first to drive to where the captain stands, the other and all behind it cross over a sufficient distance to form the corral by the wagons stopping, so as to form a gateway, for the stock to pass through, turned so that they will not interfere with each other when hitching. The next wagon drives to position, with the righthand side of cover almost touching the left-hand or back, outer edge of the wagon in front, with tongues of wagons turned out, so that all can be hitched to at one time. In this way the entire corral is formed, meeting at the back an oblong circle, forming a wall or barrier, the cattle cannot break through. The horses are caught and harnessed outside the corral, but the cattle have to be driven inside to be yoked.

Thursday, June 8.

It rained all night, seemingly without cessation; the wind did not blow, so there was no harm, but lots of good done. I am glad when the rain comes in the night-time, instead of day-time. Where the beds touched the covers, they were quite wet this morning.

Friday, June 9.

We came through a little town—Valley City. There is a very pretty attractive looking house near the road. Cash and I had come on ahead of wagons. Our inclination to enter that pretty home was irresistible, so we dismounted, took off our habits, hitched our ponies, and knocked at the door. A very pleasant lady opened the door and gave us hearty welcome. We told her frankly why we came. She laughed, and said, "I have had callers before, with the same excuse, but you need not apologise, I am glad my home is attractive to strangers."

The gentleman of the house is postmaster, and has his office in the room across the hall from the parlour. While we were there the coach arrived, and the mail was brought in. He did not know we were there, and called to his wife to "Come see this mail." We went with her, and oh, such a mess. They had emptied the mail-sack on some papers that had been spread upon the floor, and such a lot of dilapidated letters and papers I never saw before. I picked up a photograph of an elderly lady, but we could not find the envelope from which it had escaped.

Perhaps some anxious son, away out in the mines, far from home and friends and mother, will look in vain for mother's pictured face, and be so sadly disappointed. I am so sorry for the boy that will miss getting his mother's photograph. She looks like such a sweet, motherly mother. A great many of the letters were past saving; if the owners had been there, they could not have deciphered either the address or the written contents, for they were only a mass of pulp; the postmaster said it was "Because they send such old leaky mail-bags on this route; those post-office folk seem to think any old thing will do for the West, when we ought to have the very best and strongest, because of the long distances they must be carried." All that could be, were carefully handled and spread out to dry; still, they would reach their destination in a very dilapidated condition.

We have made a long drive, are within four miles of Fort Kearney. There are a great many wagons within sight besides our own long train, whichever way we look we can see wagons. The road from Kansas City comes into this road not far from Valley City, and there are as many, or more, coming that way as the way we came. People leaving war-stricken Missouri, no doubt. I have never seen a fort. I do hope Kearney will come up to my expectations.

FORT KEARNEY.

Saturday, June 10.

I was disappointed in Fort Kearney, as I so often am in things I have formed an idea about. There are very comfortable quarters for the soldiers; they have set out trees, and made it quite a pretty place, away out here in the wilderness, but there is no stockade, or place of defence, with mounted cannon, as I had expected.

Sim and I rode horseback through the fort while the wagons kept the road half a mile north of the fort. Only a few of us came by the way of the fort. A soldier gave us a drink of water from a well by the wayside. He seemed a perfect gentleman, but had such a sad expression. We were told that these soldiers were in the Confederate service, were taken prisoners, confined at Rock Island, and enlisted in the Government service to come out here and fight Indians. They are from Georgia and Alabama.

Two families have joined our train and come into corral on the opposite side, just behind the Walkers: Mr. and Mrs. Kennedy—a newly-married couple—and Mr. and Mrs. Bower, with a daughter fourteen and a son five. We only came one and a half miles west of the fort near Kearney City. I do not understand why we have made such a short drive, for the boys say the feed is not good, it has been eaten off so close.

Sunday, June 11.

We were obliged to leave camp and travel today, the first Sunday we have hitched up since we started. It was a case of necessity, as there was not feed for our large herds of cattle and horses. We made only a short drive, just to get good feed for the stock.

We are camping near a station that must seem like a military post, there are so many soldiers. Several soldiers came to our camp this afternoon; they confirmed what we heard yesterday. They are Confederate soldiers, they were prisoners, and their homes are in far-away Georgia and Alabama, and they are desperately homesick. It is a distressing sickness. I have been so homesick that I could not eat or sleep, and a cure was not effected until I was at home again. Then how nice it did seem to be home, and how good everything tasted. I do hope this cruel, homicidal war will soon be over, and these fine-looking Southern gentlemen will be permitted to go to their homes and loved ones, who, no doubt, are waiting and longing for their return. My heart aches for them.

ELEVEN GRAVES.

Monday, June 12.

We stood by the graves of eleven men that were killed last August by the Indians. There was a sort of bulletin-board about midway and at the foot of the graves stating the circumstances of the frightful tragedy. They were a party of fourteen, twelve men and two women, wives of two of the men. They were camped on Plum Creek, a short distance from where the graves are. They were all at breakfast except one man who had gone to the creek for water, he hid in the brush, or there would have been none to tell the tale of the massacre.

There had been no depredations committed on this road all Summer, and emigrants had become careless and travelled in small parties. They did not suspect that an Indian was near until they were surrounded, and the slaughter had commenced. All the men were killed and scalped, and the women taken prisoners. They took what they wanted of the provisions, burned the wagons and ran off with the horses.

The one man that escaped went with all haste to the nearest station for help. The soldiers pursued the Indians, had a fight with them and rescued the women. One of them had seen her husband killed and scalped and was insane when rescued, and died at the station. The other woman was the wife of the man that escaped. They were from St. Joe, Missouri.

Ezra met with quite an accident today; he went to sleep while driving the family wagon—he was on guard last night—the horses brought the wheel against a telegraph pole with a sudden jerk that threw him out of his seat and down at the horses' heels—a sudden awakening—with a badly-bruised ankle.

We are in the worst place for Indians on all this road. The bluffs come within half a mile on our left, and hundreds of savages could hide in the hollows; the underbrush and willows are dense along the river banks. There is an island, about a mile in length, that comes so near this side in many places that a man could leap from bank to bank. The island is a thick wood, a place where any number of the dreaded

Indians could hide, and shoot down the unwary traveller with the guns and ammunition furnished them by the United States Government.

How I would like to climb to the top of those bluffs, and see what is on the other side, but the captain says, "Stay within sight of camp." And I must obey.

A Narrow Escape.

Tuesday, June 13.

Cash, Neelie and I created quite a sensation this morning. We waited, after the train had started, to mount our ponies as we usually do. Cash and I had mounted, but Neelie led her pony, and we went down to the river to water them, Neelie found some beautiful wild flowers, and she insisted upon gathering them. Of course, we waited for her. The train was winding round a bend in the road, and the last wagons would soon be out of sight. We insisted that she must come. "The train will be out of sight in five minutes, and we may be cut off by savages in ambush."

She did not scare worth a cent. She led her pony into a little hollow to mount when we saw two men coming toward us as fast as they could ride. Cash rode at an easy canter to meet them, while I waited for Neelie, who was deliberately arranging her flowers so that she would not crush them.

"Those men are coming after us, perhaps there are Indians around." She took her time, just the same.

When the captain saw that the train would soon be out of our sight, he went to Mr. Morrison, who was on horseback, and said, "Ride quietly back and warn those girls of their danger, there are Indians around. They have been seen by the guard, on the island, and by the herders, in the hollows of the bluffs this morning. They would not be safe one minute after the train is out of sight."

They had kept it quiet, as they did not wish to cause unnecessary alarm, for they knew there was no danger, for the Indians knew they were being watched, and besides we are too many for them. Mr. Morrison started, but not quietly; he snatched off his hat, whipping his horse with it, passed Mr. Kerfoot's wagon as fast as his horse could go. Mr. Kerfoot asked, "What is the matter?"

Someone said, "Indians!"

He wound the lines round the brake-handle, leaped from his high seat on the front of the wagon, grabbed the first horse in reach, snatched Mr. Gatewood's boy out of the saddle, jumped on the horse and came tearing toward us, lashing the horse with his long whip—his hat flew off soon after he started, but he did not know it. He passed Mr. Morrison, and meeting Cash, he stopped long enough to bring his whip over her horse's haunches with all his might, and sent her flying toward the train. He next met me—for I started, when I saw them coming, and was perhaps a hundred yards ahead of Neelie—and stopped and said, "Miss Sallie, do you know that we are in the very worst Indian country there is on this road?"

He did not wait for a reply, but went on to Neelie, who was looking all about to see the Indians. He gave her pony a cut with his whip, as he had Cash's, and we went flying over the ground, Neelie's merry laughter pealing forth. Mr. Kerfoot did not speak to either of us. Mr. Morrison had turned back with Cash, and scolded all the way, she said he stuttered and stuttered, until she had hard work to keep from laughing. The captain had stopped the train, and we were greeted with loud cheering and hurrahs.

There was considerable joking about our being anxious for an adventure, and the young men were profuse in their declarations about what they would have done if we had been captured by the Indians. Everyone laughed about our "narrow escape," as they called it, except Mr. Kerfoot; he was pale and trembling. It is a shame that he should have been so unnecessarily frightened by our thoughtlessness, and I believe he thinks it was my fault. I wonder what he would have thought if I had left Neelie to come alone?

Wednesday, June 14.
One of the men found the skull of a human being today while we were stopping at noon. It seems horrible to think of one's bones being scattered about in such manner. There is a storm coming; a storm on the plains is something to be dreaded, especially a windstorm. Old men who have been freighting across the plains for years, say they have seen wagons upset with three tons of freight in a wind-storm. I am more afraid of a wind-storm than of Indians. The boys say I am not afraid of Indians at all.

Thursday, June 15.
The storm came with great violence last evening; we saw it coming in time to be prepared for it, so there was no damage done. The rain came down in torrents, and made the roads as hard and smooth as a floor, not any mud. It has been fine for horseback riding, everything seems so fresh and clean and pure, and not too warm. Mr. Milt Walker

joined us about an hour before camping time. He seems a very pleasant gentleman.

Friday, June 16.

We had a storm last night, much more terrific than the night of the 14th, yet there was no harm done, more than to frighten some of the women and children. For my part I enjoyed the coming of the storm exceedingly. I never witnessed a storm-scene so sublimely grand. Oh, for the pen of an artist, that I might picture the majesty and grandeur of the coming of that storm.

BEAUX.

Nellie Bower has a pony, and rides with us sometimes. She is a very mature young lady for her age, and very pleasant company. Neelie and I were riding together this morning, while Cash and Nellie Bower rode a short distance ahead. We had been on the road about half an hour when Dr. Fletcher and Milt Walker rode up, requesting the pleasure of our company, in a very formal manner. Of course, we smilingly bowed assent, and the doctor rode with Neelie, and Milt with me. It is the first time there has been any formality in our pairing off while riding. The boys sometimes ride with us, but they come informally, we ride as we please, and stop and climb into the wagon when we please, without saying by your leave.

I am sorry any such formality has been commenced, for when I want to lope off, and be by myself, I want to feel free to do so, rather than to be constrained to entertain a *beau*, as we did this morning. Of course, Dr. Fletcher and Mr. Walker have not gone with us thus informally. I presume we succeeded in entertaining them, for when the train turned out for noon, each gentleman looked at his watch and wondered "If it could be possible, it is noon?"

Dr. Fletcher is stepbrother of the Walkers—his mother and their father being married. He is physician for our train; an intelligent, handsome man, below medium in size. I think he must be dyspeptic, for he is always finding fault with everything. He seems to admire Neelie very much. We came through Cottonwood this morning. Stopped at noon where the feed is fine, so it has been decided that we stay here until tomorrow. The sky has the appearance of another storm this evening. We have had a busy afternoon.

Saturday, June 17.

There was a brisk shower last evening about dark, only lasted about half an hour, there was no wind. About midnight the cattle stampeded, the herders do not know what frightened them, but the first thing thought of was Indians, yet there were none visible. Some of the cattle were not found until this afternoon, so here we will have to stay another night.

The bluffs near here are quite high and abrupt. I climbed to the top this morning. I seemed to be away up yonder, when looking down at our corral the people looked like midgets. The bluffs are 150 feet high. I received a beautiful bouquet of wild flowers this evening, but do not know who sent it. The boy said, "A gentleman sent it." But he either could not, or would not, tell what gentleman. Perhaps the one that sent it thought I would know instinctively, but I am certainly in the dark.

Two gentlemen took lunch at our table this afternoon; they are father and son. Hillhouse met them out on the road; they asked him, "Do you know where we can get something to eat? We have had nothing since a very early breakfast."

He brought them to our wagons, and we soon had a lunch ready for them. Their name is Reade, the father's hair and whiskers are as white as snow, otherwise he is not an aged-looking man. They asked questions, and when they found we had not fully decided upon our destination, they insisted that Montana is the place for us. They have been there and are going again with freight. They belong with the Irvine train. Each train goes by the name of its captain, ours is known as "The Hardinbrooke train." Then there is the McMahan train, and the Dickerson train, that always camp within sight of us, for mutual protection.

We have not met any of the people from the other trains. The Irvine train—which is very large—are some miles ahead of us. The Reades were hunting cattle, had been as far back as Cottonwood, but without success. The son had a long talk with the boys before leaving camp. After he had gone, Hillhouse came around and took a seat on the wagon-tongue, near where I was engaged in the interesting occupation of the week's mending. I said, "Mr. Read thinks Montana the place for us."

We Decide to Go to Montana.

"Yes, so do the Walkers, and Mr. Hardinbrooke, and Mr. Morrison, and everyone else that are going to Montana."

"Well, why not go there?"

"I do not like for you and mother to go there, for it will be rough living I expect, but I intend to go as soon as you are settled somewhere near Mr. Kerfoot's folks."

"Just listen to the boy. Mother come here for five minutes, do. What do you think this boy is saying? That he is going to Montana when we are settled in California, or some other place."

"Well, if he is going to Montana, we are going, too. How many women are on their way there in these trains? I reckon it will not be any worse for us than it will be for them."

"All right, if you are both willing to go to Montana, we will change our plans accordingly. It is not as far as California."

And I know he is glad. So, it was settled then and there that Montana will be our destination.

Sunday, June 18.

We started very early this morning, as soon as light, about four o'clock. I think the most of the women were yet in bed. It was a glorious morning, and I did so enjoy my early ride on Dick. We had not been on the road very long when Frank joined me. I told him, "We had decided to go to Montana."

He was silent a moment, then said, "It is the place to go. I do hope we can persuade Uncle Ezra to go there, too."

"I hope he will decide to go with us, for it would be hard to part with all of you now. It would seem almost like leaving home again."

We halted at nine o'clock, had breakfast at ten, started again at twelve. Stopped again at four, and are camping on Fremont's Slough.

Monday, June 19.

We passed two graves this morning that have been made within a month. The first a man who shot himself accidentally three weeks ago. The other a woman, forty years old, who died one month ago today. As I stood beside the lonely graves, I thought of the tears that had been shed, the prayers that had been uttered, the desolation of heart that had been endured by those who had been obliged to go on and leave their loved ones here in this wilderness. How my heart ached for them. My heart went out in thanksgiving and praise to our Heavenly Father that there has been no serious sickness in all these trains with so many people. It is marvellous.

We are camped on the banks of the South Platte. The men have driven the stock across to an island. I do not know if it is because they are afraid of the Indians stampeding them, or that the grass is better.

If there should be danger, I presume they would not tell us. There is a town of prairie dogs near; several of us went to make them a visit, but the boys had been there with their guns shooting at the little things, and frightened them so they would not come out, although we waited in silence until almost dark.

I shall make another effort to see them very early in the morning before the boys are awake. I have heard they are early risers, that they come out to greet the rising sun. We met an acquaintance today—Will Musgrove—he is on his way to Central City, Colorado. He is night herder for a freight train. The most casual acquaintance seems like an especial friend, when we meet, away out here, so far from home, or anywhere else.

Prairie Dogs.

Tuesday, June 20.
Winthrop was quite sick last night with cramp colic. I was up with him the latter part of the night, so was dressed and ready for my visit to Prairie Dog Town at an early hour. The little fellows were up, standing at their doors, and greeted me with a welcoming bark. Some of them turned and darted away, no doubt to tell others we had come, for they immediately came back to peep out at us and bark and chatter, as if carrying on a lively discussion. They seemed perfectly fearless as long as we kept our distance, but if we tried to get a nearer view, they whisked away, and were gone in an instant; then they would send out two or three scouts, and if we had gone far enough away, they would come again to their doors. They have been well described by many writers. Cash and Frank joined me, while at Prairie Dog Town.

I rode horseback this morning, and Milt Walker rode with me. Winthrop is about well this evening. His was the first sickness we have had. Will Musgrove came up with us while we were halted for noon—his train is a short distance behind—he rode with me in the wagon all afternoon, and drove the horses, and mother rode Dick. We had a long talk about friends at home. He took dinner with us, and then said goodbye, and we will see him no more, for we will travel faster than the freight train.

Wednesday, June 21.
Mr. and Mrs. Morrison are large-hearted, cheerful people, who seem to be always happy and trying to make others happy. Mrs. Morrison learned that Miss Lyde Walker has her guitar, and sings beautifully, so she invited her to come to their tent and help to entertain a

few friends.

It was a very pleasant diversion. While Lyde was singing, the men and boys from all over the corral came near to listen. When she sang "The Cottage by the Sea," both inside and outside the tent, there was great applause that terminated in an encore. But no, she would not sing anymore; she murmured something about the rabble, and laid her guitar away.

If I was gifted with a talent, with which I could give pleasure to people, I would certainly do so whenever opportunity was afforded. I would be glad to promote the happiness, and dispel as much sorrow as possible, in this sorrowful world.

Thursday, June 22.

We came through a place called Star Ranch, or Old California Crossing. We are camped twelve miles below Julesburgh. Mr. Reade called this evening; we told him we had decided to go to Montana. He seemed as pleased as though personally interested. Says the Irvine train is only half a mile ahead tonight, and invited us to go with him to call upon the young ladies. We, with one accord, asked to be excused. We all felt that we are not in calling costume.

Friday, June 23.

We are camping in Colorado. Came through Julesburgh, a rather insignificant-looking place, to have such notoriety as it has in the newspapers. We met a company of soldiers with about twenty Indian prisoners. They were captured at Fort Laramie, and they are taking them to Fort Kearney. The soldiers had a fight with about one thousand Indians three weeks ago. There were no soldiers killed, though a number were seriously wounded, and they lost a good many horses. There were squaws and *papooses* with the prisoners, though not captives.

The Indians in the fight were Sioux and Cheyennes; they all look alike to me. They were the most wretched-looking human beings I ever saw, nothing majestic, dignified, or noble-looking about any of them.

An ex-Confederate soldier gave me my information about the fight. There are a great many Southern soldiers on this route. We passed another newly-made grave this afternoon. Mr. Reade called this evening.

Saturday, June 24.

I was caught in a hail-storm this morning. I was half a mile from the wagons, on a high bluff, looking over the river, watching the storm coming. I did not realise that it was so near, but all at once it came down pell-mell and gave me some pretty hard knocks. Dick seemed in a hurry to get to the train, and I let him go. We seemed to fly over the ground through the storm, but we had the benefit of it all, for it stopped just when we reached the wagons.

I unsaddled Dick and turned him out, while I took passage in the wagon, changed my wet clothes for dry ones and wrapped in a shawl to keep from taking cold. When the teams were being hitched up at noon, Hillhouse said to me, "Dick has not had water; you would better ride to the river and give him a drink."

The river was half a mile from the road, but in sight all the way. Dick cantered to the watering place, drank all he wanted, and we started back when I saw someone coming toward me. I will not say who it was because of what followed.

"I thought you were getting too far behind for safety."

"Oh, there isn't any danger; you need not bother about me."

"Bother? Oh, no." And then came a declaration that about took my breath. At first, I felt that I would like to box the presumptuous boy's ears. Then I wanted so much to laugh. But when I saw how desperately in earnest he was, I thought, perhaps, I have been to blame for not seeing how things were tending. I was perfectly amazed; such a thought never occurred to me.

Our ride back to the train was rather embarrassing to me. I tried to make him see the comicality of the whole business, but he would not see it. We passed a station where the Indians had burned all that would burn, but these *adobe*, dirt-roof houses, or cabins rather, would not make much of a blaze I imagine. Inside one of the cabins—or what was left of it—were two dead Indians that had been killed in the fray.

Sunday, June 25.

Mr. Reade came with six young ladies to call upon us this morning, also one gentleman from the Irvine train. They had gone down into their trunks and were dressed in civilization costumes. They were Misses Nannie and Maggie Irvine—sisters—their brother, Tom Irvine, Miss Mollie Irvine, a cousin—Miss Forbes, and two other young ladies, whose names I have forgotten. They are all very pleasant, intelligent young people.

The trains are keeping as close together as possible, for protection, for the Indians are on the warpath. Every station and ranch-building that we are passing these days have been destroyed.

PREACHING SERVICES.

We have had a preaching service this afternoon. Rev. Mr. Austin, of the Methodist-Episcopal Church South—the church that I am a member of—was the preacher. The services were well attended, and the sermon was fine. He compared our situation with that of 'The Children of Israel" in the wilderness. He spoke of God's care for them, and that He careth for us, spoke in an earnest manner of our dependence upon God, and our inability to take care of ourselves, or to accomplish anything without God's help and co-operation, and of the necessity of earnest prayer and faith in all circumstances of life, and always to remember that "The Everlasting Arms are underneath."

When the people were gathered, at the call of the bugle, some sat on chairs in the shade of wagons, some under umbrellas, some in carriages and light wagons. Mother and I stood near a carriage, before the service commenced, when a lady invited us to sit with her and her children—a little boy of five and a girl of three. We accepted and were introduced to Mrs. Yager, wife of the physician for the Chilicothe train, Mr. Dickerson captain. The services were held at their camp. Mrs. Yager is a Southern Methodist, too. Rev. Austin is a member of the Chilicothe train. I am glad there is at least one preacher among us.

MUSIC IN CAMP.

Monday, June 26.

Mr. and Mrs. May—a newly-married couple that came into our train at the junction of the roads—are both musicians; several of our young men have fine voices, and with Lyde's guitar, and Mr. May's violin we have had an enjoyable musicale away out here in the wilderness. If the Indians had been within listening distance, it would be interesting to know what impression the music made upon their minds, as "Music hath charms, etc." The music this evening has been the happiest feature of the day, for I have had to ride in the wagon all day.

One of the big horses went lame this morning, so Dick was put in harness and the dear little fellow has worked all day. He looks funny beside the big horse; the harness had to be taken up to the last holes to make it fit him. I would not enjoy taking this trip without a saddle-horse or pony to ride. I must be more generous hereafter and let Lyde and Mrs. Kennedy and other ladies that have no horse ride Dick oftener than I have been doing. I have not fully realised how very tiresome it is to ride in the wagon all day, and day after day.

I have always supposed that good water would be very scarce on this road; we have not found it so, there are always from one to three wells at the stage-stations, with excellent water, free for all—thanks to Uncle Sam for this provision for our welfare. In some places wood is very scarce and must be hauled long distances; we cooked dinner this evening with wood hauled from near Cottonwood. Cedar logs are fastened under the wagons, lengthwise between the wheels; as there are no stumps or rocks in the road, they carry all right, when there is no wood to pick up the log is taken down, a piece cut off and split up for use. It is surprising with what a little bit of wood one can cook a meal on these sheet-iron stoves.

Tuesday, June 27.

Among the men who are driving for the Walkers is an eccentric old bachelor named Fogy; he is very bashful when in the presence of ladies. I have often heard it said that men cannot drive oxen without swearing; it is a mistake. I have seen a whole lot of ox-driving on this trip, and today I heard the first profane oath since we left the Missouri River. It would have been funny if it had not been shocking. We have travelled all day where the bluffs come close to the river, the road is very uneven, little hills and hollows, in some of the hollows there is mud. Mr. Fogy admires Neelie very much (at a distance, of course), we often hear the extravagant compliments he pays her, and his regrets about that troublesome "if."

Soon after the start this morning, Neelie and I rode to the front to escape the dust and sand that were flying; as we came near the front wagon, we were startled by hearing a terrific. oath. The wagon had stuck in the mud and would, of course, stop the entire train. Mr. Fogy was the driver. He was greatly embarrassed and distressed when he knew we had heard him swear, and stopped stock still and let the wheels sink into the mud so that they had to double teams to get them out. He afterward told some of the boys he was effectually cured of swearing; that he never felt so cheap in his life, and if he is ever tempted to swear, he knows the remembrance of that moment will check him.

We had a refreshing shower about two o'clock, that laid the dust, cooled the air, and made everything sweet and fresh. We hoped and expected to have a pleasant afternoon, after the rain there was a calm—not a little tiny breeze or breath of air—it was just suffocating, and then came a cloud of buffalo-gnats that almost devoured us, so that horseback riding was an impossibility.

Wednesday, June 28.

Cash is on the sick-list today. I trust it will not prove to be anything serious. I greatly fear Mr. Kerfoot's family are destined to have considerable sickness before this trip is ended. They have such a sameness of diet, and it is so poorly cooked I fear the result.

When we started on this trip not one member of the family had ever prepared an entire meal; they had always had a houseful of servants to cook and do everything else for them. The first two or three weeks, Neelie and her mother tried to learn to cook, and mother and I tried to teach them. It takes great patience to learn to bake in stoves out of doors; they heat red-hot so quickly, and cool just as suddenly; they must have careful attention all the time.

They made several failures baking light bread, and, giving it up in disgust, settled down to biscuit, that are hard as brick-bats, when cold, bacon, coffee, and beans—when we stop long enough to cook them. They were well supplied with fruit at first; the canned fruit was so easily served that it is all gone. They have dried fruit, but think it too much trouble to cook. Neelie does the cooking with some assistance from her father, such as getting wood, making fires, bringing water, grinding the coffee, etc. Henrietta and Emma—the next younger sisters—wash the dishes. It is no small undertaking to cook for a family of twelve; I do not blame Neelie for getting tired, she says they have such appetites it is not worthwhile to tempt them with extras.

Neelie is the dearest, sweetest, most unselfish daughter and sister; it seems they all depend upon her, the children go to her in their troubles and perplexities, her father and mother rely upon her, and she is always ready to do what she can for any and everybody that needs her help; she is unselfishness personified.

The wind blew so all afternoon that we could not ride horseback. The roads are smooth and hard as asphalt, result of rain yesterday and the wind today. Dr. Fletcher who was called to prescribe for Cash says she will be all right in a day or two.

THE MOUNTAINS IN SIGHT.

Thursday, June 29.

We could see the mountains, as the sun was sinking behind them; they were plainly visible though one hundred miles away. It does not seem possible they are so far away. Long's Peak and others near it are

174

the points in sight. They look very much as I have imagined mountains would appear in the distance.

Mr. Walker is my informant as to names of places, distances, etc. He has been over the road and seems to know all about it. We usually ride some hours in company each day, so I have fine opportunities for asking questions, and he seems a willing instructor. He never broaches the sentimental, has never paid me a compliment in words I am glad to say, for since my late experience I would hesitate to ride with him were he not the sensible man that he is. We crossed a small stream today that was bridged and had to pay fifty cents toll for each wagon; the ford had been spoiled, or we could have crossed without the bridge.

Friday, June 30.

We stopped at noon where the road forks, the left-hand road goes to Denver. Mr. and Mrs. May, and Mr. and Mrs. Kirkland and children took the left-hand road, as they are going to Denver. Mr. May's brother, George, goes on to Montana on horseback; he will leave us in the morning and depend upon reaching stations, or emigrant camps, for food and shelter nights. I do hope the Indians will not get his scalp.

We have been feasting on antelope, the first that any of our party have killed. It is fine, much better than venison—but then I never ate venison when I was so hungry for fresh meat—we do get so tired of cured meat. We see no game except antelope and jack rabbits. The great herds of buffalo—that we read about—have not been in sight as yet.

Mr. Morrison's four-horse team ran away this afternoon with Mrs. Morrison and the children in the wagon. I had been riding with them since noon, had just left the wagon. When all the horse teams were driven out of ranks and down to the river for water, the lead horses took fright at an ant-hill—the ant-hills are big as a chicken-house—and started to run. There were several men near who caught and stopped them just as the fore-wheel went over the bank of the river. Mr. Harding was driving; he tried to rein them away from the river but they were right on the verge when stopped, one moment more and there would have been a serious accident. Mrs. Morrison did not scream nor try to jump out, neither did she allow the children to, but sat quite still and acted like the sensible woman that she is.

We are only six miles below the crossing of the South Platte.

Saturday, July 1.

We were awakened this morning at the first peep of dawn by the sound of the bugle call. Soon the teams were hitched, corral broken, and we were journeying to the crossing of the river, where we were driven into corral again. While we were getting breakfast the men were raising the wagon-beds and fixing them upon blocks as high as the wheels, and binding them tight with ropes to the coupling poles and lower parts of the wagons, ready to ford the river.

They had a top-heavy appearance, as if the least jolt would topple them over. Some of the women were very nervous about riding in wagons set up on stilts, and felt quite certain somebody would be drowned. Wagons were crossing when we drove into corral, of course we had to wait our turn—first come, first served. Some enterprising young men have the blocks and ropes there to rent, at a very reasonable hire, too, for they might have asked what they would, we had no choice but to use them.

The river is half a mile or more wide, about half way over there is a large freight wagon stuck in the quicksand, just below the track of the wagons; it has been there since yesterday; it is slowly, slowly sinking, and cannot be gotten out. It has been unloaded and left to its fate, it seems a signal of distress to warn drivers to keep farther up the river and avoid the quick-sands.

I drove the horse team over, and Hillhouse rode Dick and directed our going. The wagons of our train were all over and in corral by two o'clock without accident or mishap. Wagons have been crossing all day, and this evening we are a considerable town of tents and wagons; more than two hundred wagons within sight on the north side of the South Platte, at the eastern extremity of Fremont's Orchard—though why it is called an orchard I cannot understand, for there is certainly no fruit, neither promise of fruit about it, mostly quaking-asp and cottonwood, I think.

Our corral is just to the left of where the wagons drive out, and near the bank of the river. Hillhouse has crossed the river on Dick at least twenty times today; he seemed to know just how to help and has been in constant demand, so he and Dick are thoroughly tired out tonight. We will stay here over Sunday, and hope to have religious services tomorrow as there are several preachers with us. I have not met any of them except Brother Austin who preached for us last Sunday.

Cash is much better, able to be out, though quite pale and weak. The mountains looming up in the distance seem to be the goal to which we are tending, and now we seem to make some progress every day for we are certainly nearer than when we first saw them on the twenty-ninth of June.

Before they came in sight, we did not seem to make any progress, but travelled day after day, and seemed to camp at night always in the same place; there was such a sameness in the landscape. In the early morning when the sun shines upon the snow-capped mountains the effect is thrilling; they seem to be the great altars of earth raised up to Heaven for the morning sacrifice.

A Town of Tents and Wagons.

Sunday, July 2.

It is wonderful, wonderful to behold how this town of tents and wagons has sprung up since yesterday morning when there was no sign of life on this north bank of the South Platte, and now there are more than one thousand men, women and children, and I cannot guess how many wagons and tents. The wagons have been crossing all day, the last one has just been driven into corral at sunset.

I was sitting on the bank of the river watching with anxiety the wagons as they ploughed through the deep waters—for the ford has washed out and the wagons go in much deeper than when we crossed yesterday—when a gentleman came and introduced himself as Dr. Howard, physician for the McMahan train. He said, "Miss Raymond, I have known you by sight since we camped at Kearney, and now as I have an errand for an excuse, I hope to become better acquainted."

I could not imagine what his errand could be, for he talked of other matters for fifteen minutes or more, then said, "Miss Raymond, I have been directed to your wagons for the best and most wholesome bread that is baked on this road. Captain McMahan's nephew, Robert Southerland, has been very sick but is now convalescing and needs nutritious and wholesome food to help him gain strength. I came to ask you for a piece of good bread."

Of course, I gave him a loaf, and said, "Come get more when that is gone." He thanked me profusely.

There has been no serious accident nor any lives lost, although thousands of cattle, hundreds of horses, and more than a thousand human beings have crossed the river since yesterday morning.

Oh, for the pen of a Dickens to describe this wonderful scene, which no one ever has or ever will see again, just as it is. The moon is at the full and shining brightly as there is not a cloud in the sky, the camp-fires do not glow as they do dark nights. The men are building a great bonfire in the middle of our extemporaneous town.

177

There is to be a praise and thanksgiving service for our safe conduct through the deep waters and our protection from the Indians. The people are beginning to gather near the bonfire and I must go, too.

Later.

Our service is over; it was grand, the singing of the old familiar hymns by so many voices spontaneously was inspiring, the talks by five or six ministers of different denominations were full of love for the Master, and brotherly love for everyone.

An invitation was then given for all who had enlisted in the service of the Master to come forward and shake hands with the preachers, thus testifying for Christ. Neelie was the first one in that long procession to give her hand. Precious girl, she is always first in every good work. I noticed Dr. Howard in line, and I also noticed that Mr. Reade and Milt Walker were not among the soldiers of the cross.

The feed for stock is abundant, if it were not so, all these cattle and horses could not find pasture.

Monday, July 3.

The scenes in this great expanse of low, level land on the north side of the Platte in the early hours of this morning is hard to describe. Corrals and camps here, there and everywhere. Cattle and horses being driven into corrals to be harnessed and yoked, men and women cooking by camp-fires and on stoves, everybody seemed to be in a great hurry, all was animation and life, men riding after horses, oxen and mules; yelling, hallooing and calling, but not a profane oath did I hear. Among so many children, we rarely ever hear a child cry, and never hear a woman scold.

Our train was the third to break camp and file into the road this morning. The place that knew us yesterday will know us no more forever. Our town of tents and wagons that was teeming with life this morning is this evening deserted, silent, and uninhabited. We have folded our tents and driven or rode away. I did not mount immediately, but led Dick by the bridle, and gathered a magnificent bouquet of the most beautiful wild flowers. I had loitered by the way and did not notice that I was getting far behind our train, when I looked up and saw only strangers in the train that was passing.

I thought it was time to mount, threw the bridle over Dick's head, while arranging my flowers, so that I would not crush them. I saw a gentleman in the train throw down his whip and start toward me, as if to assist me in mounting. I waited until he was quite near, then placing a hand on either horn I sprang lightly into the saddle, turned and waved my bouquet toward him as Dick galloped off. Such a cheer as the men in the train did raise, and then such merry laughter; it was fun to hear them.

Dr. Howard says it was Colonel Woolfolk—a gallant young widower—and the men that witnessed it guyed him unmercifully on having been snubbed. We came to the western extremity of Fremont's Orchard, ten miles, and stopped for lunch. Then came the Sand Hills, where all the heaviest wagons had to double teams to get through. The captain came on four miles and selected a camping ground, and we drove to our places, to wait for the heavy wagons to get through the sand.

Hillhouse, and several others, who came on with us, went hunting for antelope. We have been feasting on antelope for several days; it is fine, but if I could have my choice I would rather live on ham and bacon all the while than to have our men go hunting in this Indian country. Since we have crossed the Platte we have no protection from the soldiers, as there are no stations on this side the river.

We suffer agony when our boys are away from camp guarding stock or hunting. I have no fears for myself nor any of us while we are all together in corral; but just a few away by themselves, how easily they might be cut off. There were Indians seen this morning by men looking for feed for the stock. It is almost dark and the boys have not come. I think the captain is getting anxious; he keeps looking in the direction the boys have gone. Ten p.m. The boys have just come with one antelope. They lost their bearings and came to the river, one mile or more above camp, and that was what kept them so late. When we scolded, they said they were obliged to stay to get at least one antelope for our Fourth of July dinner tomorrow.

WE CELEBRATE THE FOURTH.

Tuesday, July 4.

We made corral at eleven a.m., the captain announcing, "That we will stay four hours." I do not know if we stopped so soon, because it is the Fourth, or because it is so intensely warm, and the sun beams so hot, or because it was such a delightful camping-place. Whatever the cause, there we rested beneath the shade of large cottonwood trees, and it was so pleasant.

We had dinner at two. Our bill-of-fare—oyster soup, roast ante-lope with oyster-dressing, cold beans warmed over, dried fruit sauce, and our last cake and custard for desert. We used the last of our eggs, which were packed in salt; it is surprising how nicely they have kept. I believe they would have kept another month.

We had a very enjoyable feast, with an abundance of lemonade without ice. The boys put up a large swing on two large cottonwood trees; two could swing at once, with lots of strong arms to send us away up high. We began to file into the road at three p.m. Our fun was all too short. Dr. Fletcher rode with Neelie, and Milt Walker with me.

Wednesday, July 5.

Here is where we would have crossed the South Platte—if we had not forded it at the east end of Fremont's Orchard—on Lathan's Ferry. If all those wagons had crossed on the ferry it would have been a big pile of money for the ferrymen, for they charge one dollar a team.

We passed an Indian village today; it was just *tepees* and huts. Oh, dear, but they do look so uncomfortable. We are at the mouth of the Cache la Poudre—where somebody *cached* their powder. The water is so very clear and cold; it seems so nice after the muddy Platte. As there are no stations on the north side of the river, there are no wells. The Cache la Poudre is supplied by springs that flow from the snow-capped mountains that seem to be right over there.

Thursday, July 6.

As we were passing another Indian town, I peeped into two or three of their dwelling-places. They are desolate-looking homes; no sleeping-places, no tables, chairs nor any furniture, just some rolls of blankets and buffalo robes, some camp-kettles, and that was all. There were squaws and *pappooses* innumerable squatted around on the out-side of their *tepees*, the squaws making *moccasins*, or decorating them with beads. When we said "How," they grinned and held up two fingers, indicating they wanted two dollars for a pair. We did not purchase.

THE BLACK HILLS.

Friday, July 7.

We are camped at the foot of the Black Hills. They seem like im-mense mountains to me. There are four large corrals near the little village of La Porte. We rushed through with dinner, then Mrs. Hardin-brooke and I started for the top, taking our note-books with us. Before we had gone far, Winthrop and Frank joined us. Frank brought his gun; I do not know if he expected to find Indians or antelope up here. After much puffing and blowing, climbing and clambering, we reached the top. Oh, it is magnificently grand. If only I could make a pen-picture of this scene that others might realise it, as I do.

The mount upon which we stand is shaped like the quarter of a ball or globe miles and miles in diameter and circumference; we having climbed up the outside of the quarter to the top edge are looking down a steep precipice—the perpendicular side of the quarter. When a stone is thrown over, it takes it twenty-five seconds to reach the bottom, where the Cache la Poudre River runs at the base of the precipice.

How easy to step off into eternity from this place. I would not like to live near here, lest I might be tempted to do it some time. The valley over there looks as if—away back in the ages past—another quarter of the great ball that had been separated from this quarter, had been lifted by giant hands and carried away, leaving the most picturesque valley that I have ever beheld. There are three prosperous-looking farms in sight, a large herd of cattle grazing, and a beautiful grove or park at the northern end of the vale. West of the valley, and opposite where we stand, are peaks much higher than this; behind which the sun is sinking. The setting sun has crowned the mountain-tops with a crown of glory and brightness. The moon is rising out of beautiful, white fleecy clouds in the east. It is lovely beyond description.

How beauteous is this earth,
How bright the sky,
How wisely planned by him
Who reigns on high.

The sun is gone, night is coming; we must go, for we are at least one and a half miles from camp. I fired Frank's gun before starting; I aimed at the river, and hit the mark. How weak and insignificant these words seem when compared with the reality.

We Visit A Beautiful Spring.

Saturday, July 8.

The scenic beauty of the route we have come over today was ever changing. We were either coming through a narrow canon, across a beautiful vale, climbing or descending a steep hill or mountain. Nellie Bower and I had started on horseback to have the morning to ourselves, when Mr. Walker rode up and asked us to go with him to a lovely spring of delightfully cold, clear water he knew of, some two or three miles ahead. We consented, of course, and had soon left the wagons behind us. Mr. W. has been over the road before and seems to know the landmarks and places of interest.

We found the spring, as described, in a beautiful dell, where the loveliest wild flowers I ever saw are growing luxuriantly. We were soon off our horses, enjoying the cool, delicious spring water. We gave our horses a drink, and then we each gathered a large bouquet of beautiful, fragrant wild flowers. They certainly are "wasting their sweetness on the desert air."

I believe we were almost an hour ahead of the train. Mother scolded, and so did Mr. Bower, because we had gone so far ahead of the wagons, for it is said these hills are full of Indians. I am all the time forgetting about the Indians. Mr. Kerfoot will not allow his girls to get out of sight. I am glad mother is not so exacting as that, but I ought not to impose upon her good nature, and cause her to worry. I never do intentionally, but sometimes I forget.

We are camping in a beautiful basin surrounded on all sides by high hills, and where the grass is plentiful. There is only one other train with us, but then it is the McMahan train, and they are all such fine-looking young men—and of course they are brave—that I always feel safe when they are near. Our captain has forbidden our going out of sight of camp. There are canons in all directions; how I would like to explore.

Hillhouse and Sim Buford gathered some wild currants while herding; they will pass for fruit, but they look better than they taste. We have made sauce of them; with lots of sugar and cream they look inviting, and the boys seem to like them; very few will satisfy me. We can always have cream for breakfast, as the milk stands overnight, and a pat of the sweetest, most delicious butter every evening, when we travel, as the milk is churned by the motion of the wagon. Fruit is very necessary on this trip, because of the alkali in the water, dust, and air we breathe, to keep us in health.

Sunday, July 9.

I was up very early this morning; I cannot spend precious time in bed after daylight while we are camping in this delightful place and have this perfect weather. I led Dick to the spring for a drink, bathed my face and hands in the cool water, picked a bouquet for the breakfast-table, and returned to camp to find the girls in bed. They missed a glorious sight by not seeing the sun rise.

Mother and Mrs. Hardinbrooke went with me to the top of the hill nearest camp this afternoon. They picked flowers and enjoyed the view for a while, then returned to camp, leaving me to come later. I sat on a large flat rock, just below the top, as mother said, "The Indians could see me so much farther if on the very top." I promised her I would not go out of sight; that if an Indian carried me off, they could see him and know where I had gone. I did so enjoy the quiet of this Sunday afternoon; I had Mrs. Prentiss's delightful book, *Stepping Heavenward*, to read, and time passed so quickly the sun was setting before I thought of going back to camp. Some of the boys laughed and said, "We were watching, and if an Indian had put in an appearance, we'd have settled him; we knew you would not see him until he had you." I thanked them for their watchfulness.

We Cut Our Names in Stone.

Monday, July 10.

Just when we had mounted our ponies for our morning ride, Mr. Walker came and asked us to go with him to the top of a mountain we could see far ahead and to the right of the road. He said, "The prospect is very fine, indeed, from that mountain-top. I was there two years ago."

Cash and Neelie were included in the invitation, also Mary Gatewood, but their fathers would not let them go. So, Nellie Bower and I were the only ones who were allowed to accept his invitation. We rode our ponies until the ascent became too steep, and then dismounted and climbed. It was a hard climb, but we were amply paid. The view was magnificently grand. We found Mr. Walker's name where he had cut it in the soft stone two years ago, and we left our names, with date and former place of residence, cut in the stone. There were hundreds of names there, but I looked in vain for a familiar one. I wonder if anyone that we know will find ours? We passed the graves of two men this morning who had been killed by the Indians. What a sad fate; God forbid that any of our men or boys should die such a death.

We are camping near a military post—Virginia Dale. It is just as beautiful as the name would imply. There are soldiers here for the protection of emigrants passing through these hills and mountains. Cash and I were riding with the captain when we came to the station. The officer in charge came out to speak to the captain and asked some significant questions, "How long have you been in the hills?"

"Two days and nights."

"Where have you camped?"

"In that basin about eighteen miles back. We stayed over Sunday."

"Have the Indians troubled you?"

"We have seen no Indians."

He seemed greatly surprised, and said, "There has been no train come over that road within the last month without trouble, especially where you stayed over Sunday. Did not you notice those *cañons* in every direction? The Indians could surround you before you could know there was one near. The hills are full of Indians."

He told the captain where to camp, and where to send the stock for safety and protection. The captain thanked him, and we were starting on when the McMahan train came in sight.

"Ah, ha!" he exclaimed, "I see now why you have not been molested. Just keep that train in sight, and you need have no fear of Indians." And he just doubled up laughing until it was embarrassing to us.

"But why? Why will that train be a protection more than another?"

"Don't you see that portable engine lifted away up there, and all those iron pipes? The Indians think it is cannon, or some sort of machinery invented for their destruction; no doubt they believe it could kill them by the hundreds, though the mountains stood between it and them."

So that is why we have not been molested. We have heard of depredations before and behind us, but we have not seen an Indian. Blessings on the McMahan train; I hope we will not lose sight of it while we are in this Indian country.

We have passed through some very narrow canons today, where there was barely room for one wagon to pass. Great rocks were hanging overhead on one side, with a rushing stream beside and just below the road on the other. There are beautiful waterfalls in the *cañons*. I was standing watching one of the highest, waiting for the wagons to pass. The last one had gone when Mr. Morrison came and peremptorily commanded me to "Come on, Miss Sallie. The I-I-I-Indians will c-c-c-carry you off some of these days," he stuttered. Of course, I went.

The captain's orders are, "Do not leave camp this evening." We were only just corralled when I saw Lyde Walker climbing a nearby mountain. It is the first time I have known her to leave camp since we came into the Black Hills; she is very much afraid of Indians. When she came back, I asked, "Why, Lyde, did you not hear the captain's order that we were not to leave camp this evening?"

"Oh, there is no danger when the men are on guard and watching. It is when they feel secure and are not looking out for them that I am afraid. Indians do not molest people when they are expecting them."

LARAMIE PLAINS.

Tuesday, July 11.

The sounding of the bugle and the echo that reverberated through the mountain gorges this morning was enchantingly sweet, and must have driven slumber from every eyelid. We left the hills at noon and are camping on Laramie Plains. We came over some very steep, rocky roads before we reached the plains. I watched the wagons anxiously as they descended the steep, rocky mountain-side, bounding and bumping against the big rocks, expecting and dreading an upset, but all landed safely on level ground at last, and I gave a sigh of relief and thanksgiving. We have not had an uncomfortably warm night all summer, but while we have been coming through the hills the nights have been really cold, so that we have slept under blankets and comforts, like winter-time. There is no sickness in camp at all; it is marvellous how very well we are. I hope it will continue so.

Wednesday, July 12.

We crossed the Big Laramie River just before noon. Had a good crossing; the water is clear, the bed of the river is covered with gravel, the banks are low, and the water is not very deep. I rode across on Dick; the water just came to my stirrup. We will stay here until tomorrow, as there is no water for fifteen or twenty miles, and we cannot go so far in half a day. We young people planned a fishing expedition for this evening, but the mosquitoes are so thick on the bank of the river we had to give it up. Some of the boys went seining; Brother Winthrop was among them, so we will have fish for breakfast tomorrow morning.

The mosquitoes have not disturbed our rest at night, yet they have several times been very thick on the banks of the rivers, but have not been troublesome in camp. Perhaps the smoke keeps them away. The McMahan train keeps with us, so we are safe. Dr. Howard rode with us this morning; he is a widower.

Thursday, July 13.

We passed two large ponds of alkali this morning. The water had dried up, and the alkali was two or three inches thick all over the pond; it looked like ice, until we came very near.

Mrs. Hardinbrooke had a sick headache this afternoon; I took care of little Annie that she might not disturb her mother. She is a dear, sweet child and seems fond of me.

There was a rather serious accident as we were driving into corral. Mr. Hazelwood's horses were frightened and ran away, upsetting the wagon and smashing it up considerably. Mrs. Hazelwood, her sister, and two children were in the wagon; Mrs. H. was considerably bruised, the others were not hurt.

Dick drank alkali water this evening. I have been feeding him fat bacon; no doubt the grease and alkali have turned to soap before now in his stomach, and soap is not poison, so he will not die this time, and I will take better care of him the next time we are near alkali.

In the Rain.

Friday, July 14.

The men were until almost noon repairing the broken wagon. An accident that happens to one is assumed by all until results are overcome. As we were ready for the start, a little girl ran among the oxen to catch her pet crow; an ox kicked her on the forehead and cut a gash that had to have a few stitches and be bandaged, so we were delayed again.

When order reigned once more, we crossed the Little Laramie. It is very much like the Big Laramie, only not so wide nor deep; I rode Dick over, and then came on ahead of the train, keeping within sight.

When we had travelled about an hour the rain came down. I was likely to get very wet before our wagons came, for they were among the last in the train; I took the saddle and bridle off Dick, sat down on the saddle to keep it dry, and to wait for the wagon. I was resigning myself to a drenching when Mr. Grier, driver of the front wagon, came and spread a great big rubber coat over me, so that I was completely sheltered and was hardly damp when our wagons came.

Then mother drove the horses close up to the wagon in front I tossed my saddle and bridle in, hopped up on the tongue of the wagon before the wagon behind got close up, and we started without stopping but the one wagon. We could not stop until we came to feed for stock, so we were obliged to travel in the rain. We drove into corral about four p.m., and are again quite near the mountains. There are more pleasant things than camping in the rain. The water is so impregnated with alkali I fear it will cause sickness; the stock are in greater danger than we, for we can guard against it.

Saturday, July 15.

As I climbed out of the wagon this morning, I saw the most beautiful rainbow I ever looked at. The bow was complete, the colours dazzlingly bright and just as vivid in the centre as at the ends. It was not raining in camp, but raining hard on the mountain-side. The rainbow was so near we might easily have reached the end and "found the pot of gold." The rain came down all morning; we did not break camp until ten o'clock and then made only a short drive. We are camping among the hills once more, with not another train in sight. The Mc-Mahan train is behind us, but we do not know how far away they are, so we are glad to wait until they catch up. There is a mountain near that I would like to climb, but it is against orders.

Sunday, July 16.

We are all here; although some of the women last night seemed to think there was small chance of our seeing the light of this morning's sun. Had we known that the McMahan train was within calling distance—just a hill intervening—perhaps we would have rested easier and slept more soundly. It is considered a very dangerous place where we were last night and where we have travelled today. Although it is Sunday, I am sure there is not one in camp that would have voted to stay there to rest. We have heard horrible stories of the depredations that have been committed along this road and in these mountains within the last month.

We saw with our own eyes—just before we came to Rock Creek—a station that had been burned and all the inmates killed or taken prisoners; there were none to tell the story of the fight, although the bodies of all who were known to be there were not found. The buildings were not all burned, the fire either went out, or was put out by the rain, after the Indians left. They have been repaired, and soldiers stationed there now. We saw at the same station a coach that had been riddled with bullets; it was found on the road about a mile from the station, without horses, driver or passengers.

INDIANS.

It is supposed the Indians killed the driver, took the horses, and it is not known yet whether there were passengers or not, the coach being so riddled with bullets; it is feared there were passengers. A guard of soldiers go with the coaches we meet, or that pass us now. We crossed Rock Creek on a toll-bridge, and had to pay fifty cents toll for each wagon.

Just after we crossed the bridge, and where there is a sudden turn in the road, as it winds around the mountain, we saw where two men had been killed and two wagons burned last week. The tyre became loose on a wheel of the next to the last wagon in a freight train, the men stopped to tighten it, while the rest of the train moved on, not thinking of danger, and was out of sight in a few minutes. An hour later some of the men came back to see what kept them. There they were—dead and scalped—the horses gone, and wagons on fire. The Indians had taken all the freight they could use, piled wood under the wagons, and set it on fire. We saw quantities of white beans scattered over the ground, also the irons from the wagons.

We are within sight of Elk Mountain and seemingly quite near it. Sim and Hillhouse picked a nice lot of gooseberries while stopping at noon. I have been sitting in the wagon, picking off stems all afternoon; they also brought a bucket of snow. It is really refreshing, and such a novelty to have a snowball to eat in July. The gooseberries are quite plentiful around here. Cash and I went with Hillhouse and Sim to pick some this evening, but a shower drove us to camp; the boys stayed and picked as long as they could see. If we had time, we could gather gooseberries enough to supply the train for a month. They are very fine and large; they are certainly an acceptable addition to our bill-of-fare, where a sameness of diet is unavoidable. I shall always consider them a fine fruit hereafter.

About an hour after we drove into corral the McMahan train came, and their corral is quite near. We are so glad they are here; we feel safe when they are near.

Monday, July 17.

Such a cold, rainy, dismal day as this has been. It has rained without stopping from early morn until now, and it is almost sundown. This is the first all-day rain we have had this summer. It has rained all night several times, but that is not so bad.

Since we have been in this Indian country the tents have not been put up; everyone seems to think it safer in the wagons than in tents outside the corral, so we have had to sit in the wagons all day. I have read, sewed, written, picked over gooseberries and ran through the rain and visited some, yet the day has seemed long.

The herders have to take the stock two miles away to find feed, so we are consumed with anxiety, notwithstanding we know our Father's care is round and about us, and He can and will protect us. When we came here, we could see Elk Mountain, but now it is enveloped in clouds, entirely hidden from view. It is not pleasant camping when it rains all day long.

Tuesday, July 18.

The wagons started soon after daylight, before we were out of bed. We had been on the road a little while when I heard Hillhouse call to Brother Winthrop—who was driving our wagon—"Oh, just look, Wint. Isn't that a grand sight?"

I knew there was something to see, so I was soon up and dressed and sitting with Winthrop. I shivered with cold until my teeth chattered, but was well repaid for any inconvenience by the grandeur of the sight I looked upon. Why try to describe or picture anything so entirely impossible? The masses of fleecy white clouds, with the brightness of the morning sun shining upon them as they floated around and over the top of the mountain, made an ever-changing, beauteous panorama that I cannot describe. As the clouds rose higher and higher, they seemed to mass over the top of the mountain, as in benediction, glittering in the sunshine until they seemed to melt away.

I waited until the sun had warmed the air, then mounted Dick for my morning ride. The McMahan train broke corral and drove into line just behind our wagons. I had only just started when Dr. Howard rode up on his pony Joe and requested the pleasure of riding with me. The doctor is a very pleasant, cultured gentleman, and is very fond of his pony, yet Joe cannot be compared with Dick for beauty, neither for easy gait. Why, Dick is the most beautiful pony on this road. He is a bright bay with long and heavy black mane and tail, and his gait is as easy as a cradle. I can ride all day and not be tired at all. While his horse—well, I will not describe him. It might hurt the doctor's feelings.

We came to the foot of Elk Mountain, on the Medicine Bow, about nine o'clock. We find plentiful and excellent feed for the stock, so the captains have announced, "We will stay here until tomorrow."

WE CLIMB ELK MOUNTAIN.

The doctor thanked me for the pleasure our morning ride had afforded him, and asked, "Can we not make up a party to climb Elk Mountain after breakfast?"

"I hope so. I will ask some of the young people."

About ten o'clock a few of us commenced the climb. Lyde Walker, Nellie Bower, Cash and Neelie, Sim Buford, Brother Hillhouse, Dr. Howard and myself. We were well paid for the effort; we found beautiful wild flowers, and some wild strawberries not five feet from a snow-bank. The snow is in a ravine on the north side where the sun does not shine. The berries and flowers are on the bank of the ravine, high enough to catch the rays of the sun, facing the south. The view was fine; we could see a large white lake far away to the west. Dr. Howard said it was alkali.

Wednesday, July 19.

We passed the alkali lake this afternoon. It was a strangely beautiful sight—the water as white as milk, the grass on the border intensely green. I always thought grass would not grow where there is alkali, but it is certainly growing there; the contrast of white and green was vivid. The wind was blowing the water into little glittering, dancing skipping wavelets; the sight was so unusual that it was fascinating, though the water is so dreadfully poisonous.

There are several musicians in the McMahan train; Lyde says they serenaded me last night. She says they stood between our two wagons. I think she is trying to tease me.

"Ask Dr. Howard, if you do not believe me. He was one of them."

"Oh, no. I would be ashamed to acknowledge I did not hear them, and would feel like a dunce if they had not been there."

Dr. Howard gave me the bouquet he gathered on Elk Mountain, which was most beautifully arranged, and asked me "To keep it until it falls to dust." I have put it between the leaves of a book and will perhaps never think of it again.

We came through Fort Halleck today. There were eight wigwams, or *tepees*, at the east end of the town; the squaws wore calico dresses and hoops.

Cash and I made a few purchases at Fort Halleck. I paid eighty cents for a quire of writing paper, and Cash paid fifty cents for a can of peaches. Mrs. Morrison is on the sick-list today, and Delia Kerfoot has a very sore mouth—scurvy, the doctor says, caused by the alkali in the dust and air. Neelie and Frank are both complaining.

WE CROSS THE NORTH PLATTE.

Thursday, July 20.

The ground was covered with a white frost this morning, and it is freezing cold. Mrs. Morrison and Frank are better; Delia's mouth is healing. Neelie continues to drag around; she will not acknowledge that she is sick enough to go to bed, but she certainly looks sick. I wish they would call Dr. Howard; somehow, I have more faith in him;

190

perhaps because he is older and more experienced.

We are on the banks of the North Platte; arrived about three o'clock, did not stop for lunch at noon. We came ahead of the other trains, which will be here tonight. We will have the privilege of crossing first in the morning.

The men have taken the herds five miles away to get good feed. They are in danger from Indians. The captain called for volunteers. My brothers both offered to go, but the captain said, "Only one of Mrs. Raymond's boys must go."

Hillhouse said he would be the one. He was on guard last night, too.

We are in no danger here, for there are several trains here now and there will be more tonight. Oh, the anxious watching, the prayerful longing for day that we must endure this night, because of loved ones exposed to danger. What a precious privilege that we can go to the Mercy-seat with the assurance that if we ask aright our petitions will be granted. How do people live without Christ and a Mercy-seat? What can they do, when suffering anxiety, grief, or bereavement, if they cannot go to Jesus with their sorrows? Precious Saviour, what a refuge in time of trouble, what a joy to carry everything to God in prayer.

The McMahan train is near. Dr. Howard has been here; he begged me to let him see my diary. I asked to be excused.

Friday, July 21.

The night passed without alarm, and we are all here; I am thankful. Some of the men in our train were afraid to risk fording the river, and paid four dollars per wagon to be ferried over on a rickety old ferryboat that looked more dangerous than driving over.

Hillhouse and Winthrop were both engaged with the ox-team, Winthrop on the seat and Hillhouse riding Dick. When they drove into the river, I motioned to mother to keep quiet and drove the horse-team right in behind them. The current is very swift; they had all they could do to keep the oxen from going with the current, and did not know I had followed them until they came out on an island in the middle of the river. Hillhouse smiled a sickly little smile, and said, "You should not have tried that."

Dr. Howard stood near, holding his pony by the bridle. He complimented me on my skill in driving, and said, "I saw you drive in that swift and treacherous river with bated breath, but soon saw that you knew what you were doing, yet I rode Joe in just behind you to be ready for emergencies."

"Thank you for your thoughtfulness. I will not 'halloo until I am out of the woods'—the other side is to be crossed yet."

Hillhouse said, "You would better wait on the island, and I will come back and drive your wagon over."

But of course, I could not do that, after all the complimenting I had received. I drove in—with fear and trembling—for there lay a big freight wagon upset in the middle of the stream. It was more difficult than the first side, the banks higher and steeper, and the water deeper. We got over without mishap; the doctor came on his pony just behind us. I wandered off alone after lunch and climbed to the top of a nearby mountain. I found there a large pyramid of loose stones that looked as if they had been piled there by travellers, each one contributing a stone.

I selected a snow-white stone from the mountain-side and added to the pile. There is another town of wagons being made on the west side of the North Platte. The wagons have been crossing all day, and are crossing yet. Hundreds of wagons have been driven over that turbulent and rushing river, and not a serious accident occurred.

I have been on the lookout for the Irvine train, but it is not here. I think it is ahead of us, and we will not see the young ladies or Mr. Reade again on this trip, yet as we are all going to Montana we may perhaps meet again.

NEELIE IS SICK.

Saturday, July 22.

We are within sight of Pine Grove in Wyoming Territory.

Neelie was very much better this morning; almost well, she said at noon, and rode her pony this afternoon. I was riding with her when I noticed a heavy rain-storm coming. I begged her to come on and not risk getting wet.

"Oh no, Miss Sallie; I don't want to ride fast. This air is so delicious, and I think I want to ride alone for a while; you go on, and I will come very soon."

I saw it was useless to urge her. I am always careful not to expose myself unnecessarily to a drenching, so I raced on to our own wagons and had barely time to unsaddle Dick and turn him loose when down came the rain in torrents. I was so anxious about Neelie and expected her to come tearing through the rain. I looked from the back of the wagon and saw her coming—plodding along at the same slow gait, as if she did not know it was raining. When the rain was almost over, she came along—drenched, of course. She laughed at my look of dismay and paid no heed to my scolding.

Mother and I both urged her to go quickly and change her wet garments for dry and warm ones. She got off her horse and climbed into the wagon. When we stopped, I went around to see how she fared. She sat in the wagon with a blanket-shawl around her, and the wet clothes had not been changed for dry ones. She was shivering with cold.

"Oh, Neelie, my precious girl, I am afraid you have killed yourself."

"Oh, no, Miss Sallie; I am not so easily killed as all that."

"But, Neelie, you have been sick for a week, and now to get this drenching. I fear the consequences."

The family do not appear at all anxious, so there is nothing I can do but hope and trust that her naturally strong constitution may bear even this strain. I advised her to go to bed, drink hot tea, and get into a perspiration. I doubt very much if she will do it.

Milt Walker is on the sick list, too. Hillhouse went to bed with a severe headache last night, but a night's rest has entirely restored him.

We crossed three very muddy streams today, the first muddy water we have seen since leaving the South Platte. Since coming to the mountains, the water has been as clear as crystal until today; perhaps we are coming into mining country. We stopped quite early this afternoon; the McMahan train has passed and gone out of sight. I hope they will not go too far, and that they will lend us protection with their portable engine and other machinery.

Sunday, July 23.

We are resting today. I went with Mrs. Hardinbrooke, Lyde and a gentleman friend of Lyde's, for a long ramble over the mountains this afternoon. We found a most delightful spring where the water seemingly gushes out of the rock. Just below this spring was a patch of the finest wild onions I ever saw. We brought a good supply to camp. We are so starved for green vegetables that everyone seems to enjoy the onions, though some had never eaten onions before, they said. For my part I always did like onions.

THE SUMMIT OF THE ROCKY MOUNTAINS.

Monday, July 24.

We passed the summit of the Rockies today, and are camping on the western or Pacific slope tonight. The ascent has been so gradual we should not have known when we reached the top but for the little rivulets running in different directions. Quite on the summit and very near to each other we saw two little rivulets starting on their way; one to meander toward the Pacific, while the other will empty its confluence into the Mississippi, and thence on to the Gulf. Just a scoopful of earth could change the course of either where they started—from the same spring really. As it is, how widely different the scenes through which they will pass.

So, it is with human lives—a crisis is reached, a decision is made, and in one short hour the whole trend of our life is changed with regard to our surroundings, associates, environments, etc.

We came through Bridger's Pass today, crossed a toll bridge near Sulphur Springs, and had to pay fifty cents toll for each wagon. The streams are all muddy that we have crossed today. We saw two beaver dams; they look like the work of man with shovel and trowel. We are camping two miles west of Sulphur Springs.

Tuesday, July 25.

We are camping near another muddy creek near a station that was attacked by Indians ten days ago; they wounded one soldier very severely and ran off with nine horses.

After we were in corral, while waiting for the stove to be set up and the fire to be made, I was sitting in mother's camp-chair idling and thinking, when Neelie came to me. She dropped upon the grass beside me and, laying her head in my lap, said, "Oh, Miss Sallie, I am afraid I am going to be sick in spite of everything, and I have tried so hard to get well without sending for the doctor."

Dr. Fletcher is desperately in love with her and tried to tell her so one day not long ago, catching her hands while talking, which she resented as a familiarity, and has not spoken to him since. She told me about it the evening after. It happened at noon. I told her I believed he was sincerely in earnest and that she had wounded him deeply.

She told me what she had done to try to cure herself; the medicine she has taken is enough to kill her. I called mother and told her what Neelie had told me. Mother said, "You poor child, you do look sick, indeed; you must go to bed and send for the doctor right away." I went with her to the wagon, helped her to get ready for bed, and told Cash to send for Dr. Fletcher. She said she would as soon as Bush—her brother—came.

After dinner I went again to see Neelie; the doctor had not yet come, but Bush had gone for him. I stepped upon the tongue of the wagon and could, with difficulty, restrain an exclamation of disgust. Neelie interpreted my expression and said, "Cash just would do it; said I was looking so like a fright."

Cash had powdered and painted Neelie's pale face and crimped and curled her hair—and made her look ridiculous—trying to hide the sick look from the doctor. I did not answer Neelie, but went and scolded Cash; in a low tone she said, "She was so dark around the eyes, her lips blue, and her cheeks so pale I could not bear to have Dr. Fletcher see her looking so homely. She has told you about their little love-tiff?"

"Yes, but don't you suppose he can see through that paint and powder? I am afraid he will think Neelie did it, and she will appear ridiculous in his eyes." I saw the doctor coming, so came away. As I was sitting here writing, he came a while ago and said, "Miss Raymond, will you sit with Miss Kerfoot tonight and see that she has her medicine strictly at the right time?"

"Certainly, I will. Is she very sick, doctor?"

"She is in a much more serious condition than she or the family realise. It would not be wise to alarm her, but the family ought to know she will need very careful attention. I will tell them tomorrow. You need not sit up after the last dose of medicine is given, which will be at midnight. I think she will rest better if everything is quiet, and the lights out."

I know from the doctor's tone and manner he thinks Neelie dangerously ill. The doctor gave me directions about her medicine, and I went immediately to her wagon.

SIM BUFORD SICK.

Wednesday, July 26.

Last evening as I was on my way to sit with Neelie, I met Ezra. He said, "Miss Sallie, Sim is quite sick; very much like Cousin Neelie is, I think. I wonder if we are all going to be sick?"

"Oh, no; I hope not. I am very sorry Sim is sick."

When I left Neelie—a little after midnight—sleeping quietly, to come home, I noticed a light in the wagon that Sim and Frank occupy. I did not awake this morning until everything was ready for a very early start. Mother had kept my breakfast warm by keeping the stove until the last minute. I sat in the wagon and ate my breakfast after the train had started. When through I climbed out and went to see how Neelie was. I found her feverish and restless; her symptoms unfavourable.

Oh, the dust, the dust; it is terrible. I have never seen it half as bad; it seems to be almost knee-deep in places. We came twenty miles without stopping, and then camped for the night. We are near a fine spring of most excellent water—Barrel Spring it is called. I do not know why; there are no barrels there. When we stopped, the boys' faces were a sight; they were covered with all the dust that could stick on. One could just see the apertures where eyes, nose and mouth were through the dust; their appearance was frightful. How glad we all are to have plenty of clear, cold water to wash away the dust.

Neelie is no better. Such a long drive without rest and through such dust was enough to make a well person sick. I fear the consequences for both Neelie and Sim, for Sim is a very sick boy. Hillhouse told Sim last night that we would take him with us and take care of him, if he wanted to come and Mr. Kerfoot would let him. He wants to come, of course; so, he sent for Mr. Kerfoot this morning to come to his wagon, as he wished to see him on business.

Mr. Kerfoot came, and Sim asked to be released from his contract to drive through to California. Mr. Kerfoot asked, "Why do you want to leave us?"

"I believe Montana is the place for a young man to go, and besides I am very sick and can have better care with the Raymonds than I can here, for Neelie needs all your attention."

"I reckon your chances are as good as the rest of us have." And walked off.

Frank came for me, and I went to see Sim; he is very sick, has a high fever and coated tongue. He asked me to see Mr. Kerfoot. Frank went with me. Mr. K. seemed to know what we came for; he was scarcely civil. I put the case plainly, and said, "We must take care of Sim, either with or without your consent; we owe it to his father and mother, and to himself, to see that he is taken care of. He cannot be taken care of where he is."

After rearranging the boys' wagon and making room for Sim's bed and other belongings; Ezra, Frank and Hillhouse helped him to the wagon and put him to bed, while I went to the McMahan train, which was quite near, and asked Dr. Howard to come and prescribe for him. The doctor came, bringing the medicine with him. He says it is mountain fever.

The separation of the train is being talked of, and is no doubt absolutely necessary, for the herd is so large it is hard to find pasture for them all together. When the division is made, those going to California will form one corral, and those bound for Montana will form another. This will separate us from Mr. Kerfoot's family; I do hope we will not have to part while Neelie is so sick. I do so want to help take care of her.

Thursday, July 27.

Among the families that came into our train at Kearney was a family of four young ladies and their father—a widower—named Ryan. Sue, Kate, Mary and Maggie are their names. Mr. Ryan told some of the young men that he was taking his daughters to the west, where there are more men and fewer women, so they could have a better chance to get good husbands than in Missouri. It has been a good joke among the boys, and some of them have tried to be very gallant to the young ladies—as they are on the market.

George Carpenter, a driver for Hardinbrooke and Walker, when the train separated this morning, pretended to go into hysterics. He had a fit on the inside of the corral when Mr. Ryan drove off with the other half of the train. Mr. Kerfoot did not know he was fooling, and ran to his assistance; the captain passed, took in the situation and smiled. Mr. Kerfoot knew then it was a hoax, and it made him so mad he declared he would not stay in a train where the captain would smile at such conduct.

The doctor had said to him, "It is necessary that I see Neelie several times during the day, and you will be taking great risk if you leave the train until she is much better." He had decided to stay, and join the others any time before they came to the California road, west of Green River. He was so mad at the captain for smiling at Carpenter's nonsense, and because he did not rebuke him, that he made the boys bring in the horses and cattle and hitch up as quickly as possible. In an hour after the others started, they had followed. Mr. Kerfoot did not say goodbye to anyone. I do hope Neelie will not suffer for his crankiness.

We are now a corral of twenty wagons, the greater number freight wagons; they are in corral on the opposite side, while the families are all on our side. The Hardinbrookes, Walkers, Bowers, Kennedys, Morrisons, Currys—a family of five—Mr. and Mrs. Baily and their daughter, about ten years old, and a widowed sister of Mrs. Baily and her little girl, about the same age as her cousin, are with us at the back end of the corral. I do not know these people, only just to speak when we meet, but they now help to form our corral.

We came only two or three miles after the train separated, just far enough to get out of the dust. Mr. Kerfoot's family and ours have been almost as one family since we have been on the road, and I have become greatly attached to all of them and especially to Neelie. She is the dearest, sweetest girl, so very unselfish, and always ready to help any and every one that needs help. There is not one in the family but could be spared better than Neelie except, of course, her father. They all love her so, and depend upon her for everything. She is a precious daughter, a darling sister, and a true friend.

Sim is very much better; he has some fever, but not so high a temperature as yesterday. Dr. Howard is very attentive. He says it is mountain fever that Sim and Neelie both have. Dr. Fletcher called him to see Neelie; he says she is a very sick girl, but not worse than Sim was when he first saw him. Her temperature is not so high.

I wonder if mountain fever is contagious, or what it is that causes it? It seems the air is so pure and invigorating one could not get sick at all. I never felt better in my life, and mother seems so well. I am afraid it is the sameness of diet and poor cooking that is making Mr. Kerfoot's folk sick. The bread they make is hard as brick-bats when cold.

We Overtake the California Train.

Friday, July 28.

We came up with the other half of the train about ten o'clock, and have travelled in company the rest of the day. We have separate corrals about two hundred yards apart; the stock is not herded together.

Neelie has been restless with high fever and flighty when she dozes; with eyes half open, poor girl she is certainly very, very sick.

We are near a delightful spring, cold as ice, and clear as crystal. I went to the spring to bathe my face and hands, and brush my hair. Mr. Kerfoot and Frank came for water. Mr. Kerfoot said, "Miss Sallie, why don't you and your folks come and go to California, where you started to go?"

"Why, Uncle Ezra, you know the reason. We think Montana the better place for the boys to get a start, and we want to do the best we can for them."

"Tut, tut; wealth is not the chief thing in life. You can make a living anywhere, and Montana is an awful place. Why, the only law they have is mob law, and if a man is accused of crime he is hung without judge or jury."

"Notwithstanding, there seems to be a great many nice people going there, and I am not in the least afraid of my brothers being accused of crime."

"I do believe you will regret going to Montana, and I also believe it is all your doing that you are going. I think it is very unkind of you to leave us now when Neelie is so sick and needs you so much."

"We are not leaving you, Mr. Kerfoot; it is you leaving us against the doctor's orders, too."

I made a great mistake saying that, he fairly raved; he was so angry, actually beside himself with rage. He said very unkind things without the least foundation or truth in them, and which I will try to forget. I am so sorry for him. I did not answer a single angry word, and I am glad I did not. But Frank did; he was about as angry as his uncle was, and talked manfully in my defence. He gave his uncle the lie, and clenched his fists and seemed ready to fight.

I ended the embarrassing scene by walking away. Mrs. Hardinbrooke was waiting for me; we climbed to the top of a very steep point, which was hard to climb, and we were out of breath when we reached the top and were glad to sit and rest. The view was fine, the evening pleasant, and we were glad of each other's companionship, but we did not talk. I think Mrs. Hardinbrooke attributed my silence to anxiety about Neelie, and she was not far from the truth.

Saturday, July 29.

Neelie was very much better this morning; her fever gone, she was very weak, but was free from pain. Her medicine had the desired effect. She had rested quite well last night—better than since she has been sick—and all her symptoms are favourable.

The doctor seemed greatly encouraged and told Mr. Kerfoot that if they would stay here until Monday, he felt sure Neelie would be out of danger and they could move on without any risk of doing her harm. He did not dream that Mr. Kerfoot would again disregard his advice. Neelie continued better until noon, then someone proposed moving on a half day's drive, thought it would not hurt her if they made only short drives at a time.

Mr. Kerfoot listened, and finally consented. He is very much afraid of Indians, and in a few days, we will be out of the Indian-infested country. The doctor is very much out of patience with him, told me he gave Mr. Kerfoot a piece of his mind.

You must make big allowance for the poor man. He does not realise that he is endangering Neelie's life; he cannot believe it possible that such a calamity as Neelie's death can befall them while he is trusting in a merciful Father above. Yet I do wish someone might have exercised authority and prevented their going.

Sim is very much better, improving rapidly. Mr. Walker is able to be around once more. I wonder if he had mountain fever?

I have been trying to get the dust out of our wagon this afternoon; it was hard work taking everything out and cleaning off the dust. Lyde Walker pleasantly entertained us this evening with songs accompanied with guitar. The wagon the Walkers occupy is just in front of ours since the separation.

ON EMITTER CREEK.

Sunday, July 30.

We came fifteen miles today, but have not overtaken the California train. It must be that Neelie is no worse, and their traveling yesterday did her no harm, or they would have waited over today; we shall hope so anyway.

Dr. Howard rode with me this morning. We are traveling on Bitter Creek, which is considered the very worst part of all the road. I had heard so much about the desolateness of this part of the country that I expected to find a barren waste. It is not so bad as represented. There are long distances where there is not sufficient pasture for the stock, but in places the feed is plentiful. The captain and two or three men are off the road the greater part of the day hunting pasture; we stop when they find it at whatever hour it may be.

Monday, July 31.

We came twelve miles, passed one station; it was built of stone and seemed a very comfortable place. Mrs. Hardinbrooke has been quite sick today. I have taken care of little Annie. We have not had any word from Neelie. I trust that no news means good news. Sim was able to sit up in the wagon for a while this afternoon. I think with care he will be well in a few days. We have had delightful weather, since we passed the summit. The roads are quite dusty, but not like they were before we came to Barrel Springs. The water in Bitter Creek is not so nice as the mountain streams and springs, but it is not bitter, as I thought it would be from its name.

Tuesday, August 1.

We are at Point of Rocks, the place is rightly named; one who never saw them could hardly imagine such enormous piles of rock; they are high as mountains, with scarcely any dirt among them, the sides are smooth and even, the stone is soft like slate or sandstone, and the whole face of the enormous pile, as high as man can reach, is literally covered with names, dates, and places of former residence from all over the United States. I looked in vain for some familiar name. I left my name in a conspicuous place, so if any of my friends look for my name, they will not be disappointed. There are springs flowing from the clefts in the rock; and oh, with what pleasurable anticipation did I hasten to partake of the pure water, as I, of course, supposed it was.

I had been riding with the captain as he came ahead to find a camping place when the train came. I rode to our wagon, got a cup and crossed Bitter Creek to get a drink of nice, cold spring water. I took one swallow. Oh, oh, oh; the horrid stuff. I was glad there was no one with me to see the face I made. I think I never swallowed a more disagreeable dose. It was the strongest sulphur-water I ever tasted. In my haste and eagerness, I did not notice that the atmosphere was impregnated with sulphur, and the sulphur formations around the springs, because they were covered with dust.

The wind is blowing as cold as Greenland. I expect we will have to go to bed to keep from freezing. Mrs. Hardinbrooke is no better; her symptoms are the same as Sim's and Neelie's were at first, and we fear she is taking the fever. Dr. Fletcher thinks Neelie must be better, or we would have heard, as Mr. Kerfoot said he would send back for him if she got any worse.

DELAYED ANOTHER DAY.

Wednesday, August 2.

We had a very cold night; there was ice a quarter of an inch thick this morning. Several head of Hardinbrooke's and Walker's cattle were missing this morning; the men have been hunting them all day, they were found this evening in a canon four miles from camp; there were the tracks of two horses, with shoes, that had driven them there. The Indians do not shoe their horses, so there must be thieves besides Indians in this country.

And here we are another whole day's drive behind the other half of our train. Oh, I wonder if it will be possible to overtake them now, before our roads separate entirely. They must be at least two days ahead of us, if they have not been delayed.

Thursday, August 3.

The mountains in this region are very barren, composed of sand and rock, principally.

It comes nearer being desert than anywhere on the road. We have travelled all day, and have come only thirteen miles. The road has been very rough indeed. I rode in the wagon the greater part of the day, so I could take care of little Annie Hardinbrooke; her mother is very sick. I have thought so much about Neelie, whenever the wheels would strike a rock, or jolt down into a rut; how she must have suffered, if in pain or fever; how hard it must have been for her.

Lyde says Dr. Fletcher is very impatient and cross, because of the delay; he threatened to take a horse and go horseback yesterday, when he found the train would not move. She thinks he is very anxious about Neelie, and very much in love.

Friday, August 4.

The wolves howled around our camp all last night and kept Caesar—our watch-dog—barking; so, we could not sleep. Have made only a short drive, and are camping at Rock Springs, where the road forks. The men are not agreed as to which road to take; the upper—or right-hand road—is the shortest, but the lower is best supplied with pasture and water. If we take the upper road, we cannot hope to see our friends again, so Dr. Fletcher and I want to take the lower road, for we still hope that we may overtake them.

Mrs. Hardinbrooke is very sick; I fear we are going to have another case of serious sickness in our camp. I have taken care of Annie again today, which seems to be the most efficient service I can render, as Lyde and Mrs. Joe Walker take care of Mrs. Hardinbrooke when her husband cannot be with her. He takes all the care of her at night, and a most excellent nurse he seems to be. Sim is quite well, only pale and weak.

Saturday, August 5.

The decision was made in favour of the lower road. As the train was rolling out I had just mounted my pony, when Dr. Fletcher came and asked me to ride with him. He has never seemed to care for my company, nor I for his until since we have been so anxious about Neelie. Our anxiety has been a bond of sympathy, and we have rather enjoyed each other's society. We had gone a short distance ahead of the train when we saw someone coming horseback. I soon saw that it was

Frank. We hurried on to meet him. He shook hands without speaking. I asked, "How is Neelie?"

"She is very low. I came after you, doctor. Our camp is about four miles from here; we have waited two days for you, and thought you would certainly come yesterday. When you did not come, we thought you must have gone the upper road, and I was going back as far as the first station to inquire if you had passed. I am glad, indeed, to meet you, but greatly fear you will not be in time to save Neelie."

The doctor asked two or three questions, excused himself and rode away at a gallop, leaving Frank and I to follow, while I plied him with questions, which he answered patiently. He then said, "Neelie was much better for a day or two after we left you; we all thought she was getting well; she spoke of you every time I saw her, and wondered why you did not come. Since the fever came back, I have not talked to her at all. Part of the time she has been delirious, and when conscious she was too weak to talk."

Oh, dear. I do so want to see her and help take care of her.

A Fatal Shooting.

We rode a while in silence, then Frank said, "That is not all the bad news I have to tell, Miss Sallie."

I looked up quickly and asked, "What else has happened, Frank?"

"Frasier was shot and killed day before yesterday evening."

"Oh, Frank; how did it happen?"

"Hosstetter did it, but I think he was not much to blame."

Frasier is the man who spoke to Cash, Neelie and I, as we were watching the wagons ferried across the Missouri River, whose son ran away from his mother, and home, to come to his father, and go with him to Montana. Frasier had teams and wagons for freighting, and Hosstetter some capital to invest in freight, to take to Montana. Frasier advised the purchase of flour, and he would freight it to Virginia City for fifteen dollars per cwt. He said flour was worth fifty and sixty dollars per hundred in Virginia City. (So it was in the Spring of 1864, and as high as seventy-five and one hundred dollars per hundred, which was the cause of a bread riot in Virginia City.)

No doubt Frasier was honest in his advice, and would have invested in flour for himself. He charged more freight than was right, for ten and twelve cents is the prevailing price; but then Hosstetter should have found that out for himself.

When he found he had been imposed upon and learned that flour

203

is retailing at Virginia City for $15 per hundred, he was angry, dissatisfied, and perhaps quarrelsome. Frasier was no doubt very aggravating. They had quarrelled several times, and the evening of the 3d, Frasier was heard to say to Hosstetter in a threatening tone:

"You may consider yourself lucky if you ever see Montana. You need not expect to get any of this flour. It will take it all to pay the freight."

It was getting dark, and Frasier stood with one hand on a wheel as he talked. He then got into the wagon and out again, with something in his hand, which Hosstetter thought was a revolver in the gathering darkness.

He came back to the wheel where he had been standing when he made the threat, and Hosstetter thought he had come to shoot him, and fired twice, as he thought, to save his own life. Frasier fell, shot through the brain, and died instantly.

Then it was found he had a hatchet in his hand, and had come to tighten a tyre on the wheel, which he had found loose when he laid his hand on it. Frasier's eldest son of fourteen years is here. There are five children and their mother at home. Hosstetter has three children and a wife. Eleven innocent persons to suffer, no one knows how intensely, for that rash act.

Frasier's son knelt beside his father's dead body, and placing his hand on his breast, he swore a fearful oath that he would have but one purpose in life until his father's death is avenged. Oh, what a shocking ambition for so young a boy.

Frasier and Hosstetter have travelled and camped near us all the way from Plattsmouth. When the train was organised, they came into it; when it was divided, they went with the others as there were not so many of them, and the herd was smaller.

By the time Frank and I had discussed the direful circumstances connected with Frasier's death, in the presence of this greater calamity Neelie's sickness did not seem so sad an affliction as it had before, for she is not dead, and while there is life there is hope.

We came in sight of three corrals about eight o'clock, camping near together.

Tried For Murder.

Everything had a funereal appearance. Men stood around in small groups talking earnestly in a low voice, whittling sticks, the incessant occupation of most men when trying to think.

Those with whom we are acquainted bowed as we passed them, without speaking. I was soon off my horse and ready to see Neelie, while Frank took Dick to hitch him for me.

As I approached the tent where Neelie is, Mrs. Kerfoot came to meet me.

"How is she, Aunt Mildred?" I asked anxiously.

"We think perhaps she is better now. She is quiet and resting easy, but she has had a very restless night, and the doctor says she must be kept perfectly quiet; not the least excitement."

She had led me away from the tent while talking. I saw in a flash what she meant. I was not to see Neelie.

"After we left you, she kept asking about you, and when you did not come, we thought perhaps you had gone the short cut, and so we told her you had gone the short cut to Montana, and we would not see you anymore. She seemed grieved at first, but became reconciled to what could not be helped, and now, if she should see you of course it would excite her, and I know you would not do anything that might harm her, or make her worse."

"Oh, no; of course not."

Emma, Delia and Juddie had come to where we were talking. I kissed them all, said goodbye, and came away, with a heavy heart.

I unhitched Dick and, leading him by the bridle, went on in advance of the trains, selected a place for the corral, unsaddled Dick, and waited for the wagons. I did not have long to wait, and the captain was so good as to corral on the place I had selected.

I had a motive in being in advance of the other trains. I hoped to get Hillhouse and mother to consent to pull out of corral and go on if the train did not move. We are not in any danger from Indians now, and we can go alone if no others choose to go with us. I cannot bear to stay here and not see Neelie.

We could not move today, but Hillhouse says we will tomorrow morning. The men from these four trains elected judge, jury, prosecuting attorney and lawyer for the defence, and have tried Hosstetter for murder. The jury brought in a verdict of "Not guilty." He shot in self-defence, as Frasier had threatened to kill him.

Hillhouse served on a jury, the first time in his life. He is only twenty. They buried Frasier yesterday. Lyde and I visited his grave this afternoon. Hosstetter seems very remorseful; blames himself for being so hasty.

Sunday, August 6.

We were up bright and early this morning. By the time other camps were at breakfast we were ready to start, one other family with us, Mr. Curry, his wife and four boys. When Hillhouse spoke to the captain about our going on, he said he thought it advisable, as our teams are in good condition, the cattle not at all lame. We can make much better time than the train can, as so many of the cattle are lame, they will be obliged to travel slowly. There is no danger from Indians, and after we reach Green River pasture will be plentiful, without going away from camp to find it.

I climbed into Mrs. Hardinbrooke's wagon to tell her goodbye, kissed little Annie as she was sweetly sleeping. Mrs. H. seemed sorry to have us go. I met Dr. Fletcher as I was leaving Mrs. Hardinbrooke and asked about Neelie.

"She is very low, indeed. Of course, while there is life we may hope; but if she lives, they will have to stay here a week or ten days."

I did not tell him we were leaving, but said good morning, and went to find Lyde. She was worried and anxious about Milt. He has been staying behind the train to drive lame oxen almost every day since he has been well enough. He is usually in camp by 10 p. m. Last night he did not come. She said, "Brother Joe is quite sick, too. I wonder what will happen next?"

"Oh, Lyde, no very serious calamity has happened to you or yours, nor me or mine. Let us not borrow trouble, but hope for the best. Milt will be here in a little while. I know he is able to take care of himself, and he is going to do it."

WE LEAVE THE TRAIN.

The wagons had started, so I mounted Dick and was off. As I came into the road I looked back, and saw Milt coming in sight, driving his lame oxen. I left the road once more and went to Frasier's grave. His son has set it with prickly pears, so closely that it will make a pretty mound if it grows, and will be a protection from wolves, unless their hides are thick and tough. Poor boy, he must have been seriously scratched while transplanting the prickly things, but perhaps it was a relief to his mental suffering, to bear physical pain while trying to do a last something for his poor father.

I spent a dreary morning. I feel the parting with our friends so distressingly. It is not likely we will meet again in this life. I think Sim is feeling blue over it, too.

We met a squad of soldiers from Green River going to arrest Hosstetter, and take him to Fort Bridger for trial. They say his trial was not legal. He and all the witnesses will have to go by the way of Fort Bridger, and will perhaps be detained for some time. I do hope for his own and his family's sake he will be cleared. The upper road from Rock Springs goes by the way of Fort Bridger, I think, for the soldiers spoke as if it was not on this road.

We arrived at Green River about three o'clock. The river is about as wide, deep and swift as the North Platte, yet I have not dreaded any of the rivers we have crossed as I did dread to ford this one. Perhaps it was because there are so few of us, for in numbers there is a feeling of security, even in crossing deep and dangerous streams. We crossed without accident or loss, and are camping on the west bank of Green River. When we first came to the river, one of Mr. Curry's boys exclaimed:

"Well, this river is named right. If I had been going to name it, I believe I would have named it Green River, too, for it is green."

The water is very clear, yet the river has a bluish-green appearance. I do not understand why.

There are several corrals along the river, but the people are strangers, so we feel very much alone. There is a station here and soldiers' tents within sight. We are camping on blue grass, with the mountains very close. They are the highest I have seen. I would like to climb to the top, but mother says there are too many soldiers and strangers around.

At the foot of the mountain, a little way from our camp, there is a graveyard with about a dozen graves. It is a beautiful spot, with the mountain for an enduring monument. Several of the graves have been made this year, with names and dates quite distinct on the plain pine headboards. Others are entirely worn or washed off by the relentless hand of time and storm. It seems that Bitter Creek was too much for the weak or frail constitutions. Like Moses, they were permitted to look upon the better land before they died.

Monday, August 7.

The soldiers brought Hosstetter here in the night, and I suppose the witnesses came too. I wanted to go to the station to see if I could hear anything from Neelie, and the rest of the sick folks, but mother did not want me to go where there are so many soldiers, so I did not go. We started very early this morning and have driven about twenty miles. Are camping on Black Fork, where the horses and cattle are just wading in fine pasture right around camp.

We ascended a mountain this morning that was seven miles from base to summit, the way the road is. We had toilsome climbing, and I guess the teams found it a hard road to travel before we reached the top. I came on in advance of the wagons, sometimes riding and sometimes leading Dick where it was very steep, and had time to enjoy the magnificent scenery that lay spread out on all sides. The snowy range could be seen in the distance, glittering in the morning sunshine. The wild currants are here in abundance. I am going fishing with the boys, so I must be off.

WILD CURRANTS GALORE.

Tuesday, August 8.

We caught fish enough for breakfast last evening, and gathered currants enough for sauce, but I spoilt the sauce by putting the sugar in, when I put them on to cook, they hardened and were not fit to eat. I have been experimenting today and have succeeded in making a nice cobbler.

I did not sweeten at all before baking, but made the sauce sweet enough to sweeten all. I also made a fine sauce by cooking the currants only a very few minutes, and putting in the sugar after they were cooked. We will have currant dumplings for dinner tomorrow. We have picked a lot, enough to make sauce and pies and other good things for a week. The currants are a beautiful fruit, and some are as large as small cherries. We are waiting at Camp Plentiful, in the hope that some of the wagons from the train will drive in before night.

There are three wigwams within sight of our camp. Sim and Hillhouse went hunting today. On their way back they stopped at the wigwams and found them occupied by white men with squaws for wives.

Wednesday, August 9.

Somehow, I felt a little suspicious of those white men living with squaws, and feared some of our horses might be missing this morning, but my suspicions were groundless. Our horses and cattle were all here, well fed and ready for a long drive. We were off bright and early, without seeing any one from the train.

We passed the Bridger Road, where our friends going to California will turn off, so we are not likely to see them again, perhaps for years, perhaps never again in this life.

There is a very fine ranch at the junction of the roads, where we stopped at noon. Two men from this ranch visited our camp this evening. They were rather fine looking, genteel in appearance, dressed in civilization style, but for some unexplainable reason, I was afraid of them. They tried to be very cordial and polite. They engaged Sim in conversation, and plied him with pertinent questions, such as:

"Who owns those big American mares?" (Referring to our horse team).

"They are the property of a widow."

"Whose bay pony is that?"

"It belongs to the widow's daughter."

"Who is the owner of that chestnut sorrel?"

"Mr. Curry, father of those boys playing over there."

They asked many more questions. Where we came from? Where we are going? What we expect to do, etc.

Sim answered them patiently and civilly. He thinks they are horse thieves, but hopes they will not be mean enough to steal from a widow. As if horse thieves care who they steal from. No doubt, their ranch is stocked with stolen horses and cattle, for they have things as they choose away out here, where there is no law, except the law of might.

God's Word says, "*As the partridge sitteth on eggs, and hatcheth them not; so, he that getteth riches, and not by right, shall leave them in the midst of his days, and at his end shall be a fool*" (Jer. 17: 11).

We are camping on Ham's Fork, where the currants and fish are very plentiful, and the pasture very fine. We had our currant dumplings for dinner. They were lovely. No one can imagine how we appreciate this fruit by the wayside, except those who have been deprived of the strawberries, raspberries, blackberries and cherries, each in their season, and confined to the sameness and tameness of diet, which people making this trip are necessarily confined to. This fruit would seem inferior among other cultivated fruits, but where it is, it seems a luxury provided for our benefit.

Thursday, August 10.

We went fishing at noon. It is such fun to fish in water so clear that we can see the fish biting at the hook. They do not seem at all afraid, and sometimes there will be two, three, or four grabbing at the hook at the same time. Such shoving, pushing and crowding as they all try to get the tempting bait. How eager and unsuspecting they are. Soon the strongest or fleetest, or rather the most unfortunate one seizes it. Away goes bait, hook and all, and then out comes a fish on dry land. I give a shiver of pity for the unlucky fish, as I call to the boys: "I have another."

It does seem such a cruel thing to take them from their pleasant home in the deep, clear, cool water. But then, "Life is sustained by death." And thousands upon thousands of lives are taken daily to nourish and sustain human life. We are in a beautiful place, where all things necessary for camping are plentiful, and we are all alone, no corral within sight; the first time we have been entirely alone.

Friday, August 11.

One or other of the boys stood guard last night. It proved an unnecessary precaution. There was no disturbance either from horse thieves, Indians, or wild beasts. We are living fine since we crossed Green River. We have fresh fish for breakfast and sometimes for dinner. Wild game of some kind for dinner, with currant pudding, cobbler, or dumplings, with rich cream for dessert. We may possibly go hungry next Winter at Virginia City, but there is no danger of starving while we stay on Ham's Fork.

The weather is perfect. I have been riding my pony the greater part of the day, sometimes one of Mr. Curry's little boys with me, and sometimes alone. I have enjoyed the delightful atmosphere—it seems so pure and invigorating; the scenery is beautiful, and it has been a glorious day.

MR. CURRY'S HORSE STOLEN.

Saturday, August 12.

It was considered unnecessary for anyone to stand guard last night, as we had come two days' travel from where the suspicious characters live. So, all went to bed, retired early, slept soundly, and even neglected to put Caesar's rug in its usual place—under our wagon—so he went into the tent with Mr. Curry's boys to find a comfortable bed, leaving the camp entirely unguarded. One of our big horses wears a bell. I was awakened in the night by hearing an unusual rattling, and the horses came galloping up to the wagons.

Dick whinnied. I raised the wagon cover and spoke to him, and he commenced cropping the grass. The other horses were in sight, but not eating. They seemed frightened, and just then Caesar came tearing out of the tent and ran toward the road barking fiercely. The moon was shining brightly. I looked out at the back of the wagon, but could not discover anything wrong, but evidently there was something wrong, for Mr. Curry's horse was gone this morning.

Mr. Curry, Sim and Hillhouse have been hunting the horse all day, but without success, except to find certain evidence that it had been stolen. They found the camp-fire, where three horses had been tied for some time. They then found where four horses had travelled, so they concluded there were three men after the horses.

The boys think it was the merest accident that our horses are not gone too, but I believe it was providential care that kept them for us. Mr. Curry is anxious to stay and try to recover his horse. I believe, as the boys do, that it will be a waste of effort, for if men are mean enough to steal a horse, they will manage to keep it. But we do not like to offer too many objections, as it might seem like selfishness on our part, as we are not the losers.

Oh, dear, why don't people be good, and do as they would be done by? How much happier this world would be if there were no thieves nor wicked people in it. I know it is hard for Mr. Curry to give up his fine horse without making an effort to get it back. Yet I feel sure he will not get it. For if he found it, he could not force the thieves to give it to him.

Anxiously Waiting at Ham's Fork.

Sunday, August 13.

It was decided this morning that Hillhouse, Sim and Mr. Curry would go in pursuit of the horse thieves. Sim is just recovering from a severe sickness, and is not able to go on such a trip, but he positively refused to stay in camp and let Hillhouse and Mr. Curry go without him. I believe it will prove a wild goose chase, so mother and I exacted a promise from Hillhouse that he will not stay away tonight. We are looking for him. It is getting dark. Surely, they will not leave us here in this wilderness with only two boys and Caesar for protection. If we are left alone, I shall take my turn, with Winthrop and Alex. Curry standing guard in camp. Sim rode Dick this morning, the others walked. What they expect to do if they find the thieves (which they are not likely to do) I do not know.

Mr. and Mrs. Kennedy, Mr. and Mrs. Bower, Nellie and Alton, and Mr. Grier's teams passed here today. They left the train the next morning after we did. The train had not started then. They said Neelie was about as when we left, and Mrs. Hardinbrooke was no worse.

Monday, August 14.

Hillhouse came in about an hour after dark. He was very tired and hungry; had walked since early morning until he started back at three o'clock. He tried to prevail upon Sim to return, and let him go on with Mr. Curry if he must go. But Sim would not listen to such a proposition, although he is still weak from his late sickness. Mr. Curry thinks he will find his horse at the ranch near the junction, although the trail they were following led away from, instead of toward it. If he finds it, he will go back to the train and get the men to help him get it either by fair means or by force.

He then proposed that they keep Dick, but they said he would not reach camp before midnight on foot and he might lose his way, but Dick would take him the shortest route if he would just let him go his own way, which he did, and he brought him safe about an hour after dark.

I am so sorry for Mrs. Curry. She tries to be brave for her children's sake, but anyone can see she suffers, and Alex says she does not eat at all, just takes a cup of tea once in a while.

Tuesday, August 15.

Another day has come and gone, and the wanderers have not returned. Hillhouse said he did not expect them today, but would look for them tomorrow, for they will not have anything to eat after today, and will be obliged to leave the foot hills and come to the road, whether they find the horse or not, to get something to eat.

A party of emigrants stopped near us today at noon, and one of the men came to our camp. We, of course, asked if they had seen the Hardinbrooke train. They passed the train Sunday. They were still where we left them at the west end of Bitter Creek. He saw and talked to the captain, who told him to tell us, if he caught up with us, "The sick folks are all better, and they expect to come to Green River Monday." They may catch up with us yet.

I do not know what we would do with ourselves if it were not for the currants. We are making jelly, and as it takes lots of currants to make a little jelly, we have not suffered from enforced idleness, with our suspense and anxiety.

Wednesday, August 16.

There are three varieties of currants here. The yellow ones are not very plentiful. They are the largest and best. I have made a pickle jar full of the loveliest jelly. It is the colour of gold and as clear as crystal. The red currants are very plentiful and more like the tame currants, though they do not yield as much juice.

We gather the bushes by the armful, and carry them to camp, and sitting near each other, we pick off the currants.

Though we do not talk much, we like to be near each other. Another day and they have not come, and another night of anxiety before us.

Thursday, August 17.

I was awakened very early this morning, as soon as it was light, by hearing Hillhouse bustling about making a fire in the stove, as if in a hurry for his breakfast. I dressed as quickly as possible, and hastened out to see what it meant—for it was only four o'clock. When I asked for an explanation, he said:

"I am going to hunt those men. I can't stand this any longer. I have laid awake almost all night thinking about them."

"What can you do? You will be lost yourself."

"No danger of that. I will go back on the road as far as Green River, get some of the soldiers and some of the boys that know them, and we will hunt until we find them, or know what has become of them. I may meet them on the road and return tonight, but I will not come until I bring them with me, or know their fate."

I could not object to his going, but oh, how my heart sank at the thought.

We made all haste to get breakfast, and Hillhouse was all ready to start when Mrs. Curry and the boys came out. Mrs. Curry seemed both glad and sorry he was going, said she hardly knew which. I had supplied him with pencil and paper, and he promised to send us word every opportunity. He mounted Dick and rode away without saying goodbye.

He had gone almost out of sight. One moment more and a bend in the road would hide him from our view. When, lo, there is a gun fired not far off.

My thought was Indians, and I looked to see if Hillhouse was hurt. He was waving his hat furiously and came tearing back to camp. Then I heard Mrs. Curry cry out:

"Oh, it is my husband." And she dropped in a heap on the ground, and cried out loud.

They were plainly visible by that time, coming over the hill and down to the creek and through it, before anyone could show them where they could cross without getting wet.

All was excitement for a while. The meeting between Mr. Curry and his family was very touching, indeed. I think Mrs. Curry had about lost all hope of ever seeing him again.

How famished and worn out they did seem to be. Sim was utterly exhausted. I do not believe he could have gone another half mile. We gave Sim a bowl of bread and milk, and a cup of coffee. Then the boys helped him to bed in our wagon, because it is on springs and we expected to start before he waked. Within one hour after they reached camp Sim was sleeping the sleep of exhaustion. We did not ask any questions, nor let him talk at all, before he went to sleep.

Mrs. Curry prepared the best breakfast the camp could afford for her husband, and as the family had not breakfasted, they all sat down together. She came for Sim to take breakfast with them, but he was sound asleep, and I would not have had him awakened for the best breakfast ever prepared. Perhaps Mr. Curry can stand eating such a meal after starving so long, but I believe it would kill Sim in his weak condition, for he is not fully recovered from his recent illness.

We made all haste to start once more, and by eight o'clock were on the way. We had left the camp where we spent five such anxious, distressful days. Sim did not awaken until after ten o'clock. We gave him some fish and bread and milk, which we had ready for him. When he had eaten, he lay in bed and told mother and I the following narrative of what had befallen them since they left camp:

SIM'S STORY OF THEIR WANDERINGS.

"After Hill left us that first afternoon, we walked on as fast as we could, as long as we could follow the trail. Then made a fire, ate some supper without anything to drink. We had not seen water since noon.

"We rolled up in our blankets and lay down with our feet to the fire and tried to sleep. I am sure I did not sleep an hour, I was so tired and nervous. As soon as it was light enough to see, we were up and ate a dry breakfast, for we could find no water in the vicinity. We were soon following the trail. Before night we had eaten all our grub, and found no water. Oh, what would I have given for a cup of cold water? It seemed that we must find water or perish. We dragged on as long as we could see; then lay down and slept from exhaustion. When we awoke it was light.

"I was so weak that Mr. Curry had to help me to get on my feet. I declared I could go no further. Mr. Curry prevailed on me to try, for we must be near Green River. I made a desperate effort, and dragged on for half a mile perhaps, Mr. Curry carrying my blanket, when I positively could go no further, and told Mr. Curry to go on and leave me and try to save himself. Mr. Curry was desperate. He said: 'I must find something to eat.' He covered me with the blankets and went to look for some kind of game.

"When he had gone about a hundred yards, he saw a bird about the size of a partridge sitting on a limb ready to be shot. He took careful aim and shot its head off. He hastened back to where I lay, made a fire, skinned the bird, and held it on a sharpened stick before the fire and roasted it thoroughly. I would have eaten it when half done, but Mr. Curry would not let me have it until well cooked, for fear it would make me sick.

"I never tasted fowl that tasted so good as that did, although we ate it without salt. After eating I felt better, and made another effort to move on. We had gone only a little way when Mr. Curry stopped, listened a moment, and exclaimed: 'There, hear the rushing of the river?'

"I could not hear it at first, but soon I heard the glad sound too. It gave us courage, and with renewed energy we pushed on, and before eleven o'clock we reached the river. We slacked our thirst, cautiously, at first, then had a bath and were refreshed.

"While I rested on the bank, Mr. Curry looked up and down the river for the trail, which had gone into the river. He did not find it. We then started for the road, which we came into in about an hour, just below the ranch at the junction.

"A party of emigrants had stopped for noon, who gladly gave food and refreshment to us weary wanderers. While I was resting, Mr. Curry investigated the ranch, looked among the horses in the pasture, peeped in stables, but did not find his horse.

★★★★★★

Those men at the junction did steal Mr. Curry's horse. The men in the Hardinbrooke train saw them in their corral, and asked, "Where did you get that horse?" They answered, "From a man by the name of Curry. Paid $150 for him."

★★★★★★

"After Mr. Curry had given up getting his horse he was all eagerness to get back to his family, but considering how very weak I was, he consented to stay with the kind people we had fallen in with until morning, so we travelled with them, and I rested in a wagon all afternoon.

"At the first peep of dawn Mr. Curry was up and awakened me. I felt refreshed and ready for our early walk. Mr. Curry explored the grub-box, found some bread and meat, which he appropriated, leaving greenbacks to pay for our entertainment.

"We expected to reach camp by ten o'clock p. m., but I gave completely out, and we were obliged to lie down and rest when about five miles from camp. I slept until awakened this morning before it was light by Mr. Curry, who was so anxious to be on the way I wondered that he let me sleep so long.

"We came over the foot-hills, instead of by the road, and saved about a mile in distance. We saw Hill riding away from camp and felt sure he was starting to try and find us. Mr. Curry fired his gun to attract his attention, and you know the rest."

He turned over and went to sleep again, and slept until we stopped for noon. We made a long drive today and are camping at the foot of Bear River Mountain.

We had a hard rain and hail storm this afternoon. It was very violent while it lasted, and we halted by the roadside until it was over. It was over in half an hour.

Mr. Curry has suffered with a severe headache and high fever all day, the result of that hearty breakfast this morning after fasting so long.

BEAR RIVER MOUNTAIN.

Friday, at noon, August 18.

I am on the summit of Bear River Mountain, in the border of a beautiful grove of pine and quaking-asp, near a spring of the most delicious ice-cold water. I must be some miles ahead of the wagons that I left toiling up the steep mountain side. Yet I do not feel that I am alone. Oh, no. I feel that God is here in his might, majesty, power and glory. I feel His nearness now, and as I gaze from these dizzy heights upon the country spread out beneath my feet, I am lost in admiration, the scene is so grand, so magnificent, that I forget my own vanity and nothingness. I feel that I am standing upon an altar raised by Nature's grateful hand up to Nature's God, and that I could offer myself a willing sacrifice.

This is emphatically one of the high and sacred spots of earth. How manifold, how wonderful are the works of Nature: Everywhere something worthy of our highest admiration is presented to view; everywhere do we see the manifestation of an invisible and omnipotent Creator. The terrific storm, the broad prairies, the majestic forest, excite within our bosoms emotions of awe and admiration, yet there are no places on earth that I have seen which have a tendency to inspire me with such tender feelings, such elevated, pure, holy thoughts as mountains. Oh, it seems that one could never sin, or have an evil thought, in such a place as this. Behold the mountains as they stand upon their broad bases, contemplate them as they rear their snowy tops in awful, majestic grandeur above the clouds, view them as you will, and they ever present the same untiring pleasure to the mind.

Men and women will travel thousands of miles and make the greatest exertion to climb the rugged steeps of mountains, to enjoy for one short hour the charming prospect. I have wondered at this sometimes, as I have read of their hazardous exploits in trying to obtain a point where they could have the finest view, but I never shall again.

A country destitute of mountains may be fertile and productive of all that conduces to human happiness, yet it will lack the essential of attractive moral grandeur.

It may enchant the imagination for a moment to look over prairies and plains as far as the eye can reach, still such a view is tedious and monotonous. It can in no wise produce that rapturing delight, that pleasing variety of the sublime and beautiful of landscape scenery which mountains afford.

Let those whose tastes are on a level with the ground they tread feel proud of and admire their prairie fields, but give to me a mountain home.

The wagons are almost at the top, and as mother has driven up the steep ascent, I will drive down the western slope, and have mother ride Dick, and enjoy the delightsome scenery as we descend the mountainside, which looks very steep from here.

We were all the evening crossing the mountain, and it was a hard drive. We are camping at the foot of the mountain near a spring in Bear River Valley, within calling distance of the Chilicothe train.

We passed two freight wagons on the mountain-side that were rather badly smashed up. One had upset, and crackers in a broken-up condition, and other debris from family groceries were scattered about.

We learned that the wagons are Dr. Yager's, and he has gone somewhere to get the wheels mended. We are quite disappointed that he is away, for Sim is not so well as he was yesterday, has had fever and been flighty and in a stupor this afternoon. He needs medical treatment, and we hoped to have Dr. Yager prescribe for him.

We passed eight graves on the mountain, one a young lady twenty years old from Monroe County, Missouri. A beautiful resting place for the dead. Mrs. Yager is quite sick, and seems sadly disheartened.

Thinks crossing the plains and mountains in a wagon (they have a very comfortable carriage) is a sad, discouraging, never-to-be-repeated experiment. I am sorry she could not enjoy the fine prospect on the mountaintop, for she is a lady who would appreciate such grandeur to the fullest under favourable circumstances.

We reached level ground without accident, and were glad to come up with friends we had met before on the road.

We Meet Captain Hardinbrooke's Brother.

Saturday, August 19.

We left the Chilicothe train this morning. As it will take all day to get the wagons mended, they cannot start today. We came on to Bear River, reached here a little after noon, and will stay here until tomorrow.

We crossed a toll bridge on Smith's Fork, and met Captain Hardinbrooke's brother at the bridge. He is going to meet the train. He did not know of Mrs. Hardinbrooke's illness. He asked very especially and with some confusion, "Is Miss Walker well?"

Ah, I think know who he is going to meet, and understand some things that have not been very clear to me before. "Ah, ha, Miss Lyde, you have guarded your secret well, but see if I have not guessed it now?" Well, he is very nice looking, and if he makes as good a husband as his brother, he will no doubt be worth coming to Montana for. I wish you joy, and that I may be present at the wedding festivities.

The boys have gone fishing, all but Sim. Poor boy he is too sick again. I feel very much out of patience with Mr. Curry, because of the tramp he led Sim when in so weak a condition.

Sunday, August 20.

We passed a grave this morning that was made yesterday for a young mother and her new-born babe. Oh, how sad. With what an aching heart must that husband and father go on his weary way, leaving his loved ones by the roadside.

We crossed another toll bridge. It seems to me that emigrants are greatly imposed upon by these men who claim toll. They throw a very poor excuse of a bridge across a stream that could be easily forded if let alone, but they spoil the crossing by digging ditches and throwing in bush and timbers to obstruct the fording, then build a cabin, close to the bridge, and squat to make a fortune by extorting large toll from emigrants, who have not the time to stop and contend for their rights.

It seems a shameful business.

While stopping at noon we saw a company of Indians coming down the road toward our wagons. My first sensation was fear, but upon reflection I knew that is not the way they go on the warpath, and by the time they reached camp I was ready to say "How," and try to talk to them. There was one that could understand English and talked quite well. They are Bannocks, the tribe that was conquered in Idaho some years ago. Their chief was with them. He held a stiff neck and tried to look dignified. They are going on a buffalo hunt. It seems that the whole tribe are going, squaws, *pappooses* and all.

We have been meeting them all afternoon and are camping with them all around us tonight. They all seem to want my pony. I have been asked at least twenty times this afternoon to "Swap." I gave all the same answer, "No swap." Why, I would not give my Dick for twenty of their ponies.

The squaws and *pappooses* are around our camp tonight begging biscuit, I do wonder if they are so hungry?

We crossed the steepest, straight up and down mountain today that we have crossed yet. It seemed that the wagons would turn a somersault as we were making the descent.

Sim was too sick to sit up, and he would slide down in a heap, bed, bedclothes and all, against the seat and grub-box. We stopped twice to have him helped back into place. When we reached level ground, he was all piled up again. Poor Sim, he is very sick. I do wish we could come across a physician. We have administered simple remedies, but seemingly without effect.

There is an old lady ninety-three years old in a train camping near us tonight. She is cheerful as a lark, sings sometimes, and is an incessant talker. She says she is going to Oregon, where she expects to renew her youth. She looks very old and wrinkled in the face, but is very active in her movements, and not at all stooped. The people she is with are not at all refined or cultured, but I do like to talk to the old lady, she is so quaint. It makes mother seem quite a young woman to see her with an old lady more than forty years older than she is. Why, she seems just in the prime of life, and we had thought her growing old.

MORMON TOWNS IN IDAHO.

Monday, August 21.

Since we crossed the last steep mountain the horse flies have been very troublesome, the first that have bothered us all summer. I wonder

219

if the Indians brought them?

We came through two villages today; they are about five miles apart. The first Bennington, the last Montpelier—pretty large names for such small places. They are Mormon towns, although this is Idaho Territory. The women appeared sad and sorrowful enough to be the wives of Mormons. I did not see one of them smile. Our wagons were thronged with women and children selling butter, eggs, cheese and vegetables.

They sold eggs at seventy-five cents per dozen, butter seventy cents per pound, cheese fifty cents, potatoes twenty-five cents, and everything else in proportion. The prices seemed enormous to us, but I presume we would have purchased if they had been double what they were, for we are about starved for such things. Just think of spending a whole summer without garden productions.

This is a beautiful valley. Too good to be possessed by a community of bigamists. What a stigma upon the Government of these United States that whole communities are allowed to live criminal lives with impunity. I wonder how many are paying the penalty for bigamy in the penitentiaries of the United States? What is crime in one place, under the same government, I would think, would be crime in all other places, if the one did happen to be an isolated case, while the other is in large numbers, or wholesale. I suppose I am not well enough versed in law and politics to understand why it is crime in one place and not in the other. We are camping eight miles from Montpelier. Sim is much better today.

Tuesday, August 22.

Here we are at Soda Springs. I am surprised to see so small a town, for it is quite an old place for this western country, at least ten or fifteen years old, and does not have a post-office. The town is beautifully situated, the landscape views are glorious. The soda springs are bubbling up out of the ground in many places in this vicinity, and I expect there will be a city here some ay. There are medicinal springs here that possess wonderful curative properties, or people think they do. We wanted Sim to test them, but he said:

"I am getting well as fast as possible, and I don't care to drink that nauseous water. I prefer the pure, unadulterated snow water from the mountain springs."

This is the junction of the Oregon and Montana roads. There are three camps within sight of us.

Wednesday, August 23.

As we drove into the road this morning there was a train of eight wagons came into line just behind our wagons, and have travelled with us all day, stopping at noon when we did, and they are camping near us tonight, though we have separate camps. They are from Missouri, and are going to Virginia City. They seem to think as we all came from the same State, and our destination is the same place, that of course there is a bond of fellowship that is mutual, but to be frank, I must confess I do not care to go into a strange place in their company, for I fear we would be judged by the company we keep, and I think it would not be very favourable, so we will try to get away from them as soon as possible.

The weather is perfect. This is a beautiful valley. The men say the land is extremely rich. We are camping on the Blackfoot. We have not been able to shake our Missouri friends.

WE MEET MEN RETURNING TO THE STATES.

Thursday, August 24.

We came to a toll bridge over the Blackfoot this morning, where the toll was one dollar per team, and fifty cents for horseback riders. There had been an excellent ford just below the bridge. The men collecting the toll had spoiled it by digging ditches on both sides near the bank. The water was clear, and they were plainly visible. Hillhouse mounted Dick to see if we could ford it. One of the men screamed out at him: "You will mire your horse if you try that."

"I'll risk it." And he rode in below where the ditches were dug. The pony's feet were not muddy. Hillhouse found we could easily ford the creek below the ditches, which we did without accident.

It does seem a shame that we should have to pay toll for crossing a stream like that, after fording South Platte, North Platte and Green River.

The Missourians refused to pay the exorbitant price, and offered them fifty cents per wagon. They swore they would not take a cent less than one dollar. But the travellers were too many for them, and they drove over and did not pay a cent. The toll men were fearfully angry, and made great threats, but the men dared them to do their worst and laughed at them.

I do hope we will get ahead of these people tomorrow. They are not the kind of people I like to travel with.

We have met as many as twenty men today going back to the

States from the Virginia City mines. George Mays was with them. I mentioned about his leaving the train to go through on horseback, expecting to get his meals at stations and emigrant trains, when his brother with his bride went to Colorado. Says he worked just one day and got five dollars for it, and took the back track the next day.

"Mining is the only work a man can get to do, and it would kill an ordinary man in less than a week."

He is distressingly homesick. He is going to Denver to his brother.

Friday, August 25.

We were up at the first peep of dawn, had breakfast, and were hitching up to start, when the folks in the eight wagons began to emerge and light their camp fires, so we have left them some distance behind. We have been meeting men all day returning from the mines. They give a doleful account of the hard times in Montana. They say: "There are a few fortunate ones who are making money like dirt, but they are the exception, about one in a hundred."

One man was very anxious to buy Dick. I told him: "This pony is not for sale," and rode away before he could say anything more. The boys say we have met as many as two hundred men today returning from the mines. I believe we are all somewhat discouraged this evening. We have always heard such flattering reports from Alder Gulch and Virginia City.

Friday, August 26.

We have overtaken Mr. Grier, Mr. Bower and Mr. Kennedy. Some of Mr. Bower's cattle have eaten a poisonous herb—wild larkspur, I believe it is. One ox has died and several are poisoned, but will not die. They got the poison weed the day before yesterday, when they stopped at noon. I am glad we have overtaken them, but sorry for their misfortune. Hillhouse has just now come in, and says Joe, one of our big white oxen, is poisoned. He came for remedies and to sharpen his knife to bleed him. No doubt he got the poison the same place Mr. Bower's cattle did when we stopped for noon. Sim, Hillhouse and Winthrop have gone to his relief.

MOTHER AND I SAVE JOE'S LIFE.

Later.

The boys came back very much discouraged after working an hour, and said: "The blood will not flow, and he is swelling frightfully. I fear he will die, for when the blood will not run and the animal

222

begins to swell, they cannot be saved."

Mother said: "We will not let him die without further effort, at least. Come on, Sarah, let us try what we can do for him."

We melted a quart of lard and put it in a long-necked bottle (that we had brought for the purpose of drenching horses or cattle), cut up a lot of fat bacon into strips, put on our big aprons, and taking a bucket of cold water, we were ready. Hillhouse said: "Don't give him water." I answered, "You never mind, who is doing this?"

We were not long finding poor Joe. He seemed to be suffering dreadfully. His nose was as hot as fire. It actually burned my hands when I took hold of it to drench him with the lard. He seemed to know we were trying to help him, and did not resist at all when I put the bottle in the side of his mouth to pour the lard down his throat. He looked at us with his great, soft, patient eyes in such a docile, knowing manner, I felt sure he would not bite me, so I put my hand away down his throat to make him swallow the strips of fat bacon. He swallowed them as patiently as if he knew what they were for. We then bathed his nose with the cold water, without letting him drink any, and before we came away, he seemed relieved, and the swelling had stopped and he breathed much better. I believe he will live.

Saturday, August 27.

Joe did not die. This morning when Hillhouse went to see about him, expecting to find him dead, he was grazing, and seemed as well as ever, except his nose, which looks as if it had been scalded.

We came to Snake River ferry this morning, six miles from where we camped last night. We paid eight dollars for our outfit crossing on the ferry. As Nellie Bower and I were standing on the bank of the river watching the wagons being ferried over, holding our ponies by their bridles, a gentleman came near. Lifting his hat and bowing politely, he said to me: "I will give one hundred dollars in clean gold dust for that pony."

"This pony is not for sale, sir, at any price."

We came from the ferry about two miles, and stopped for lunch. I told Hillhouse what the man said.

"If I were you, I would certainly sell him, so many seem to want him. He will very likely be stolen."

"Oh, I can't sell my pony."

After lunch the men folks went to fish in Snake River. They had been gone but a few minutes, when the man that wanted Dick rode into camp. He rode straight to our wagons, and said:

"I will give you one hundred and ten dollars for that pony."

I had begun to relent somewhat. I felt that it would not do to be sentimental under existing circumstances. We had spent almost all our money for toll, ferrying and other expenses on the road. It might prove to be a serious matter to be in a strange place without money, and if we fail to get employment, we will be obliged to sell something, and there is nothing we can spare so well as Dick. I knew the man had offered all and more than I could expect to get for him.

But as Hillhouse was gone fishing and I could not think of selling my pony myself, I said to the man:

"My brother is not here, and I cannot let him go."

"Tell your brother to bring him to the ferry, and I will send you the pay for him."

"I think you need not expect him, for I am sure he will not come."

He went away without Dick, and Hillhouse did not take him back, so I have my pony yet. We came five miles and camped, as too long a drive is not good for the poisoned cattle. I wish there was a longer distance between us and the man that wants my pony.

Mr. Grier sold his riding horse at the ferry. He says:

"There is a party of half a dozen gentlemen going to the States horseback. They are all supplied, except the man that wants your pony. He has waited, trying to find a horse with an easy gait, and Dick is the only one that has suited him. Oh, he will be back again. Miss Raymond, and make another offer, and if you do not let him have him, I don't know what he will do, for he seems determined to get him."

If he does come, I will not dare to refuse him, but I do hope we are out of reach of temptation. Dick is as fat as when we started. I comb and brush him every day, and he shows his keeping. He always looks nice and sleek. He is a bright bay, with heavy black mane and tail.

DICK IS SOLD. OH, DEAR.

Sunday, August 28.

It was scarcely daylight when that hateful man was here again after Dick. I had just finished dressing when Hillhouse came to the wagon and said:

"Shall I let Dick go?"

"Do as you think best." And I threw myself on the bed for a good cry. I had not stopped crying when he came back, and throwing a buckskin purse into my lap, said:

"There is your pony." There was one hundred and twenty-five dollars in gold dust in it. I sobbed out loud. Hillhouse looked at me with contempt in his expression, but said nothing. I could not help crying.

I know he would never sell anything that he loved, and I love that pony. I let the purse roll out of my lap down into the bottom of the wagon, and have not touched it yet. Of course, I knew the wagon-bed was tight, and there is no danger of its being lost. We came to Silver Lake today. We are having a fine shower of rain, which we were needing very much. It was some time coming, so we had dinner over and were ready for it when it reached us.

Monday, August 29.

We have travelled today over Snake River desert, nothing but sand and sagebrush. We watered at noon at a toll well, called Hole-in-the-sand, and paid ten cents a head for watering stock. I wonder what we will have to pay toll for next?

We are camping on Camel's Creek. There is a family camping near us from Bannack, going to the States. The lady is a sister of Mr. Esler, one of the quartz kings of Montana, so she says; I presume everybody knows about him, but I must confess I never heard of him until now.

His sister is taking his motherless babe back to its grandmother. Mr. Esler's, wife died more than a month ago. The babe is about four months old, and as sweet as can be. I could not keep my hands off it, and that is how I came to get acquainted with its auntie. She is a great talker, seems to think I am going to Montana husband-hunting, and volunteered a deal of advice on the subject, especially I must not tell that I am from Missouri, as Missourians are below par in Montana. She is from New York. Oh, dear, it makes one tired to see a full-grown woman so frivolous.

Tuesday, August 30.

We watered the stock at noon at Hole-in-the-rock. Didn't turn them out to graze, as there was nothing for them to graze on.

Mr. Bower has lost another ox, and was obliged to buy a yoke of oxen to get his wagons over the ranges. There are two mountains to cross before he reaches his home in the Madison Valley, fifteen or twenty miles the other side of Virginia City. Of course, he had to pay a most exorbitant price. Joe, our ox that was poisoned, seems as well as ever, except his nose has peeled off as if scalded into a blister.

We are camping at the foot of the last range we will cross before we reach our destination.

Mrs. Kennedy and I have become quite well acquainted the last few days. She was a bride of only a few days when they started to the West. Her husband drives one of Mr. Bower's teams. They are going among strangers, to make them a home and fortune. She is a very intelligent and well-educated young woman. I do not know her husband very much.

Mother's Birthday.

Wednesday, August 31.

Mother's birthday. She is fifty-three years old. We have not been able to celebrate it especially, yet she is not likely to forget it, though spent in climbing a Rocky Mountain range. We have been now four months on this journey. Have lived out of doors, in all sorts of weather. It has been very beneficial to mother. She was looking frail and delicate when we started, but seems to be in perfect health now, and looks at least ten years younger.

I have not heard her utter one word of complaint, either of physical suffering or outward discomfort, such as the heat or cold, mud, dust, rain, nor any of the things that make camping out disagreeable, and so many people grumble about. "*What can't be cured, must be endured,*" is her motto, and the one care has been that we all keep in good health, and she would ask nothing more.

We are camping in Pleasant Valley, a depression right on top of the mountain, just large enough for a good-sized ranch. It is a beautiful place, the scenery is magnificently grand. There is a fine grove of beautiful trees at the lower end of the vale. The sides and upper end are hedged in by straight up and down hills or mountain-sides, about fifteen feet high. The grass is a luxuriant green and very plentiful.

There is a station here, occupied by a family that used to live in Virginia City. They have two very bright little girls, who have spent the early evening hours with us. They are perfect little chatterboxes to talk. They have a married sister living in Virginia City, the wife of a Mr. Wheeler, who is a candidate for some office. The little girls had forgotten whether for sheriff or Member of Congress.

Thursday, September 1.

This is brother Mac's birthday. He is twenty-seven years old. I wonder if he has thought of it, and remembered us. I presume he has. It has been some weeks since we have had an opportunity to post a letter to him. There have been depredations by the Indians, which have no doubt been largely reported in the newspapers, and he cannot know that we have escaped. His anxiety and suspense must be hard to bear. I know I should suffer agonies were our circumstances reversed.

As we were descending the mountain, we met a freight train loaded with people returning to the States. After we had passed them about half a mile, Hillhouse was walking in front of the wagons, and found a miner's shovel. It is bright and shining, but not new. It is worn off some. The men tell Hillhouse it is a good omen, that he will make money by the shovelful. He laughed, and said: "I reckon I'd better keep it, then, to shovel it up with."

Friday, September 2.

When I awoke in the night, I heard the rain pattering on the wagon-cover. This morning the mountains were all covered with snow, and presented a magnificent picture. Those nearest our camp are covered with pine trees of an intensely dark green. The snow on the boughs and beneath the trees glittered in the sunshine. The scene was constantly changing, as the warm sun melted the snow from the boughs, and before night it was all gone except on the highest peaks, where it stays all summer.

The roads have been sloppy and muddy today, though the water has all run off or evaporated, so that it is comparatively dry where we are camping, notwithstanding there was so much snow and water on the ground this morning. It is too cold for comfort this evening. We are hovering around the stove with our shawls on.

SWEET WATER CAÑON.

Saturday, September 3.

We came through a deep, dark *cañon* this morning, and passed the grave of a man that was robbed and murdered last week. It is the deepest and darkest *cañon* we have travelled through. Ten men have been robbed and murdered in it in the last two years. We were in no danger of being molested. Only men who have their fortunes in gold about their person are intercepted, robbed and killed. How awful it seems. Why will men be so wicked?

In several places in the *cañon* the road has been widened with pick and shovel, perhaps two or three days' work done, and we had to pay ten dollars toll for our two wagons passing over it. We stopped at noon on Black Tail Deer Creek. Are camping on the Sweet Water, about twenty-five miles from Virginia City. This is a beautiful place. There are fine large trees along the creek, high mountains around a lovely dale. It is just large enough for a fine farm. There is a deserted cabin here, where someone commenced improving a farm, became home-sick and discouraged, and left it for someone else.

Sunday, September 4.

We are camping within seven miles of Virginia City, near a freight train of about fifty wagons, with from seventy-five to one hundred people all together, men, women and children, returning to the States.

To hear these people talk of the disadvantages and disagreeable things with regard to life in Montana, would have a tendency to dis-courage one, if it were not so palpable that they are homesick, and everyone knows that when that disease is fairly developed, everything is coloured with a deep dark blue, and even pleasant things seem ex-tremely disagreeable to the afflicted person. The ladies seem to have the disease in its worst form, and of course they make the gentlemen do as they wish, which is to take them home to mother and other dear ones.

We have had a very pleasant day, about as pleasant as the day we started on this journey, the first day of May. It is cheering that the first and last days of our journeying should be so lovely. After four months and four days of living outdoors we are all in the most robust health. Yet we shall be glad to have a roof over our heads once more, even if it is a dirt roof.

Monday, September 5. Noon.

Here we are camping in the suburbs of the city, in Alder Gulch, where the miners are at work. How I wish my descriptive powers were adequate to making those who have never seen gulch-mining see as I see, and realise the impression made upon me as I first looked into the gulch at the miners at work. There is a temporary bridge (very shaky) across the gulch that wagons may pass over.

Standing on this bridge, in the middle of the gulch, looking up and down, and even beneath my feet, the scene is a lively one. So many men, it seems they would be in each other's way. They remind one of bees around a hive.

And such active work. It seemed that not one of that great mul-titude stopped for one instant shovelling and wheeling dirt, passing and repassing each other without a hitch. It made me tired to look at them. The ground is literally turned inside out; great deep holes and high heaps of dirt. The mines are said to be very rich.

2 p. m.

We dined at noon today. Had beefsteak at fifty cents per pound and potatoes at twenty-five cents. I do not know if the price had anything to do with it, but it certainly tasted better than any I ever ate before.

I interviewed a woman—or rather she interviewed me—that lives near where we are camping. She said her name is Neihart. Her husband is a miner and earns seven dollars per day. Judging from the manner in which they seem to live, they ought to save at least five of it. I presume I did not make a very favourable impression, for after I came back to camp, she called across the street to her neighbour—so we could hear what she said:

"Some more aristocrats. They didn't come here to work. Going to teach school and play lady," with great contempt in her voice.

I laughed at the first impression made, and tried to realise that teaching is not work.

THE END OF OUR JOURNEY.

Mrs. Curry, Sim, Hillhouse and I are going to town as soon as Mrs, Curry is ready. We held a council whether we should get out our street suits and last summer's hats, or go in our emigrant outfits, sun-bonnets and short dresses, thick shoes and all. Decided in favour of the latter. No doubt the people of Virginia are used to seeing emigrants in emigrant outfits, and we will not astonish them.

Evening.

We were not very favourably impressed with Virginia City. It is the shabbiest town I ever saw, not a really good house in it. Hillhouse and I, after hunting up and down the two most respectable looking streets, found a log cabin with two rooms that we rented for eight dollars per month. Mrs. Curry did not find a house at all. We thought as so many were leaving there would be an abundance of vacant houses, but there were enough living in tents to fill all the houses that were vacated.

Mr. Curry's folks and Mr. Kennedy's will go to Helena. Mr. Bower has a ranch on the Madison Valley. Mr. Grier will stay here for a time, anyway.

The cabin is on the corner of Wallace and Hamilton Streets, next door to the city butcher. The cabin has a dirt roof. There is a floor in it, and that is better than some have. It is neat and clean, which is a comfort. Men have not bathed in it.

We found quite a budget of letters at the post-office, the most important of which are from brother Mac and Frank Kerfoot. Mac's letter:

229

Cincinnati, August 10, 1865.

Dear Mother, Sister and Brothers:

It is with fear and trembling that I pen this letter. I have not heard from you for more than a month, telling me you had decided to go to Montana. The papers are full of accounts of Indian depredations. I have realised to the fullest extent that *"Hope deferred maketh the heart sick."* In your last letter you had decided to go to Virginia City, so I will direct this letter to be held until called for. I am glad you are not going any farther West. I cannot conceive why you wanted to go to that far off wild Western country. I do wish you had stopped at Omaha, or St. Jo, or even Denver. It would have been better than Montana.

With sincerest love to all,

Your son and brother, Mac.

But oh, the sad, sad news comes In Frank's letter. Neelie is dead. Oh, the anguish of soul, the desolateness of heart, that one sentence gives expression to. Frank's letter:

Green River, Wyoming Ter., Aug. 18.

Dear Miss Sallie—I write to tell you of our very great sorrow. Precious Neelie is gone. We are all sorely bereaved, but how Uncle Ezra's family can ever get along without her, I cannot see. Any member of the family, except uncle, could be spared better than Neelie. She got very much better, and the doctor said if uncle would stay there another week, he was sure Neelie would be well enough to travel without danger of a relapse, but if she had another relapse she could not be saved.

The Hardinbrooke train left Monday morning. Mrs. Hardinbrooke was much better. The Gatewoods and Ryans stayed with us. Neelie was much better. She sat up in bed some. That night Uncle Ezra did not sleep at all, he was so afraid of Indians. The next morning, as Neelie had a good night's rest, and was feeling stronger, nothing else would do but we must move on to Green River, where the soldiers are. We started about nine o'clock, and drove twenty-five miles without stopping. It was very hot and dusty. Uncle drove the family wagon and watched Neelie carefully. After a time, she seemed to be sleeping quietly, so he thought she was all right. But it was the sleep from which there is no waking in this life.

Dr. Howard and Dr. Fletcher were both at Green River, and

they both worked all night trying to arouse her, but without success. At early dawn Neelie's sweet spirit took its flight, and we are left desolate.

Miss Sallie, do you remember Carpenter? the young man that made Uncle Ezra so mad by pretending to go into hysterics when the Ryan girls were leaving the train? When he heard that Neelie was gone, he went out on the mountain and found a large, smooth, flat stone, white as marble, but not so hard, and engraved Neelie's name, age, and date of her death on it, to mark her resting place. He worked all day upon it, and at the funeral he placed it at the head of her grave, and if you ever go over this road it will not be hard to find Neelie's grave. We gathered wild flowers and literally covered her grave with them. Darling Neelie, our loss is her gain, for we all know that she was an earnest, devoted Christian. We will start on our now sorrowful journey tomorrow. I wish you were here to go with us, but hope you will be successful where you are, and happy too.

Mrs. Hardinbrooke was much worse after they came here. That hot, dusty drive was hard on well people; for sick people it was terrible. When Neelie died, she was very low, but she has rallied, and the rest of the train will move on tomorrow. But Mr. Hardinbrooke will stay here with his wife until she is entirely restored, and they will go to Virginia City on the coach. All send love to you all. Aunt Mildred asked me to write you.

Very sincerely your friend,

Frank.

I believe I am homesick this evening. It is so dreary to go into a strange place and meet so many people, and not one familiar face. But I must not complain, for we are all here, not even Caesar missing. My heart aches so for the Kerfoots. I do not know how they can bear this terrible bereavement under such trying circumstances.

Tuesday, September 6.

Mr. Curry's folks have started to Helena. Mr. Bower's to the Madison Valley, and Mr. Kennedy with them, to drive his team, leaving Mrs. Kennedy with us until tomorrow, when they will take the coach for Helena.

We moved into our cabin this morning. It does not seem as much like home as the wagons did, and I believe we are all homesick if we would acknowledge it.

The boys found a checkerboard nailed on the window where a pane of glass was broken out. We pasted paper over the place. They made checkermen out of pasteboard, and Sim and Winthrop are having a game. Hillhouse is reading the Montana Post. Mother is making bread, and initiating Mrs. Kennedy into the mysteries of yeast and bread-making.

As Hillhouse was on his way to the butcher shop, he passed an auction sale of household goods. The auctioneer was crying a beautiful porcelain lamp. He stopped to make the first bid. "One dollar" he called. There were no other bids and he got the lamp—his first purchase in Virginia City. (He has it yet.)

When he brought it home, with the meat he went to get, mother said: "What is the use of the lamp without the chimney?"

So, he went to purchase a chimney after dinner and coal oil to burn in the lamp. He had to pay two dollars and fifty cents for a chimney, and five dollars for a gallon of coal oil, so our light is rather expensive after all. And thus ends our first day in Virginia City, and brings "*Crossing the Plains and Mountains in 1865*" to an end.

By S. R. H.

LEONAUR

ALSO FROM LEONAUR
AVAILABLE IN SOFTCOVER OR HARDCOVER WITH DUST JACKET

THE WOMAN IN BATTLE *by Loreta Janeta Velazquez*—Soldier, Spy and Secret Service Agent for the Confederacy During the American Civil War.

BOOTS AND SADDLES *by Elizabeth B. Custer*—The experiences of General Custer's Wife on the Western Plains.

FANNIE BEERS' CIVIL WAR *by Fannie A. Beers*—A Confederate Lady's Experiences of Nursing During the Campaigns & Battles of the American Civil War.

LADY SALE'S AFGHANISTAN *by Florentia Sale*—An Indomitable Victorian Lady's Account of the Retreat from Kabul During the First Afghan War.

THE TWO WARS OF MRS DUBERLY *by Frances Isabella Duberly*—An Intrepid Victorian Lady's Experience of the Crimea and Indian Mutiny.

THE REBELLIOUS DUCHESS *by Paul F. S. Dermoncourt*—The Adventures of the Duchess of Berri and Her Attempt to Overthrow French Monarchy.

LADIES OF WATERLOO *by Charlotte A. Eaton, Magdalene de Lancey & Juana Smith*—The Experiences of Three Women During the Campaign of 1815: Waterloo Days by Charlotte A. Eaton, A Week at Waterloo by Magdalene de Lancey & Juana's Story by Juana Smith.

NURSE AND SPY IN THE UNION ARMY *by Sarah Emma Evelyn Edmonds*—During the American Civil War

WIFE NO. 19 *by Ann Eliza Young*—The Life & Ordeals of a Mormon Woman During the 19th Century

DIARY OF A NURSE IN SOUTH AFRICA *by Alice Bron*—With the Dutch-Belgian Red Cross During the Boer War

MARIE ANTOINETTE AND THE DOWNFALL OF ROYALTY *by Imbert de Saint-Amand*—The Queen of France and the French Revolution

THE MEMSAHIB & THE MUTINY *by R. M. Coopland*—An English lady's ordeals in Gwalior and Agra during the Indian Mutiny 1857

MY CAPTIVITY AMONG THE SIOUX INDIANS *by Fanny Kelly*—The ordeal of a pioneer woman crossing the Western Plains in 1864

WITH MAXIMILIAN IN MEXICO *by Sara Yorke Stevenson*—A Lady's experience of the French Adventure

www.ingramcontent.com/pod-product-compliance
Lightning Source LLC
Chambersburg PA
CBHW032050080426
42733CB00006B/220